ARISTOTLE AS TEACHER

Other Books of interest from St. Augustine's Press

Aristotle, *Aristotle – On Poetics* (translated by Seth Benardete and Michael Davis

Aristotle, *Physics, Or Natural Hearing* (translated by Glen Coughlin)

Plato, *The Symposium of Plato: The Shelley Translation*

Averroes, *Averroes' Middle Commentary on Aristotle's* Poetics (translated by Charles Butterworth)

Averroes, *Averroes' Middle Commentaries on Aristotle's* Categories *and* De Interpretatione (translated by Charles Butterworth)

Michael Davis, *The Poetry of Philosophy: On Aristotle's* Poetics

Ronna Burger, *The Phaedo: A Platonic Labyrinth*

Thomas Aquinas, *Commentary on Aristotle's* De Anima

Thomas Aquinas, *Commentary on Aristotle's* Metaphysics

Thomas Aquinas, *Commentary on Aristotle's* Nicomachean Ethics

Thomas Aquinas, *Commentary on Aristotle's* On Interpretation

Thomas Aquinas, *Commentary on Aristotle's* Physics

Thomas Aquinas, *Commentary on Aristotle's* Posterior Analytics

Leo Strauss, *Xenophon's Socrates*

Leo Strauss, *Xenophon's Socratic Discourse: An Interpretation of the* Oeconomicus

Stanley Rosen, *Plato's* Symposium

Stanley Rosen, *Plato's* Statesman*: The Web of Politics*

Stanley Rosen, *Plato's* Sophist*: The Drama of Original and Image*

Stanley Rosen, *Platonic Production: Theme and Variations*

Stanley Rosen, *Essays in Philosophy: Ancient* (vol. I of two volumes)

Joseph Owens, C.SS.R., *Aristotle's Gradations of Being in* Metaphysics E–Z

Josef Pieper, *The Platonic Myths*

Josef Pieper, *Enthusiasm and Divine Madness: On the Platonic Dialogue* Phaedrus

Seth Benardete, *The Archaeology of the Soul: Platonic Readings of Ancient Poetry and Philosophy*

Peter Kreeft, *Socrates' Children: Ancient* (vol. I of four volumes)

Peter Kreeft, *Socratic Logic: A Logic Text Using Socratic Method, Platonic Questions, and Aristotelian Principles*

ARISTOTLE AS TEACHER

His Introduction to a Philosophic Science

Christopher Bruell

St. Augustine's Press
South Bend, Indiana

Manufactured in the United States of America

1 2 3 4 5 6 20 19 18 17 16 15 14

Library of Congress Cataloging in Publication Data
Bruell, Christopher, 1942–
Aristotle as teacher: his introduction to a philosophic science / Christopher Bruell. – 1st edition.
pages cm
ISBN 978-1-58731-050-8 (hardbound alk. paper)
1. Aristotle. Metaphysics. I. Title.
B434.B78 2014
110 – dc23 2014009627

∞ The paper used in this publication meets the minimum requirements of the American National Standard for Information Sciences Permanence of Paper for Printed Materials, ANSI Z39.481984.

St. Augustine's Press
www.staugustine.net

Table of Contents

Preface

In the customary divisions of our colleges and universities, philosophy is treated as one discipline among many. It distinguishes itself from its fellow disciplines, however, at least in this: that there are truly no teachers of it. Or, rather, its only true teachers are the genuine philosophers themselves. A young person who seeks to get an inkling of what philosophy originally meant must therefore sit at the feet of the masters, which he can do only by reading—and not just reading but studying—their books. And anyone who should wish to help him must be willing to serve as a mere intermediary to these books. Indeed, the willingness of such helpers will be in vain, if they are not already themselves sitting at the feet of the masters, having become again, or being still, young and innocent or ignorant enough to do so.

Someone might object that this is to make philosophy merely a thing of the past. But not all that is past is irretrievably past. And, as for philosophy in particular, it may, for all that we can know, have a future.

Introduction

The pages that follow these brief remarks were written to aid in the reading, that is, the understanding of a philosophic work. What does it mean to endeavor to understand the work of an author whose powers of comprehension and composition far exceed our own? We must raise this question at the outset, lest we become guilty of the sin which some older commentators (of Homer and Aristotle) were accused of by Swift's Gulliver: as he claimed to have learned, they "always kept in the most distant Quarters from their Principals in the lower World, through a Consciousness of Shame and Guilt, because they had so horribly misrepresented the Meaning of those Authors to Posterity" (*Gulliver's Travels*, Part III, Chapter VIII "A further Account of Glubbdubdrib"). We must raise this question at the outset, in other words, and also reflect on it, if we are to avoid misrepresenting the meaning of our author not only to others but to ourselves. Yet this is just what, at the outset, we cannot reflect on, at least in any satisfactory way: we lack the necessary experience. Here we must, we can learn only by doing. Still, some preliminary observations may be in order.

We note first that the speech of our author is likely to be more precise, and even considerably more precise, than that to which we are accustomed. We readily grant that the thought of the great thinkers is broader and deeper than our own. But we sometimes fail to reflect that it could not have achieved such breadth and depth, as thought, if it were not also more precise than ours. And the precision, the care and exactness, of a man's thought is almost certain to be reflected in his oral or written speech.

This means that we must always be attentive to what he actually says: not what, at first or second glance, he appears to be saying, but exactly what he says. In the best case, we will read his work in the language in which it was written. But, where an older work is concerned, we cannot even then be content to rely solely on the text of the work that a modern editor or editors have given us. Grateful as we must be to those editors, who have performed the indispensable labor of producing a text through the painstaking examination of often divergent and sometimes unconstruable manuscripts, we know or soon discover that they have, here and there, made questionable choices among alternative manuscript readings and that they have even introduced into the text changes based on conjectures of their own. In the better editions, the conjectures are identified as such and the more important of the rejected manuscript readings are reported. We must take full advantage of these reports to see whether a superior manuscript reading has not, on occasion, been passed over. For the most precise speech is not necessarily the most readily graspable. It may even, on our first or second look at a particular passage, be barely intelligible. And yet that same passage, when once we have wrestled with it, may disclose an unexpected and important meaning. In other words, it would not and perhaps could not have disclosed that meaning to us, the underlying thought, if we had not wrestled with it. For to understand, to appropriate a thought, if only to be in a position to judge for ourselves of its validity, is not merely to hear or read some expression of it. We must, rather, repeat the thought on our own. And therefore the adequate expression of it, which may have to be difficult or puzzling for just this reason, will be designed to elicit such a repetition from us.

To put this another way, speech that is intelligible in itself—and only precise speech is truly intelligible—is not necessarily intelligible to us. It becomes so when we grasp the problem it addresses. Accordingly, our author is likely to be more concerned to expose us to questions or problems that we may have been insufficiently aware of than to hasten us toward their solutions. Now, if those problems are themselves complex, as they are likely to be, we must expect the discussion of them to be no less complex. It may have to be carried out in stages: at the conclusion of each stage, the treatment of the problem will seem to have been completed; but it will seem to have been so only until a hitherto unobserved difficulty makes its appearance and compels us, following the author's lead, to reconsider the whole matter. And this means, given the interconnectedness of the problems, that a philosophic work will have a plot, which may contain as many surprising twists and turns as that of a good work of fiction. Even key terms, of use throughout the work, may disclose new meanings, therefore, as its progress sheds further light on the context to which they belong. Precision of speech is not the same thing as rigidity of terminology.

We must be no less attentive, then, to the argument of the work as a whole, to the movement of that argument or the plot, than we are to the difficulty of particular passages. And we must be prepared to be led by that plot into territory that is at first as unfamiliar to us as are the problems that the plot unfolds. We should not conclude from this, however, that the problems with which a philosophic work is concerned are, in themselves, alien to us. Since "the great thinkers . . . see pitfalls where we are sure of our ground," they are more likely to be the very problems with which our thought, unawares, is already burdened. And the land to which such a work can lead us may well be none other than that in which, without truly seeing it, we already dwell.

Aristotle as Teacher
His Introduction to a Philosophic Science

Among the works of Aristotle that have come down to us is the book or collection of books to which the name "Metaphysics" has been given: The works that come "after" the physical works (those devoted to natural science). As Aristotle refers in the Metaphysics itself to one who stands higher on the scale of knowing than the natural scientist (G3 1005a33–b2; E1 1026a10–13, 27–31), we may take "after" in the title given to the work to mean "higher." But the higher knowledge in this sense is the more fundamental; and the more fundamental is also the more elementary. We will assume then that the Metaphysics is an elementary work in the sense indicated: indeed that, whatever other purposes it may serve, it is intended also to introduce its readers to science and the problem of science. And we will attempt to see what the work discloses of its author's thought when it is read in the light of this intention—as Aristotle's introduction to a philosophic science.

A1) To the question that must be put at the outset—why should one take an interest in science at all?—Aristotle answers, "All human beings yearn by nature to know." These are his first words in the work. Knowledge is of course necessary to all animal life; and it is supplied in the first place by sense perception. But Aristotle observes that we human beings value the perceptions of the senses, of sight especially, for themselves even apart from their use in guiding our actions. Still, the knowledge supplied by the senses is not yet science.

The latter requires a long development, whose intermediate stages are experience and the "arts" (technai) and whose preconditions include, in addition to sense perception, the remembering of what we perceive and an ability to learn, which is linked to hearing in particular. From many memories of the same matter, a single experience is formed which, for example, enables us to treat similar instances of illness in the same appropriate manner. That is, the one form, which sets all such instances apart from others, is already effective in the experience that distinguishes instance from instance. But when that form is itself grasped as the universal applicable to the similar instances, the stage of art has been reached. We are then able to give an account (logos) of the appropriateness of the treatment in a given case—by showing that the case falls under the universal in question—so that teaching, too, becomes possible. And it thus comes about that, whereas the other animals live by perceptions, or the imaginations to which they give rise, and memories and have but a small share in experience, human beings live also by reasonings and art.

But this means that it is life more generally, and not the yearning for knowledge as such, that chiefly motivates the development of the arts. And the first to be discovered therefore were those that attend to our necessities or our amusement. Yet when it comes to practice, art that lacks experience is likely to be inferior to experience without art: art is what it is by its grasp of the universal, but practice concerns the particulars that fall under the universal, which it belongs to experience to grasp. And, even so, art is thought to be superior to experience in knowing, as Aristotle observes, and its possessors are held to be wiser than the experienced, since the latter know the "what" but not the "why" or the cause.

We may therefore be entitled to discount the fact that the theoretical sciences, those directed neither to pleasure nor to the necessities, were discovered only when provision for all such concerns had already been made. And there is the additional consideration that the development of those sciences requires leisure—so that they were discovered first in the places where leisure was available to some. For this reason, for example, the mathematical arts were first put together by Egyptian priests. There is, however, a difference between art and science for which Aristotle refers us to a discussion in his Ethics (Nicomachean Ethics Z3–4), where he had stressed that science has as its object what cannot be otherwise than as it is: what is, and is as it is, by necessity. What he wishes to stress now is that what is honored with the name "wisdom" is held by "all" to be concerned with the first causes and the principles (beginnings). Would the Egyptians have agreed that those causes are as they are by necessity?

Aristotle concludes this discussion of our natural yearning to know by agreeing that wisdom is a science concerned with some principles and causes.

A2) Since it is this science that we are seeking, we must raise the question: with which or what sorts of causes and principles is it concerned? From the expectations that we hold regarding wisdom and the wise—it is on the basis of these that Aristotle attempts to cast some light on the question—they would seem to be the highest universals. (See Physics A5–7.) One who knows the universals knows "somehow" all of the things lying under (underlying) the universals. And the first things and the causes are the preeminent objects of science because it is through them and from them that the other things, those lying under the causes, are made known. Moreover, in every science, the one who is more precise as to the causes, and more able to teach on their basis, is held to be the wiser. And, among the sciences, those whose objects are fewer, since they are of higher universality and more removed from sense perception, are more precise than those whose objects are constituted by some addition to the universals in question. Arithmetic is more precise in this way than geometry, for example. Still, in adding here that the science concerned with the causes is also more able to teach, Aristotle leaves the question of the character of the causes open.

Certainly, the science that we seek is a theoretical one, choiceworthy on its own account, or for the sake of knowing, rather than on account of what might come from it. This is so, despite the fact that, if the good is one of the causes, the sought-for science would be the one most capable of ruling. It would know that on account of which each thing is to be done: the good of each or, altogether, the best in all of nature. Insofar as we are merely seeking it, of course, we do not know this—nor even, on the basis of the science itself, why it in particular is choiceworthy. Any confidence that this is the case must rely either on our natural yearning to know or on some pre-theoretical knowledge of the good, or on some combination or cooperation of these sources. Perhaps some light is cast on the matter by the example of the first philosophers, to whom Aristotle first directs our attention in this context.

The first philosophers were motivated by wonder or perplexity, especially about the "greater" things: for example, about what happens to the moon, or with the sun and stars, and about the genesis of "the all." In perplexity and wonder, there is awareness of one's ignorance. This much the philosopher (lover of wisdom) shares with the lover of myth, for myth is composed of wonders. The lover of myth, too, is "somehow" a philosopher (Critias 110a3–6). As for the philosophers proper, if they philosophized in order to get out of their ignorance, it is manifest that they pursued scientific knowledge in order to know, and not on account of any usefulness it might have. And if their investigations attain their end, the result must simply be that they cease to wonder about what was perplexing them when they began: for example, the two turns (at the solstices) that the sun makes in its annual course through the heaven. In the same way, a man who has become a geometer no longer wonders about the incommensurability of the diagonal of a square to its side, since he has seen that it cannot be otherwise.

According to the sketch of the origin of philosophy that Aristotle gives here, this sort of prudence began to be sought at just about the point when all of the necessary things, as well as those serving ease and amusement, were present. That is, he makes no explicit reference to an intermediate or contemporaneous stage, in which another sort of prudence may have been sought (Nicomachean Ethics Z5 1140a24–28). Yet those who first ventured to philosophize were confronted with the objection, of which the poets made themselves spokesmen (Republic 607b5–6), that their activity is not pleasing to the divine. Aristotle responds to the objection, on the behalf of the first philosophers as well as his own. But one must wonder whether they responded to it—as they must have done, to themselves if not also to others—in the way that he does: that is, whether they accepted all of the premises of his response.

If they did not accept one or more of them—and who would have been more aware of their non-acceptance than Aristotle?—

his tendering of the response that he makes here would be an additional indication of the reserve with which he has sketched the origin, and therewith the nature, the permanent character, of philosophy or what we have called "philosophic science." Still, the sketch has served to deepen the consideration, from which he began, of our natural yearning to know. For it is only on the basis of a grasp of what it would mean truly to know, that we could even begin properly to assess what our stance toward knowing is.

A3) The objection that confronted the first philosophers may have to be traced to the character of the causes with which they were concerned. Whatever is at any time held to be wisdom is, of course, admired; and there is universal agreement, as Aristotle has stressed, that wisdom is concerned with the first causes and the principles. Yet in his own name, he went only so far as to agree that the science with which, for his part, he identifies wisdom is concerned with some principles and causes. (A1) Moreover, an initial effort to cast light on the character of those causes and principles ended inconclusively (A2). Perhaps the general agreement referred to conceals a disagreement as to the character of the causes that are truly primary. If so, it would belong to the first and highest tasks of a philosophic science to adjudicate the disagreement. But the dispute may have arisen in the first place due to the fact that the causes recognizable by science as causes (whether primary or not) are not the only ones imaginable. Can it be left, then, to science to adjudicate a dispute to which it is, by its very nature, a party?

Aristotle prepares now to push forward into the thicket of this difficulty. Against the background of the demand for a science of the primary causes, he reminds readers of the fourfold division of causes in his Physics, whose treatment of them he refers to as "adequate"—perhaps to distinguish it from its restatement here. (See Physics B3 194b23–35.) In accord with the intention of the more fundamental work, however, he goes on now to raise the question whether there is some genus of cause different from those four; and he suggests that it will be conducive to the present inquiry to look into the matter. Either we will discover a different genus of cause or (in the case that we do not) we will have more trust (and more reason to trust) in the four that have been mentioned. Yet it is by taking up the views of his philosophic predecessors on the question of principles and causes—that is, the views of scientists—that he proposes to look into it. So far, then, as the surface of the ensuing discussion is concerned, there is only the presence at its margins of "the very ancient . . . first theologians" and of another poet, who are mentioned in passing, to remind us of the deeper difficulty. As to what it would mean to discover a genus of cause different from the four of the Physics, we are left to figure it out on the basis of whatever the discussion may reveal about those.

Most of the first philosophers thought that principles in the form of matter are the sole principles of all things, on the ground that what all the beings consist of, what they are first generated from, and what in perishing they return to at the last, is the element and the principle of the beings. As for this element or principle itself, its being was thought to remain (the same) while undergoing changes in (secondary) characteristics sufficient to account for the emergence in it of the beings, as we know them, as well as for their persistence while they persist and their disappearance when they perish. Since at best only analogues of the basic process of generation and perishing can be observed, it could not have been observation that led these philosophers to their fundamental thought—as distinct from their views as to whether the material principle is one or many and as to its form, where opinions differed and where observation (as the case of Thales shows) would have been able to play a significant role. It was rather their conviction that there must be some nature, one or more, from which the others (the perishable things) are generated, while that nature is itself preserved. In other words, they were convinced that there can be no genesis or destruction of nature as a whole. This "ancient" conviction was shared by "all": it is as old as philosophy itself (Physics A4 187a27–29, 32–35; On Generation and Corruption A3 317b29–31). Aristotle thus corrects a misconception that could have arisen from his earlier remark to the effect that the first philosophers were perplexed with regard to the genesis of "the all" (A2). On the other hand, some people go so far in the opposite direction as to think that even "the very ancient . . . first theologians"—who, in speaking of some watery beings as "fathers" of genesis, may have reminded them of Thales—held an opinion like his about nature. Aristotle remarks here only that it is "perhaps" unclear whether theirs was an opinion about nature, that is, whether they conceived of the simply first cause as Thales did. But at the beginning of the next chapter (A4), he quotes some lines of the poet Hesiod that begin, "first of all things, chaos came to be."

According to the fourfold division of causes with which the present chapter began, the being, or defining character, of any being is to be distinguished from its matter, or what underlies it. The philosophers who recognized only material principles of things denied in effect the meaningfulness of this distinction. To have acknowledged it would have been to deny to matter as such that intelligible or transparent fixity that qualified it in their eyes to be the first principle of nature. Yet those among them who posited only one such principle were compelled themselves to distinguish between the being of their principle and the (other) characteristics of that being, since it is not the whole of what is said by them to underlie the other beings that remains, while those beings undergo the changes to which they are subject.

Perhaps it was this difficulty that led Empedocles and Anaxagoras to posit a plurality of material principles. For that enabled them to assert that the principles or elements undergo no generation (change) other than repeatedly combining and separating (in such manner that the other things are produced and then again destroyed): that, in respects other than combination and separation, the elements remain always or perpetually free from generation and destruction. But as the formulations employed here by Aristotle imply, the solution was less complete than it might have appeared to be. It gives us in fact, as principles, again wholes (the elements in their respective states of combination or separation) only parts of which always remain.

The obvious presupposition of the difficulty, as it was experienced by the first philosophers, is that the things for which the principles or causes must account are in motion (Physics A2 185a12–14, B3 194b16–23). The question had to be faced, then, of what is responsible for the motion. We have seen that the fourfold division of causes suggests that the being of a thing is to be distinguished from its matter. We must now note that it suggests in the same way that its matter is to be distinguished from what Aristotle calls the source of the beginning (principle) of (its) motion. Or, as he says now, to seek the latter is to seek "the other principle"—other, that is, than the material one. Aristotle knew, of course, that even some of those who posited but a single material principle thought that they had provided at the same time for motion by identifying, as that principle, one that is itself moving (Physics A2 184b15–18), just as he knew that wood, one of his examples here, has an internal principle of motion by his own scientific doctrine (Physics B1 192b8–23, 193b8–11). But the problem remains of understanding the necessity that draws the movement from what underlies it, that is, from the material principle proper. In the absence of that understanding, the latter would lose the intelligibility it was thought by the first philosophers to possess, precisely as a natural principle.

Rather than accept such a loss, therefore, some of those who spoke of one principle—indeed, the most demanding of them—were apparently willing to go so far as to deny motion to the principle, and therewith to the whole of nature. As can be seen, however, from the example of Parmenides, the greatest of these thinkers, the denial could not be sustained. Now, Parmenides was able to take cognizance of a cause of motion only insofar as he posited no longer one cause but two "somehow." Those who, from the outset, made the (material) causes more than one were all the more able, therefore, to give an account of motion. Yet Parmenides must have retained awareness keener than theirs of the less than fully satisfactory character of the account. We are reminded of that account, and thus of the problem linked to it, by what Aristotle says about Empedocles' use of the four elements, toward the end of the next chapter (A4). Immediately thereafter, he turns to a discussion of Leucippus and Democritus, who reduced the material principle—if one can put it this way—to its principle, fullness or solidity, and admitted as modifications (differentiae) of it only those that could affect it as such: shape, station, position. And he concludes his discussion of them there with the remark that they, too, left aside the question of how motion was to come to (such) beings, although—as is shown perhaps by their admission of the being of the void (On Generation and Corruption A8 325a23–31; compare Physics A3 186a16–18)—they were not quite so easy-going in this respect as were the others who did so.

A more widely felt ground of dissatisfaction with attempts to identify the source of motion with a material principle is discussed by Aristotle in a passage that intervenes between the two we have been considering. It is the putative insufficiency of principles of this sort for generating the nature of the beings, some of which are—while others come to be—in a good and fine condition. That fire (to which appeal had been made as a moving principle), for example, or earth, or another of the principles of this sort, is responsible for this is perhaps not plausible—nor that "they" (the first philosophers) thought so. Nor would it have been fine to entrust so great a thing to chance and luck. So when Anaxagoras or another said that there is mind in nature (as a whole)—just as in animals—which is responsible for its fine order, as well as for all of the arrangement, he appeared like one who is sober, as compared with his vainly speaking (or drunken) predecessors.

A4) What particularly struck Aristotle about those who held the opinion expressed by Anaxagoras is that they attempted to put together the cause of what is fine, as a principle of the beings, with the sort of cause that is the source of their motion. (We are treating here under A4 the last sentence or half-sentence of A3. The chapter divisions are unlikely to go back to Aristotle himself. We use them chiefly for ease of reference: to be free to move back and forth in the chapter under consideration without having to offer more precise indication of the place within it of the textual reference of each remark. On the other hand, we try to remain open to the possibility that whoever was responsible for the chapter divisions, and also the arrangement of books, had a grasp of the articulation of Aristotle's argument, and therefore an understanding of his intention, that is superior by far to ours.) And he suggests that Hesiod may have been the first to seek such a thing, along with anyone else who included eros or desire among the beings as a principle of them: Parmenides, for example. We note in passing, however, that according to the latter, unlike Hesiod, the emergence of eros is the result of contrivance on the part of someone or something (compare page 12 above).

Eros is surely not mind (Theogony 120–22), but it may be of such a nature as to aim at the good and yearn for it (compare Physics A9 192a16–19), and thus bring the good about. Why, then, does it remain necessary to distinguish between the causality of the good and that of what, as desire or deliberation, moves towards it (Physics B3 194b29–33)? It would "perhaps" be fine to say of Empedocles—who was first to divide the moving cause (so as to be able to account also for what is not fine and in order) and who was again first to speak of four material elements—that he was first to speak of the good as a principle.

That would in fact have been fine to say of him, if what is responsible for (bringing about) all of the good things is itself the good. But to put it this way is to put the cart before the horse. Movement towards the good is knowable as good from the end that it approaches. That end is then the principle in light of which any movement can be determined to be good, or indeed bad or indifferent. And, precisely as this principle, it is extrinsic to the movement proper or to its source, "lying over against" the latter as a distinct sort of cause (A3 beginning). When speaking in A3 of the putative insufficiency of the principles hitherto discussed to account for what, in the nature of the beings, is good and fine, Aristotle had given the impression (984b8–11; compare 984a16–19) that it would be necessary, for that purpose, to introduce another principle: the one "coming next" (after matter and the source of motion). Now, after the remark regarding Empedocles that we are considering, he says that "these"—a group that must include Empedocles, as well as Parmenides and Anaxagoras—had gone only so far as to grasp two of the causes which he distinguished in the Physics, matter and the source of motion, and even those only dimly and in no way clearly.

By way of elaboration, he speaks of the failure of Anaxagoras and Empedocles to make a proper use of mind, and love (philia) and strife, respectively. Anaxagoras had used mind only when he was at a loss for a necessary cause of what comes to be; and Empedocles had been unable to distinguish consistently between the motion for which love (as cause of the good things) and that for which strife (as cause of the bad ones) is responsible. At least the latter failure, if not also the former, may have to be traced to the fact which Aristotle's fourfold division of causes has already called, with the utmost restraint, to our attention: that motion and what is good must each be traced to principles proper to them and distinct from one another (compare A7 988b6–11). This much, the atomists to whom he devotes the last part of the chapter saw with sufficient clarity.

A5) "Among" these thinkers and "before" those already discussed, the so-called Pythagoreans, through their involvement with mathematics, came to the thought that the principles of these sciences are principles of all of the beings. Aristotle indicates that he does not follow a strictly chronological order (compare A6 beginning). Yet a departure from that order is not necessarily a sign that the thinkers he treats later than it would call for are superior, in his view, to those he chooses to treat before them (see the reading of ms.E at 987a10). It is more likely that in "the investigation (that he is conducting) now of the causes" he has proceeded in the way most suited for casting light on these.

The philosophers discussed hitherto have given him occasion to consider two sorts of causes (A4 end), that is, two of the four causes mentioned in the restatement (at the beginning of A3) of the fourfold division of the Physics. This means that he has not yet taken up the cause which the restatement placed first: the being (of a thing) and what it was (for the thing in question) to be—or what the listing in the Physics had called the form and the paradigm. In turning now to the Pythagoreans, all of whom held as principles what look, at least, like forms (the numbers or their elements—the even and the odd or the limited and the limitless—or also the other contraries), Aristotle thus appears to be preparing the ground for a consideration of this sort of cause. Yet, as it turns out, the Pythagoreans seem to have regarded the contraries, or the numbers, as material principles. Or, as Aristotle says more precisely of the first group of Pythagoreans he discusses, they "too" plainly held what they took as principle, namely number, to be so both as matter for the beings and (at the same time) as their characteristics and states.

We will try to grasp the bearing of this puzzling suggestion by returning to the philosophers to whom our attention is directed, at just this point, by the otherwise superfluous "too." They are those of the first philosophers who, as we heard in A3, thought that the sole principles of all things are the material ones: what the beings consist of, are generated from and, in perishing, return to. For those philosophers, who recognized no formal cause, must have taken their principles to supply the character of the beings, as well as their matter; just as the Pythagoreans in question took number to supply the matter of the beings, as well as their characteristics and states. Now, as we have seen, the philosophers could not have supposed material principles to supply what they wished them to supply, had they not made a distinction between what is unchanging in the being or nature of their principles and its changing characteristics (A3 983b9–10). Yet to admit this distinction at the level of the material principles themselves, is to set in motion what they looked to as the fixed source of all natural fixity or limits. Was it not to avoid exposing their principles to this danger that they had refused recognition to a formal cause, to begin with?

But the recognition of a formal cause—that is, one which is distinct from matter—would threaten to set in motion in this way not only matter but also the forms in matter that give to beings their characteristics and states and that, in doing so, become subject to changes within matter (A9 992b1–8), at least to the extent of becoming perishable. Thus the Pythagoreans, with their form-like principles, would have had a motive no less powerful than that of the philosophers—it is at bottom the same motive—for refusing to acknowledge a distinction that would expose their principles to this danger. And it is in this light, then, that we can perhaps understand the suggestion that they "too" attempted to make their principles do the double service of supplying both matter and form to the beings, as well as the bearing of the suggestion on the preparation of the ground for a consideration of the formal cause. In becoming aware of the resistance that a clear-cut recognition of that cause met with from seemingly opposed camps, we may begin to appreciate what the recognition of it entails.

That recognition was reserved for Plato. It is necessarily, as we have seen, at the same time the first full recognition of the character of the material cause or of the problem of "matter." (Compare A6 988a7–10.) The problem of matter, in turn, is at the same time the problem of being, or more precisely, of the transparency or intelligibility of being. But the latter problem presents itself also on the level of Pythagorean forms, that is, of forms that are taken to be beings in their own right (whether as separate from the perceptible things or not: compare A6 987b22–24, 27–28 and 29–31). To bring this out, Aristotle turns again to Parmenides, less now for his denial of motion in particular to (material) being (A3), than for his denial to being of plurality of any sort. For to admit plurality within being (as one does, for example, in making the contraries beings) is to run the risk of making of it an unintelligible mixture of being and non-being. Aristotle has explained the difficulty more clearly in the Physics (A3 186a32–b11), but without a comparable intimation of its gravity. And just as Parmenides was more rigorous on the plane of reasoning (the logos) than the Pythagoreans, he was more conscious than they were of the necessity of adhering to the phenomena or to what is in accord with sense perception. (Compare On the Heaven B13 293a23–27, which is perhaps the text alluded to on the occasion of the mention of their invention of the "counter-earth," as well as G7 306a16–17 in the same work.) In concluding this chapter, Aristotle refers to what is to be learned from his predecessors "and the others" (compare A4 end).

A6) He turned next to Plato, not simply to his thought but to his whole activity (pragmateia).

Since Plato had grasped the formal cause in its distinctness from matter, he had to consider the consequences of what he had come to see for the possibility of science. We spoke rather loosely earlier of the formal cause or of forms as "giving" character, or their characteristics and states, to the beings. More precisely put, that cause is the perceptible or intelligible character of a being, nothing more. Or better, the character insofar as it is shared by a class of beings. Or better still—since, as shared, character is expressible in speech through name and definition—it is the account (logos) of the character (A3 983a27–28 and Physics B3 194b26–27). Thus the formal cause tends to coincide with the "universal," whose importance for science we have to some extent already seen (A1–2). But if discovery of the universal, by Plato himself or by Socrates, laid bare the true foundation of science, then it exposed at the same time the fragility of its foundation, since the universals have no existence apart from the particulars (Z16 1040b26–27).

In this situation, Plato brought in the so-called "ideas" to complement—in fact, to replace—the universals (Z16 1040b30–34). Unlike the latter, the ideas or forms were said to be themselves particulars, that is, beings in their own right, separate from the perceptible things. According to what Aristotle says here, it was the practice of dialectics that led to their introduction, presumably through the discovery within perceptible being of what is not accessible to the senses (Theaetetus 186d2–5 and context). But it is obvious that that discovery could have been no more than a precondition for this step; and Aristotle acknowledges as much by failing to attribute the step either to the Pythagoreans or to Socrates. For the Pythagoreans had already begun to ask "what is" questions and to offer definitions (A5 toward the end). Yet, although they too made the "numbers" beings, they identified them with the things, rather than separating them—something they evidently saw no need to do. And Socrates, who was the first to set his mind on definitions, sought to grasp in or through them only the universals—whether because he did not concern himself with the whole of nature or for some other reason (compare M4 1078b27–30).

A7) Plato's activity, insofar as it consisted in bringing in the "ideas," was not entirely dissimilar to that of the Pythagoreans, which led to their invention of the "counter-earth" (A5 986a8 and context): in each case, the step taken was meant to dispose of a problem of which its author or authors were aware. But while Aristotle made this perfectly plain with regard to the Pythagoreans, he merely alluded to Plato's problem without bringing fully to light either its true dimensions or its root (A6 987a34). Paradoxical as this may seem, the reason may have to do with the gravity of the problem and with the fact that it preoccupied not only Plato but Aristotle himself. For in combating, throughout the Metaphysics and even elsewhere, the Platonic solution to it, Aristotle placed himself under the obligation of indicating the outlines, at least, of that genuine solution that he would put in the place of the Platonic one—assuming that it is in his possession. And if he hesitated for some reason to do this with complete openness (Z16 1040b34–1041a4), he would for the same reason have been reluctant to obtrude before readers who were not seeking it on their own the problem that requires the solution. But this is precisely what he would have done if, prior to attacking the ideas, he had brought fully to light the problem that they were meant to dispose of. Had he failed even to allude to that problem, on the other hand, he would have made the task that he sets for himself in the Metaphysics even more difficult to discern than it already is.

If, as we have supposed, Plato's introduction of the ideas or forms is evidence of the clarity with which he grasped the formal cause, the acceptance of them by his followers (in the usual sense of that term) is by no means evidence of their possessing the same clarity in its regard. And, at a certain point in this chapter, Aristotle ceases to speak of Plato himself, but rather of his followers, whom he calls here "those who posit the forms" (compare A6 988a2). This enables him to say that none of his predecessors has given a clear account of that cause—and therefore to conclude more generally, from his summary examination of their views (A3–6), not merely that they have proven unable to go beyond the causes which he distinguished in the Physics, but also that they grasp only dimly whatever they grasp of those. He seems to mean by this that they fail to grasp the causes in their distinctness from one another, which is, indeed, a necessary consequence of what he has stressed hitherto: their failure individually to take account of all of them (A5 987a10–12, for example). As if by way of illustration, he speaks at some length of the attempt to which he had alluded earlier (A3 end 984b20–22) to combine the final cause, or the good, with the source of motion. He mentions now also an attempt to combine the good with the formal cause. Was it not, more generally, such attempts at combination of causes that he had had in mind in raising the question (page 12 above) whether his predecessors had been able to discover a genus of cause different from those distinguished in the Physics? For, if Aristotle's predecessors fell short of him, it was less in this, that they had not taken into account all of the causes, than in the fact that, as a result, they were almost irresistibly led to ascribe more efficacy or transparency to those which they did recognize than was warranted. For to fail to grasp the causes in their distinctness from one another is to fail to grasp how modest a truly scientific account of causality must be. And from this we can begin to understand why an examination of the views of the scientists, as scientists, was necessary: that is, how Aristotle could have expected it to bear on the deeper difficulty that he had called to our attention.

A8) The examination, or a certain phase of it, has been brought to a close in A7. And this is confirmed in A10, where Aristotle, in repeating the general conclusion that he had drawn in A7, refers to that conclusion as what had become clear "from what has been said previously," that is, in the discussion preceding that of the intervening chapters (A8–9). More precisely, he refers to it as what had become clear "also" in that earlier discussion (993a13; compare 993a24–25). And we see indeed, from the very end of A7, where the discussion of these intervening chapters is introduced, that it is presented as a continuation of sorts of the examination of Aristotle's predecessors with regard to their understanding of the principles or causes. The same ground is to be gone over and the same thinkers, or most of them, are to be considered. We should not be surprised, then, if conclusions previously reached are confirmed in it and reaffirmed as a result of it. Yet it is only a sort of continuation. Aristotle indicates as much in the same introductory remark at the end of A7: let us consider . . . "after this." And in referring in A10 to what, though shown in the intervening chapters, had been made clear "also" previously, he implies that there is another portion of the contents of A8–9 of which this could not be said. Something new, then, was to have been brought out by going over once more the already ploughed ground—or, if not something new, something which had not yet been made clear.

Aristotle had begun his examination of his predecessors (in A3) with those philosophers who thought that principles in the form of matter are the sole principles of all things, and he had taken up first those among them who spoke of one such principle. In turning first to these same thinkers here, he characterizes them now as positing that "the all" is one and that it has as its matter some one nature which is bodily and possesses magnitude (compare A5 986b10–17). And the first of several criticisms that he now makes of them is this: that they posit the elements only of the bodies and not of those (beings) that are without body, although (as ms.E has it, with some support from Alexander) there are beings without body. Now, what Aristotle has criticized here is not merely the view of the elements or principles or causes taken by the thinkers in question, but also their view of what is comprised in "the all."

After making this criticism, he goes on to explain what the thinkers were doing, in the following terms: they were discoursing as natural scientists, or from the point of view of science, about "all things" and endeavoring, in particular, to give an account of the causes of generation and perishing. The explanation serves to introduce a criticism of the way in which they go about this. They do away with the cause responsible for motion (see A3). As a scientist, Aristotle criticizes the endeavor of scientists. It is no longer his purpose to challenge their view of "the all" or of "all things"; nor does his new task appear to require this of him.

It does appear to require each of the two further criticisms that he makes of them here: that neither "the being" (of a thing) nor (its) "what is" is posited by them as a cause of anything; and that, in their readiness to accept any of the simple bodies other than earth as their principle, they have failed to look into how these bodies—fire, water, earth, air—are generated from one another. For these two criticisms stand in a certain relation to one another. The acceptance of any of the simple bodies as principle of generation, other than earth, amounts to an attempt to understand all bodies, including the mature and complex, in terms of the smallest element in their composition. And Aristotle wonders whether this can be done. He raises the question whether that which is "later in generation" may not be "prior in nature"—but this is to question whether its character can be understood fully by recourse to the process leading up to it. Moreover, as he mentions in connection with his critique of Empedocles, to whom he turns immediately after the thinkers he is now dealing with, the generation of the four simple bodies from one another, which is something that we see, suggests that none of them—not fire (whose parts are smallest) nor earth (whose parts are largest)—remains always the same body. (Compare Physics A7–9.) And, if this is the case, what we have with each of these "elements" is nothing truly elemental but rather something that is perceived in the form of fire, for example, or something perceived in the form of earth: that is, what we cannot give an account of without recourse to the formal cause.

These additional indications of the inescapability of recourse to the formal cause, to the formal cause properly understood (see pages 18 bottom – 20 top, above), provide perhaps the key for understanding the treatment that is now accorded to Anaxagoras. For Aristotle turns to him here, as he had done also in A3, immediately after Empedocles. But he interprets him now in such a manner as to bring out also or especially what Anaxagoras "wished" to say. That is, after pointing out the absurdity of the doctrine that all things were originally mixed together—if that Anaxagorean teaching is taken literally—he goes on to suggest an interpretation of it which brings it close to "'what is now more clearly seen to be the case'—now, when the distinction of form and matter has been clearly recognized," as Ross puts it (see his note ad loc.). According to this interpretation, what it means for everything to have been mixed together is that it was not true to say anything of that being—to attribute to it any particular color or taste, for example, or another of the similars (shared characters)—for it was not even possible for it to be of any quality or quantity or character. These can be attributed truly only when particular forms are present to being; and this, in turn, appears to presuppose the existence or activity of what alone, according to Anaxagoras, is unmixed and pure: mind. What we heard of mind, though less intelligibly, in A3 is thus vindicated. Yet even with the properly interpreted Anaxagorean doctrine, we are, as Aristotle insists here, still in the domain of accounts of generation and perishing and motion. For it was for the being subject to these, and just about for this being alone, that the thinkers we have just been considering sought the principles and the causes.

To have a prospect of going beyond this domain, we must turn again to the so-called Pythagoreans (as Aristotle does in this chapter) and to those positing the ideas (as he will do in the next). The reconsideration of the two groups, from the new point of view, is introduced by the following remark. As for those whose theoretical endeavor concerns all of the beings, and who posit that some of them are accessible to sense perception but others are not, clearly they endeavor to look into both of these classes. Therefore, Aristotle continues, "one" would linger rather over what they say, finely or not finely, apropos of the investigation of the matters now before us. (Compare A5 986b12–13.) The Pythagoreans, for example, took their principles from beings not accessible to sense perception (for the objects of the mathematical arts apart from astronomy are without motion).

As it turns out, however, their whole conversation and activity concerns nature. That is, they use their principles and their causes to account for the generation of the heaven and for what happens with the parts of it, what they suffer and what they do. And in using the principles and the causes in this way, they proceed, according to Aristotle, as if they agree with the others, the natural scientists, that being (tò on) is just what is perceptible to the senses and what the so-called heaven encompasses. (Compare A3 beginning and Physics B3 beginning.) Moreover, although the causes and the principles that they speak of are sufficient for ascending to the higher of the beings—more than they are suitable for accounts concerning nature—Aristotle offers no suggestion as to how that ascent might be made. Instead, he makes a number of remarks about the impossibility of accounting on their basis for motion, for the characteristics of the simple bodies (such as fire or earth), and for the being and generation of those in the heaven.

It is sufficient, as Aristotle says at the beginning of the next chapter, to have touched on the Pythagoreans to this extent. Perhaps this is because the consideration of them here is but the prelude to an apparently much more important discussion to follow—of those who came under the influence of Plato's recourse, for causes, to beings imperceptible to the senses. Yet if we count the mention of Plato at our chapter's end, Anaxagoras emerges as the central figure treated in it. And Aristotle has referred not just once, in the course of that treatment, but twice to what Anaxagoras "wished" to (but did not) say. (Compare the otherwise similar treatment of Empedocles in A10.) Might not such silences as Aristotle thus points to be due to the audacity of the unexpressed or unacknowledged thought?

A9) As we have already heard, Plato too looked to intelligible rather than perceptible beings as causes. That is, he too looked to causes "sufficient for ascending to the higher of the beings." And Aristotle turns now to those who, following Plato's lead, posit the ideas. Yet he no longer complains, as he had of the Pythagoreans, that they use their causes merely to account for the being and the generation of "these beings here." Rather, he takes it for granted that it is for this purpose that recourse is had to the ideas. And the most pressing question that he finds to put in their regard is the following. What contribution do they make to the perceptible beings, to those which are always (compare Z16 end) or to those which come to be and perish—what contribution either to the existence of these beings or to a science that would account for them? For, as he suggests also in this context, wisdom seeks what is responsible for the beings manifest to us (compare On the Heaven G7 306a16–17). And the principal criticism, therefore, that he makes here of the recourse to the ideas, a criticism to which even those directed against the alleged proofs of their existence must take second place, is that it does nothing to further that search. To the contrary, it has had the result that philosophy, for those now professing to engage in it, has been reduced to mathematics and the whole investigation of nature has been done away with.

In making these uncompromising, not to say harsh, criticisms of "those who posit the ideas," Aristotle refers to them for the most part in the first person plural. He thus indicates that he makes his critique as a member, or former member, of the school. (Only later on, in a more or less word for word repetition of parts of this chapter [M4–5], is this use of the first person replaced by that of the third.) At the same time, he identifies in this way one typical addressee of his work, whom he invites to take the first steps in a development that he has undergone himself. He does so, moreover, as his prefatory remarks to it (B1 995b5) are drawing to a close, on the threshold of the main body of the Metaphysics. And all of this tends to confirm our impression that the critique of Plato or of Platonism occupies a significant place in the structure of the work as we have it. What, then, is its essential function there?

In attempting to answer this question, we will pay particular attention to what has taken place in the text since our earlier consideration of it (page 21 above). We have already drawn the conclusion—from what Aristotle said (A6 987a32–b7; compare M4 1078b12–17), together with what his argument (in A3–7) has shown—that it was a concern for science that must have prompted Plato to introduce the ideas. They were a response to a problem that he, or Socrates before him, had discerned in the foundation of science (whether a response meant truly to dispose of the problem or merely to call attention to it). And what may have come more fully to sight in the meantime is that very problem, in its full extent or dimensions. But if this is so, new light must have been cast as well on the way in which the ideas are supposed to have solved it.

What philosophy or science sought from its inception, as Aristotle has shown that to us, are the causes of the beings manifest to us, causes sufficient to account for these beings: for their coming to be, their existence as they are, and their perishing. In other words, what science sought—and sought in the expectation that they would be within the reach of our understanding—are the first causes of the beings (A3 beginning; compare A1 end). In the event, and for reasons that came somewhat haltingly to sight, it became necessary to modify, to moderate that expectation. This then seemed to entail that we modify as well what we take to be a truly scientific causal account. And since such an account had proven to be possible only within rather narrow limits, it followed that science would cease to be science in the moment that it stepped beyond those limits or, more generally, the limits of what can truly be known. But in the meantime we have been given reason to suspect that it does step beyond these limits. And we must therefore raise the question whether it is not, for some reason, compelled to do so.

Science can content itself with its rather modest causal accounts only so long as it can be confident, and reasonably so, that the causes it can grasp, or the causes to the extent that it can grasp them, cannot be overturned—in such a way as to invalidate its account of them—by the operation of more powerful causes of unknown origin. That is, it can be duly modest or cautious only if it can assume that "being is just what is perceptible to the senses and what the so-called heaven encompasses." And as we have seen, it does make this assumption. But with what right? And if the right or the justification is lacking, if the assumption in question is audacious in more than one way, does not science or philosophy come into a fatal contradiction with itself?

It was in this situation, then, if we have now followed correctly the somewhat involved indications of the text, that Plato is presented as having introduced the ideas (compare B2 997b6–7). He implies by doing so that an ascent to "the higher of the beings" need not be (dogmatically) excluded, if they are of the character that he ascribes to the ideas: if they are permanent or necessary, unchangeable, and intelligible to us. This is then the solution that Aristotle passes judgment on, a judgment that he expresses both by what he says of the ideas and by his silence in their regard or his refusal to consider them in this light. And this leaves him, as he embarks upon the delineation of his own path, with the task of vindicating his right to an assumption which, as his deed at least suggests, he shared with his fellow natural scientists.

A10) As we have already seen, Aristotle repeats in this last chapter of A the general conclusion that he had drawn in its 7th chapter about his predecessors. He is more open here than he had been in the earlier passage as to the fact that to grasp the causes only dimly, to fail to grasp them in their distinctness from one another, is in a manner to fail to grasp them at all. In other words, none of the causes had been fully grasped by the predecessors in question. By way of example, he speaks of the formal cause, making it clear now that this cause—that in virtue of which a thing is (what it is) or the thing itself—is the same as the definition (logos) of the thing. According to what he suggests here, the function of the formal cause was grasped, but imperfectly, by Empedocles. Not even the considerable latitude that Aristotle avails himself of in speaking of his teacher is sufficient to permit the mention of Plato in connection with an imperfect grasp of the formal cause (compare A7 988a34–b6).

At the very end of the chapter, he indicates that he wishes to return to these same matters, what might (still) perplex one in their regard. (Compare A7 988b20–21.) He has something further to say about them which may be of some help in regard to (other) perplexities to be mentioned later (in Book B).

a 1) Between Books A and B (these are common designations of the first and second books of an ancient Greek text), we find in the

Metaphysics, as it has come down to us, a very short Book a. The unusual designation of the book, together with its somewhat puzzling contents, prompted questions already in antiquity as to whether it was intended by Aristotle to be a part of the work and even as to whether it was written by him. As such questions can no longer be answered on the basis of extrinsic evidence, we are left with no alternative to examining the book ourselves to see whether what we are able to learn from it has any bearing on the argument of the larger work, as that argument has thus far come to sight. For prior to examining it, we cannot exclude the possibility that it has such a bearing and that its unusual designation was intended to suggest as much: that the argument of A is to be continued here, if on a somewhat different—whether lower or higher—level.

The book begins with a statement (in the editions of Christ and Ross) or a heading (in that of Jaeger, who relies here on the ancient commentators) to the effect that the theoretical pursuit of the truth is in one way difficult, in another easy. A sign of this is that, while no one is able to attain it, neither do they all miss it, but each says something about nature. The same point can be put also in this way: that the easiness of the pursuit is shown by the fact that the whole (matter) is grasped (the reading of ms.E at 993b6), its difficulty by the inability (of the very same thinkers who grasp the whole) to make clear a part. Still, through their grasp of the whole (matter) or of nature, they have laid the necessary basis for subsequent efforts, including Aristotle's own.

We have been considering from the outset what the Metaphysics may disclose of its author's thought, when it is read as his introduction to a philosophic science. We borrowed this term from the Topics (A2 101a27–28), where it is used in the plural. The term occurs now in the singular (according to the reading which should be preferred at 993b20, that of ms.Ab): "It is correct to call the philosophic science a theoretical one of the truth." Aristotle thus returns to the beginning of the chapter (and the book), where he referred to the endeavor he shares with his predecessors as "the theoretical (pursuit) about the truth." (Compare also 993b16–17.)

He had spoken of the truth twice before that in connection with what they, too, were doing. In turning to examine them as to their views on the question of principles and causes, he had described them as "having gone before us to the investigation of the beings and philosophized about the truth" (A3 983b1–3); and in preparing to summarize the results of that examination, he had referred to them as "having spoken about both the principles and the truth" (A7 988a18–20). In the counterparts here to those earlier statements, there is no longer any "and": as objective of the endeavor, he speaks of the truth alone or of what appears to be the same, nature. What, then, is meant here by "truth"?

Truth, one can say, is nothing other than being (tò on) in one of its meanings (D7, E2 and 4), perhaps its most authoritative meaning (Th10; compare E4): it is being, as known. If this understanding of truth seems impossible to reconcile with its place as the objective sought by a philosophic science, one can say that truth is being, as knowable—with the proviso that what is knowable may prove to be just what is, in some way, already known. (According to a suggestion made in this context, what the mind of our soul must bring itself to see are the aspects of things that are by nature the most manifest of all. But what is most manifest by nature is reached by beginning from what is manifest to us: A9 992b30–33, Z4 1029b3–12, Physics A1 184a16–23.) Now, following closely on the heels of the identification of truth (being, as known or knowable) as the objective of a philosophic science, is the remark that we do not know "the true" without the cause. Truth, then, or nature is being, as caused or insofar as it is caused.

This is the conclusion to which we are led by the course of his argument, but Aristotle does not himself pronounce it. And it is indeed not free from difficulty, as he begins to bring out with his very next remark to the effect that that, in virtue of which others are (or are something), is (or is that something) more than they are. For it follows from this that the cause responsible for things being true is itself what is most true, if in a new, let us say, a derivative sense of "true."

Now, what is responsible for things being true, in the original sense of "true," is what is responsible for their being, simply, for the fact that they are: they are true as known or knowable, but what is knowable is being, as caused. Let us consider first, then, the case of perishable beings. What is responsible for their being, for the fact that they are, is unable to sustain them in being (for they perish); and with their perishing, its being, as their cause, perishes too. One might even go so far as to say that its being, as cause, is conditioned on their being or caused by it, by the fact that they are, for as long as they are. And, as caused, its being a cause becomes something true also in the original sense of true: something knowable. But its truth in this sense too is only a perishable, an impermanent one. It is understandable, therefore, that Aristotle himself speaks here, not of the cause or causes of perishable beings, but of the principles of the beings that always are. It is those principles that are necessarily always most true, for there is no cause responsible for their being, but they are responsible for the being of the others. That is, as they are the preeminent beings, so are they also the preeminent truths—in the derivative sense. But are they knowable? And here we see perhaps another reason for the doubts that Aristotle had expressed in the latter portion of A9 as to the possibility of what some had asserted to be available: a science of all the beings, based on knowledge of their elements, elements not understood as the elements of perceptible being only (see especially 993a2–10).

a2) If what a philosophic science seeks is nature or truth, if truth is being insofar as it is known or knowable, but being is knowable insofar as it is caused—if, in short, we do not know the true without the cause, a philosophic science is possible only to the extent that the causes are knowable. Aristotle turns back, therefore, to the causes of perishable things which, as such, are themselves perishable. (Compare On the Heaven G7 306a9–11.) But if even perishable causes are to be knowable, they must be limited in number and not just in kind. Can perishable causes be limited in number?

According to what Aristotle suggests here, it is clear that they are. He seems to think in the first place of causes coincident in time with their effects. (Compare Posterior Analytics B12.) The matter, for example, of which such a thing as flesh is composed may consist of earth, which consists in turn of air, which consists of fire; but it is not possible for this to go on without stopping. The reason seems to be that there is some perceptible first matter—perceptible at least in its effects, as heat is perceptible in flesh—of which any perceptible being is composed. Nor with the source of the beginning of the motion—when, for example, a human being was moved by air that was being moved by the sun, which was being moved (as Empedocles might have suggested) by "strife"—is it possible that there is no limit (to this regress). For there to be any movement of moved beings at all, there must, it seems, be a first mover of that movement. The case is similar with the "for the sake of which" of actions: that it cannot go on without limit that walking, for example, is for the sake of health, this in turn for the sake of happiness, happiness for the sake of another end, and so on always, with each further end (of the same action—in this instance, walking) being for the sake of another one. And he closes this survey of the kinds of causes—of how it stands with each of them as to a limitation in number—with the bare assertion that the case is the same with the formal cause. That is, instead of indicating at this point how the limitation manifests itself also here, he explains more generally why there must be a first cause, if there is to be any cause at all. Or is the general explanation applicable strictly to the formal cause alone, and to the others in this strictest sense only insofar as they presuppose, all of them, the formal cause? (The partial repetition of the explanation, later on in the chapter, occurs in the context of a return to the case of the formal cause.) This question is left open for the time being.

Towards the end of the general explanation, Aristotle suggests that all of the terms belonging to a series with no beginning are intermediates, except for the last one, which he calls the "now" (term). He thus points to another way in which perishable causes, considered now not as coincident in time with their effects but as preceding them, would appear to be unlimited in number (for any given effect). And it seems to be the question of whether or not this is so, that he now takes up, if in a somewhat puzzling manner. He considers first and most extensively not the causes (in the "upward" direction) but their effects (in the "downward" one: for the meaning of the terms here, see On Generation and Corruption B11 338a8–9), as to whether they are unlimited in number. If they are, each effect (there being no last one) would be also a cause. For he assumes that there is a beginning to the series, a first cause, as if the necessity that there be such a beginning had been shown also for causes considered in this way, as one might have been led to believe that it had been shown for causes coincident with their effects in time.

As for the effects flowing from such a beginning, he asserts that it is not possible for them to go on without limit so that, for example, from fire comes water, from this earth, and so on always, some other kind of thing coming to be (from what precedes it). The reason that he gives is that something comes to be from another, in the relevant sense, in one of two ways: either as a man comes from a boy, or a knower from a learner, or as air comes from water and vice versa. But, in each of these cases, it is more evident that the "from which" ceases to be or to be what it was (the boy and the learner by undergoing transformation, the water or air by perishing) than that the resulting effect is not itself a cause of further effects, even of an endless series of them. Aristotle insists, however, that there are no such series here. The boy who has become a man and the learner who has become a knower do not become anything further, though of course the latter will one day lose his knowledge and the former will die. But separating these beings and whatever new being may emerge from their decay is the "in-between" that is constituted by (their being in) their own end or completion (compare B4 999b8–12). And as for water and air, which are not strictly speaking beings (Z16 1040b5–10), they turn back into one another, the perishing of each constituting at the same time the coming-to-be of the other. (See On Generation and Corruption B11 337a34–b3, 338a4–17, 338b14–19; but consider also 338a17–b5 in the light of 337b3–13.)

To this conclusion, he adds the remark ("at the same time . . .") that it would be impossible for the "first" to perish if it were everlasting, as the "fact" that coming-to-be is not unlimited in the "upward" direction (might lead one to suppose that it must be), and that it is necessary (therefore) that the "first," from whose perishing something has come to be, not be everlasting. And he thus supplies his own exclamation point to the doubts that his procedure will already have raised regarding the assumption of an "upward" limit to precedent causes: since a perishable cause, which will as such also have come into being, must have been preceded by another perishable cause (On Generation and Corruption A2 316b26–27, A3 317b16–17 and A5 322a5–6), and so on indefinitely.

Having completed in this way his treatment of precedent causes—as to whether or not they are limited in number—he returns to those coincident in time with their effects. (The return is as or even more quietly effected than his departure from their consideration had been.) More precisely, he returns only to the consideration of final and formal causes, which are thus paired here, as they had been treated one after the other also in the earlier survey. (Compare A3 beginning as well as Physics B3 beginning.) And, in addition to indicating now how a limitation as to number manifests itself with regard to the formal cause, he speaks of what the absence of limitation would mean in these two cases, in particular.

The final cause or the "for the sake of which" is indeed an end, such that the others are for the sake of it, while it is not for the sake of another one. If then there is no such end, "the for the sake of which" will not be; and this, according to what Aristotle asserts here, amounts to the removal of the "nature of the good" and the exclusion of mind from among the beings. But neither can the formal cause or the "what it was (for something) to be" be "led up" to another definition, which would presumably define an element of the original definition and thus come "before" it. For on this basis, there is always one that comes "more before," and where there is no first (term), nor therefore that which comes next (to the first), there is no later (term or definition) either. But what is done away with by the absence of limitation in this case is nothing less than science itself. For actual knowledge requires a descent to the particulars, to the actual beings (M10 1087a15–21, Categories 5 2a11–14, 34–b6). And how can the mind grasp these, in their unlimited multitude? It is necessary, therefore, that it grasp the matter in a moving being—that is, in the being that it grasps—as belonging to a certain class of beings, as some kind of thing. It is necessary in short that it grasp, in that particular matter, the formal cause. But nothing (the original reading of mss.E and J at 994b26) can be, that is, be something, by dint of a formal cause that is "led up" without limit (see also the reading of ms.J at 994b27 as well as Posterior Analytics A22 83a39–b8).

a3) It is especially this last chapter of Book a (a remark towards its end) that leads Ross to suggest "that the book, or fragment of a book, is an introduction not to metaphysics but to physics or to theoretical philosophy in general" (Vol. I, p. 213). According to the last part of the remark, what one must investigate first is this: what is nature? For it will thus become clear what the objects of natural science are and whether the theoretical pursuit of the causes and the principles belongs to one science or to more than one. Apropos of this part in particular, Ross observes that it "seems clearly to promise an immediate inquiry into the meaning of 'nature'"—a promise that he finds no subsequent book of the Metaphysics to have picked up on (Vol. I, p. 221). But even if what he suggests about the remainder of the work should prove in this point to be correct, the reason may well be that the question "what is nature?" has already been answered in it. Ross's earlier suggestion concedes, moreover, the suitability of Book a for serving as an introduction to a work devoted to "physics or to theoretical philosophy in general," devoted, that is, to what we call "philosophic science." And if Aristotle exercises, as we have already had occasion to note, a measure of reserve in the expression of his view of what nature is or what it does and does not consist of, the reason may be that he wishes to hold open the possibility, not of "metaphysics" (an unAristotelian term), but of theology as a science (E1 1026a18–23; compare A2 983a4–11). If theology is a science, it will, according to him, have as its objects beings that are separate (from perceptible being) and without motion (1026a15–16). And he adds in the context that it is necessary that all the causes be everlasting, but especially these; for they are causes of those of the divine beings which are manifest to us (1026a16–18). But is there any being (or cause) of this sort, alongside of or beyond the naturally constituted ones? If not, physics, the science of nature, would be the first science (1026a27–29).—All of the recent editors join Alexander in excising from the text the very last lines of the chapter, partly for the reason that they are repeated (not without notable changes) in B1. But the lines have a meaning in our chapter which they do not have in their other setting. It is here that the answer to the question that they raise (of whether the theoretical pursuit of the causes and the principles belongs to one science or to more than one) is made dependent on a prior answer to the question "what is nature?" Their repetition in B1 on the other hand (995b4–6), with its reference back to our passage, confirms that Book a belongs to the remarks that Aristotle regards as prefatory to the whole work and that it brings these remarks to their conclusion.

Our chapter has the primary function of considering a question that its predecessors have made it necessary to raise: to what extent can precision reasonably be demanded of a science of nature or of discourses concerning nature. And Aristotle suggests that our expectations, in this if not also other regards, are shaped by habit. It is the laws that make clear the power that habit is able to confer even on mythic and childish conceits.

B1) "It is necessary—(looking) toward the sought-after science—that we go through first the matters about which there is need to be perplexed first." With this sentence, which opens a chapter and a book of the text as we have it, Aristotle announces that he intends to make a new beginning to the work as a whole. But in what sense or respect is it new? He has been treating of perplexities for the greater portion of the first two books, as he has also acknowledged in part (A7 end, looking forward to A8–9; A10 end, looking forward to a1–2). And the matters that he now intends to take up, or to take up again, are in the first place those concerning which some have held divergent opinions: that is, opinions which differ from those that he has intimated, at least, or pointed to in the books that we have already considered. So, if he is compelled to return to those matters now, it can only be because—as the teacher that he also is—he cannot afford to assume that his intimations have been heeded or that the reasons for the opinions that they point to have been grasped. And what is genuinely new then is, in the first place, the reason that he now gives why a prior grappling with the perplexities in question, or indeed with all the difficulties simply, is needed. It is needed not merely for the identification of the bonds from which one must free oneself in order to reach a goal already clearly grasped, but also or rather for clarity as to the end or goal itself, what a philosophic science seeks.

The second chapter of Book A had brought the opening discussion of the work to a conclusion with the claim that the nature of the sought-for science had been stated, along with the target or goal that it and the whole pursuit, that is, philosophy (compare A3 984a28) needs to reach. The discussion that followed had then uncovered wave after wave of difficulties confronting philosophy as originally conceived (A3–6, A8–9, a1–2). It had thus suggested that the claim at the end of A2, which had appealed to that original conception (982b11 and following), was premature. Aristotle now acknowledges that it was, at the same time that he has indicated his intention of taking up the self-imposed task of showing that this is the case, or showing it again.

Insofar as the Metaphysics is Aristotle's introduction to a philosophic science, it is this task to which the remainder of the work is devoted. More adequately stated, the task to which it is devoted is that of showing what such a science seeks and of uncovering—is this the same as vindicating them?—the assumptions on which it actually rests. To carry out the task, he must indicate the revisions which each of the two models of a philosophic science presented in the opening discussion (as well as in his prefatory remarks more generally) would have to undergo in order to comply with its genuine requirements: philosophy as originally conceived, on the one hand, and a divine science (A2 983a4–11), on the other. But in the latter case he cannot point to the needed revisions so visibly and unambiguously as to jeopardize the survival of a "metaphysics" whose attractiveness offers the broad back on which the skeletal form of a philosophic science might have the prospect of riding into and through ages even less hospitable to philosophy than his own.—B1 then is given over to listing, B2–6 to elaborating the perplexities that are to be considered and presumably also, in subsequent parts of the work, resolved. By thus postponing the work of resolving them, Aristotle secures for himself in the meantime the prerogative of a judge, who is allowed and expected to listen impartially even to arguments that he would never have stooped to express in his own name.

What he calls the "first perplexity" is a question which (as he notes) had been mentioned, as requiring resolution, also in the prefatory remarks (a3 end): whether the theoretical pursuit of the causes belongs to one science or to many. Why is this perplexity the first? In the prefatory remarks, it had been linked to the question of the objects (or object) of natural science as, like that question, requiring for its answer the prior investigation of what nature is. Here in B1, it is linked rather to the question whether it belongs to the science (which makes a theoretical pursuit of the causes) to look into the first principles of being only or (to be concerned) also about the principles that all employ in demonstrations. But when this question is taken up for resolution in G3, Aristotle says that some of the natural scientists undertake to say something also about the principles of demonstration—adding that it is plausible for them to do so, since they alone intended their investigation to be both about the whole nature and about being. And although he suggests there that the investigation of these principles belongs more appropriately to one who stands still higher on the scale of knowing than the natural scientist, he justifies his appeal to such a knower by the remark that "nature is (only) some one genus of being" (1005a34). This, too, is an answer to the question "what is nature?" however much it may diverge from the answer to it that had been intimated earlier (A8 989b33–990a5).

The last question belonging to the first cluster of perplexities is whether there is one science of all the beings or more than one and, if more than one, whether they are all of the same genus or differ in rank. Immediately thereafter, moving on to the next cluster, Aristotle brings forward, from among the things necessary to search out, just this: whether one must say that only the beings perceptible to the senses are or also, beyond or alongside of them, others—that is, whether beings are (all) of one sort or there are more genera of them than one. By way of example (of non-perceptible being), he refers to the forms as well as to the "mathematicals," which are put (by some) between the forms and the beings perceptible to the senses. A third cluster then returns to questions concerning science: what it pertains to the theoretical pursuit about the beings to consider. But these are at the same time, of course, questions about being: for example, whether it is the genera which are the principles and the elements (of the beings) or rather the constituent parts into which each (of them) is divided.

The theme of being and its causes remains the focus as Aristotle turns, in the fourth cluster, to questions that one must devote in the highest degree not only one's searching, but also one's activity to. (Compare A5 986a8, A6 987a29–30, and pages 20–21 above.) They include the following: whether there is, besides matter, something that is of itself a cause, or not; and (if so) is it separable (from matter) or not; and whether there is something besides the whole spoken of whenever something is predicated of matter, or nothing—or (is this so) of some beings and not of others, and (if it is) which beings are they (such that there is something besides the whole that each is). We note that one of the alternatives thus pointed to is that of a cause, besides matter, which is not separable from matter (compare H1 1042a28–29). Aristotle asks here, in addition, whether the principles—both those in the speeches (logoi) and those in the substratum (what is underlying)—are limited in number or kind; and whether the principles of the perishable and imperishable beings are the same or different, that is, whether they are all imperishable or those of the perishable beings are themselves perishable. (Compare a1–2.) There is, in addition, the question that is the most difficult of all and has most perplexity: whether, as the

Pythagoreans (held) and Plato said, the one and being (tò on) is, not something different, but rather (the) being (ousia) of the beings (onta); or is this not the case, but rather something different is the substratum (of the one and being), as the natural scientists hold.

Among the perplexities that it is necessary to consider, Aristotle had mentioned at the outset of the chapter not only matters where some have held divergent opinions, but also anything, apart from those, that may happen to have been overlooked. And so he adds now, among others, the questions whether the principles are universals or on the level of the particularity of the things (see M10), and (whether they are) potential or actual (beings); in addition, whether the potentiality in question concerns motion or something else (see Th1). These, too, are according to him matters that may furnish much perplexity.

B2) At the end of B1, referring to all of the perplexities that he had listed there, Aristotle said that it is not only difficult to find a path to the truth about them, but not even easy to spell them out finely in speech. He had already alerted us to the fact that something of importance is to be learned from the perplexities themselves (995a33–b2). It is all the more necessary, then, to attend to the way or ways in which he articulates them.

For example, while he had asked in B1 whether the theoretical pursuit of the causes belongs to one science or to many, he asks now whether the theoretical pursuit of all the genera of causes belongs to one science or to more than one. As the sequel makes clear, the genera in question are the four sorts of causes that, drawing on the Physics (B3), he had distinguished in A3. He had then gone on, however, to consider whether there is some genus of cause different from those (A3 983b1–6, A7 988a18–23, A10 993a11–15). In other words, it had been a question whether "all the genera of causes" comprise just those four. And even if that question has been answered in the meantime (A7, A10), he did not make it clear until now that, in asking whether the theoretical pursuit of the causes belongs to more than one science (as he did not only in B1, but also in a3), he presupposes the validity of that answer. Perhaps, then, he did not presuppose it hitherto. But a question of which that answer is a presupposition will be a different, a narrower question than an apparently identical one of which it was not a presupposition. And what is to be learned from perplexity in its regard can be expected to vary in accord with this difference.

The chief reason why the question in its new form must be asked is suggested by something that Aristotle only now brings to our attention: to many of the beings not all of the sorts of causes or principles are present. The beings that lack motion—for example, the subjects of mathematical demonstrations (which, however, may not be beings in their own right)—are obviously unaffected by the cause designated here as a "beginning (principle) of motion" or even by the nature of the good. The good is a cause by being an end for the sake of which "the others" both come to be and are. But the "others" in question are actions and not, as had been suggested earlier (A3 983a31–32), coming-to-be more generally or all motion or change. For the understanding of the latter, and therewith in the final analysis also of actions (see also Physics Th2 253a7–20), we must have recourse to the beginning (principle) of the motion, not to mention matter (compare Physics B7 198a14–21, as well as Posterior Analytics B11 94a20–23) which, as the matter of perceptible beings, is itself in motion. Because therefore the science that we seek is a science of only some of the beings (A8 988b22–27, 989b21–27, 989b33–990a5), namely of those that are in every respect beings or beings in their own right, it may also be a science of only some of the causes. In other words, there may be more than one science of the causes, if not necessarily a different science for every different principle.

That it is this that distinguishes the science we seek and makes its possessor the preeminent knower of the thing we seek to know, this and not any difference in rank intrinsic to the causes themselves, Aristotle indicates by the suggestion which he now makes for the case of a being (an artifact) to which all of the sorts of causes are present: if there is indeed a different science for every principle, each of them has reason in that case to be called wisdom. What this suggestion portends for the scientific significance of the formal cause in particular—on whose preeminence in knowability Aristotle emphatically insists here—is not yet clear. But we have come a long way from the point at which a simple coincidence of causality and knowability could appear (at least) to be assumed, as is underlined by the reference in this context to the earlier passage in question (A2 982a4–b10, especially a30–b2; compare page 9 above).

The last question considered in the chapter is taken out of order: whether one must say that the beings perceptible to the senses are the only ones or also, beyond or alongside of them, others—that is, whether beings are (all) of one sort or there happen to be more genera of them than one. Or rather, given the substantive connection of the question placed here ahead of it with the preceding question or questions, we might say with better right that our question was taken out of order in B1. There is presumably no longer any need to make it follow immediately on the question whether there is one science of all the beings or more than one, since the further question that had been coupled to that question in B1 (whether, if they are more than one, they are all of the same genus or differ in rank) is now absent.—The consideration of the question to which we have turned entails, as B1 has already indicated, that of this further one: whether the forms are causes and beings in their own right, as well as what are called here "the intermediates." The latter were called in B1 "the mathematicals," and Aristotle says now that those who speak of them (as beings) say that they are what the mathematical sciences are about. But it is a question here whether what the mathematical sciences are about is rightly conceived of in this way.

It is astronomy—of these sciences, the one most akin to philosophy (L8 1073b4–5; compare A8 989b32–33)—that is of greatest interest to Aristotle in this connection. What astronomy is "about" is of course this (perceptible) heaven here. (The reading of ms.Ab at 997b35 must be accepted against the combined testimony of mss.E and J and Alexander: it is confirmed by 997b15–23, which draw the parallel with what optics and the mathematical harmonics are "about.") As is brought out more than once in our passage, there is no heaven besides the perceptible one for it to be about. Yet, while astronomy is about the perceptible magnitudes that comprise the heaven (for example, the stars), it is not "of" them: the arguments or demonstrations that it makes are not of them (of the stars, for example, which they reduce to points) or their movements. The movements and spirals of the heaven lack the regularity of those treated by astronomy (they are not "homoiai," the reading of mss.E and J at 998a5: compare A6 987b17 and context), just as perceptible lines have neither the straightness nor the curvature of those treated by geometry. And it is presumably this difficulty, which comes to sight in connection with the mathematical sciences and which Aristotle is here at pains to articulate, that gives rise to the question (that, as he admits, might perplex one in their regard) of which or what sort of beings they are about.

If the thread that we have been following has not misled us, the passage that intervenes between the one we just discussed and the one we discussed first, which opened the chapter, must provide some sort of bridge between the two. The first of the several questions that it takes up concerns the principles of demonstration or axioms, the common opinions which all use in demonstrating anything. As it is first put here, the question is whether it belongs to one science or to more than one (to be concerned) about them. But this variant proves to be but a way of approaching the question as it was posed in B1: whether there is one science of these principles as well as being or a different one. For all sciences, so far as they are demonstrative, use the axioms—which means that the latter are not derivable from subject matter specific to any of them, including that which knows the beings. But are they not derivable from being itself (as G3 1005a27–b1 could appear to suggest) and, for that reason, within the province of a science of the beings? A consideration of what it would require to demonstrate them is sufficient to cast doubt (on that suggestion). A demonstration of the axioms as properties of any genus of substratum whatsoever would have to employ, and thus presuppose the validity of, at least some of them. This is not necessarily to deny that it belongs to philosophy especially, to a philosophic science, to pursue in some way the question of the truth or falsity of these most universal principles of all things.

The discussion of the next question—whether there is one science of all the beings or more than one—proves to be an occasion for considering further the relationship of a science that demonstrates (the properties) that accrue to some genus of beings and a "science" of the common opinions (as the axioms are again called here) that the first must use in its demonstrations. It is less a question of whether they are two sciences or one, than of how such heterogeneous components (as are here seen to belong to any science as such) comprise a genuine whole.

The consideration of the third and last question in this series exposes another aspect of the problem. If the theoretical pursuit of the beings is concerned also with (the properties) that accrue to them—and how can it fail to be concerned with this?—it must somehow combine demonstrative knowledge (of the properties) with knowledge of the being of the beings in question, of their "what" or definition, which does not seem to admit of demonstration. As in the passage with which the chapter closes, Aristotle uses here mathematical examples. But he does not yet go so far as to question whether "the solid," of which mathematics demonstrates the properties, is a genuine being.

B3) The words with which the chapter begins (peri te toutōn oun) are the same as those with which the enumeration of the third cluster of perplexities had begun in B1; and the perplexity to which it is devoted belonged there to that cluster, as its last member. One (but not all) of the perplexities that preceded it within the cluster has been treated in the meantime in B2. The third cluster as a whole had followed (in B1) a second "cluster" that consisted of the question whether one must say that only the beings perceptible to the senses are or also, beyond or alongside of them, others—that is, whether beings are (all) of one sort or there are more genera of them than one. That question was the last one taken up in B2, where its treatment resumed or continued a consideration of the scientific role and significance of the formal cause. The question to be taken up now has thus been brought into close proximity to that fundamental consideration (see M1–3).

It is a question concerning the principles: whether one must hold the genera to be elements and principles (of the beings) or rather the constituent parts from which, in the first place (reading "prōton" at 998a23 with the mss.), each (being) is. On the one hand, the elements from which the beings were and are composed seem to be also their principles—the elements and not the genera of the beings: for example, the elements (one or more) of bodies, to which the natural scientists have recourse. And accordingly one becomes familiar with the nature of any of the other things too (artifacts), if one is willing to observe its nature, that is, the parts from which it was composed and their mutual arrangement. On the other hand, to the extent that it is through their definitions that we become familiar with each of the things, and the genera are principles of those definitions, they are of necessity principles also of what is defined (or definable). And if to take hold of scientific knowledge of the beings is to take hold of (scientific knowledge) of the forms in terms of which the beings are (able to be) spoken of, (one approaches the same or a similar conclusion) since, of the forms at any rate, the genera are principles.

We thus come to opposite conclusions about the principles, depending on whether we start from the beings themselves and their parts or elements or from the knowledge of the beings that is implicit in what we say about them. But this is to admit that we are in an impossible position. The principles with which we are concerned are the principles of the beings, and scientific knowledge must be knowledge of the beings through their principles. Nor can one speak of the principles in both ways. There is (only) one account (logos) of the being (of anything); and a definition (that proceeds) through the genera will be different from one that speaks of the constituent parts from which (something) is (compare the last portion, 206c7 and following, of the Theaetetus).

At the outset of the chapter Aristotle had intimated that, if they are to be held to be principles of the beings, the genera would have to be held also to be their elements. Or, as he says more plainly towards its end, a principle—that is to say, a cause—must be (something) besides the things of which it is the principle and be capable of being (even if) separated from them. Now, the second half of the chapter is devoted to the treatment of a secondary question—more a matter of dispute than a genuine perplexity (compare B2 996b26–27)—that had been appended to its primary question also in B1: on the assumption that the genera are indeed principles, is it the first or highest of them which one must recognize as such or the very last (genera or species) predicated of "the indivisibles" (here, the individual beings or things)? And what emerges in the course of the discussion of this question as the criterion for disposing of it, is the capacity respectively of the one sort of class to be something besides the individual species or of the other to be something besides the individuals, simply, the particular beings or things (compare B1 995b30–31). In the spirit of a new beginning that seeks to take firm possession even or precisely of ground—like what pertains to the formal cause—that may already have been won, Aristotle does not here exclude that a universal is something besides, indeed separable from, the particular of which it is predicated, although he points to the question of whether there is any basis on which one could hold this to be the case.

B4) The perplexity taken up next had been brought up in B1, too, immediately after that or those to which B3 is devoted; but Aristotle stresses now its connection with what preceded it. And he adds the comment that it is most difficult of all perplexities and most necessary to pursue theoretically. In introducing it in B1, he had said merely, of it and the other questions belonging to its cluster, that one must devote to them, in the highest degree, not only one's searching but also one's activity (see page 40 above). The designation "the most difficult of all," that is, "having most perplexity," was used, later on in B1, of another member of the same cluster: having introduced the cluster as he did, Aristotle could not well have spoken there of the necessity to pursue any of its questions (to the end) theoretically. It is when he comes to that question again, later on in B4, that he says that it is the most difficult of all to pursue theoretically and most necessary (to pursue) for knowing what is true. There remains then only the awkwardness that this cannot be said, as it appears to be said in B4, of two distinct perplexities at once: the one or ones at the beginning of the chapter and the one taken up later on, to which the label "the most difficult of all" had been applied already in B1. The awkwardness would be removed if the apparently distinct perplexities should prove to be the same, or if the perplexity before which the argument has now come to a stand should prove to be capable of presenting itself in a number of different guises.

As it is put near the beginning of B4, and as it was put also in B1, the question is whether there is something besides the (particular) whole (spoken of) whenever something is predicated of (some) matter (compare B1 995b34–35). In B1 Aristotle had in this context asked first whether there is, besides matter, something that is of itself a cause; and he had not excluded there that such a cause, though "besides" matter, is inseparable from it. But according to a suggestion that he has made in the meantime (in B3), a principle or cause must be not only besides the things of which it is the principle, but also capable of being separated from them. Perhaps this is the reason why he begins here with the question whether there is something besides the particulars: that is, besides the wholes that are spoken of whenever something is predicated of matter. Yet it would be more precise to say that he begins now with the question of how it is possible—if there is not something besides the particulars and they are limitless (in multitude)—to get hold of scientific knowledge of those limitless (multitudes); for (it is) to the extent that (there is) something one and the same and to the extent that some universal is present that we become familiar with all things. The intervening argument has indeed alluded (in B2) to a further reason for regarding the formal cause as in a manner separate from the particulars it helps us to understand (compare pages 43–44 above with page 20) but, in doing so, has only strengthened our inclination to doubt that it is a cause, in the usual sense of bearing responsibility for the coming into being of the particulars as they are or for their persistence in being.

In posing this question of how it is possible to get hold of scientific knowledge of the particulars, that is, of the beings, Aristotle traces our familiarity with them to "something one and the same" and to the presence of "some universal." Does he mean to suggest that a universal should be understood as "something one and the same," that is, as itself a particular? (Compare 999b33–1000a1.) We recall that in the latter portion of B3 he had appeared to us to leave open that a universal (or a genus or species, in virtue of its universality) might be something besides and even separable from the particular of which it is predicated. But looking back to that passage now, he suggests, on the basis of the perplexities spelled out there, that this is impossible: that the genera, whether the very last (the species) or the first, should be, besides the particulars. And to his formulation of the condition of possibility (for the acquisition of scientific knowledge) that he has mentioned here—that there must be something besides the particulars—he objects therefore that, if this is necessary, it would be necessary for the genera to be, besides the particulars.

If the quest for scientific knowledge is not to be abandoned then, another foundation for such knowledge must be sought. Yet rather than point to one, or before doing so, Aristotle asks a question that presupposes the availability of the foundation whose impossibility he has just insisted upon. Not content with mere supposition, moreover, he proceeds to argue for its availability, having first called that again into question only in order, it seems, to have the opportunity to make the arguments that he does. They begin with a review of the consequences that would flow from its not being available.

He says that if there is nothing besides the particulars, nothing would be accessible to mind but all things (merely) to sense perception; and (there would be) scientific knowledge of nothing, unless someone asserts that sense perception is scientific knowledge. Here, however, someone might assert this: that sense perception supplies scientific knowledge (compare Theaetetus 186e9–10 with 151e2–3) or at least a fundamental ingredient of it (Posterior Analytics B19 99b35–100b5); just as one might deny that particulars are inaccessible to mind (Nicomachean Ethics Z11 1143a25–29), even if its grasp of them—in this, too, it is not easily distinguished from sense perception—is completed only when they are no longer grasped merely as particulars (compare M10 1087a19–21 as well as Posterior Analytics B19 100a15–b1). In addition, (if there is nothing besides the particulars) he says (there would be) nothing everlasting or without motion (see page 37 above); for, as he also says now (compare A9 991a9–10), all of the beings accessible to sense perception perish (see B2 997b17). This follows indeed from what he adds—that they are in motion—if, as he says in the course of the next argument, the third, no motion is limitless or without an end. In the meantime, he has completed the second argument by objecting that, if there is nothing everlasting, (it would) not be possible even for generation (coming-into-being) to be. But to this one might respond that the fact appealed to is more evident than the condition alleged for it. Moreover, in turning to that fact in the third argument and to what may (or may not) be necessary to conclude from it, that is, by starting there from the fact of generation as well as movement rather than from its alleged condition, Aristotle appears to grant the validity of this response. And his representation in the fourth argument of the (everlasting) existence of (some) ungenerated matter as a mere supposition, is consistent with the conclusion that he did draw in the third, to say nothing of what he had already indicated in a2. (Compare also On Generation and Corruption A3 318a23–27 with 317b33–318a2 and a9–10.)—Among what appear to be counter-arguments following on this attempt to establish the existence of something besides the (particular) whole or, more precisely, the existence besides it of "the shape and the form" (compare D8 1017b23–26), there is the following remark. It is absurd (to think) that there is a single "being" (ousia) of, for example, all human beings; for then all beings whose "being" is one (will be) not one, but rather many and different (the reading of the mss. at 999b21–22); but this too (to think that those beings are simply different) is unreasonable.

* * * *

"In addition, concerning the principles, one might be perplexed also about this. . . ." Aristotle is apparently still following here the order of B1, at least roughly: both Ross and Jaeger refer us at this point to 996a1–2. But the question asked there was whether the principles, both those in the speeches and those in the substratum, are limited in number or kind. We took this to be the question about the causes that was treated originally in a2 (see especially 994a1–11, b16–27 and 27–31): whether for each being (or coming-to-be) there is an unlimited and hence unknowable multiplicity of causes, of any kind, or of kinds of causes. And the question taken up here in B4 concerns rather the sort of oneness to be ascribed to each of the (causes or) principles. Indeed, the introduction to it—"one might be perplexed also"—appears designed to prepare us to hear a question that has not been raised before (compare B6 beginning). Recalling therefore the distinction drawn in B1 between perplexities where some have held divergent opinions (from those already intimated by Aristotle) and others which may happen to have been overlooked, we are not altogether surprised to find a more promising antecedent of the one treated in this place in B4 among those listed in the latter part of B1, where (we take it) Aristotle has turned to perplexities of the latter sort (996a9–12 and following). It is true that the question which we have particularly in mind there (996a9–10) is taken up explicitly in B6 (1003a5–17), as Ross and Jaeger again indicate, and (in Beta at least) only there. But the treatment of the question taken up now in B4 helps to prepare us for that later discussion. And by inducing us through his imitation of the order of B1 to look first to the question treated in a2 as its antecedent, Aristotle calls our attention to that question as one that he will <u>not</u> treat here: that is, he gives some indication of what he refrains from discussing in a context in which searching has been emancipated from "activity" (see pages 47–48 above).

In the wake, then, of the attempt that we have considered to establish such a foundation for scientific knowledge as would consist in the existence of something besides the particulars, the question that Aristotle does take up is whether the principles are one (only) in kind—in which case, there would be nothing one in number, not even the one itself and being (tò on). Or are they one in number and is each of the principles (just) one? He explains what he means, by reference to the beings accessible to sense perception. In their case, as he thereby indicates, the question does not arise: the principles responsible for the many similar beings, beings which are the same only in kind, are themselves the same in kind but numerically different (compare L5 1071a20–24).—Which are the beings, then, as to which one must wonder whether their principles are one not just in kind? (Compare Physics A9 192a34–b2.)—According to Aristotle, each of the alternatives he has mentioned entails an unacceptable consequence. If the principles are one merely in kind, how will there be a scientific knowing of the beings, which requires (as he appears to suggest here) that there be a "one on (or over) all" (hen epi pantōn) that is itself something (ti)? If, on the other hand, the principles of the beings are one numerically, there will be nothing besides the elements (as he calls the principles in this context—see page 46 above). For to say "numerically one" differs in no way from saying "particular": that is what we mean by "a particular"—what is numerically one—but by "(a) universal", what is on (or over) those (particulars). In this concluding formulation, it is no longer clear that (the) universal (or "one on or over all") is taken to be itself something.

* * * *

Aristotle turns next to a perplexity which is not less (of a perplexity) than any, although there may be no necessity, still less the greatest, to pursue it theoretically. It has accordingly been neglected both by those now and those formerly (who have looked into such matters), though not by Aristotle himself, who has not only mentioned it in this place in B1 (996a1–4) but treated it in the same context, if somewhat allusively, in a1 (993b23–31). But in the meantime the question which this one followed in B1 and to which the consideration of it was linked in a1–2 (see pages 31–32 above) has been replaced by another one. We must try to see, then, how it looks now: in the light cast by the consideration of whether each of the principles is one numerically or only in kind.

It is the question as to whether the principles of the perishable beings and those of the imperishable ones are the same or different. It has as its presupposition therefore the existence of imperishable beings (compare a1 993b28). The presupposition is denied however by the man who figures most extensively in the discussion of the question and who can be taken to represent the view of the philosophers (compare 1001a12–13), as distinct from that of the theologians (who are considered as well). Empedocles does not make some of the beings perishable and others imperishable, but all except the elements perishable. And only to this extent (the reading of mss.EJ at 1000b18; compare 1000a24–26) does his speech retain consistency with itself, according to Aristotle: of perishable beings, are even the elements or principles imperishable? We stumbled across this aspect of the question in our consideration of a1; it was then explicitly included in the formulation of the question in B1 (996a3–4); and it comes up again as the question is discussed here, where the alternative that the principles of perishable beings are themselves perishable is rather quickly dismissed as entailing an impossibility. Yet if the particulars are all accessible to sense perception (999b1–2) and the beings accessible to sense perception all perish (999b4–5), what follows for principles which are one only in kind, as those of the beings accessible to sense perception are (999b28–31)? As numerically different—that is, as particulars themselves (see 999b33–1000a1)—must they not be perishable? The difficulty expressed by Aristotle in the form of a question remains then: how will there be perishable beings (or the perishable beings), if their principles will be done away with? And the earlier portion of the discussion may already have pointed to it.

To the circle around Hesiod and to the other theologians, as well as to Empedocles, one of those who speak on the basis of demonstration, Aristotle had put the question of how it is—if the principles are the same—that some of the beings are perishable and others imperishable, and through what cause (this occurs). According to the theologians, gods are the principles; but there are also gods that have been generated from gods (that is, from the principles); and whatsoever (coming from the principles) does not partake of "nectar and ambrosia" becomes mortal. Thus, from the same principles, come both mortal and immortal beings—the division between them being effected by an additional principle or cause, through its absence or presence. Of this cause, we are told by the theologians only the name or names, which mean nothing to us. Aristotle also makes this objection: if the absence of the cause is sufficient to account for the mortality of the perishable beings, its presence cannot render others everlasting, others whose very dependence on it shows that they are, in themselves, perishable.

As for Empedocles, he was as little able as the theologians to identify a cause of generation and being that would not also, for the same beings, bring about their destruction (compare 1000b25–26)—not by its absence, as he saw it, but by continuing to act as it does. Recognizing this therefore (despite what he said), he not only refrained from any attempt to provide for imperishable beings; he also introduced a second principle, a "destructive" one, to temper the action of his "productive" principle (compare A4 985a29–31). Only through their cooperation, as he saw it, are "the things" (that is, the world as we know it) possible. But that cooperation is in fact a productive tension that prevails only when, and so long as, neither of its elements is simply dominant, as each is in turn. One might suppose, then, that at least the periodic return of order is necessary, and Empedocles himself suggested as much. As Aristotle notes, however, he failed to make clear a cause (or ground) for that necessity. (Compare Physics Th1 252a5–10 and 19–32; compare also A3 984b8–19 above in the light of 984a8–13, and On the Heaven G2 301a4–11.)

* * * *

Having treated the questions whether the principles of perishable beings are themselves perishable (compare On the Heaven G7 306a9–11) and whether the principles of the beings are one numerically or only in kind, Aristotle returns now to the matter that is, as he puts it here, most difficult of all to pursue theoretically and most necessary (to pursue) for knowing what is true. As we learned from its first treatment in the chapter, it is or entails the question of whether there is anything besides the particulars.

If the principles are one merely in kind, Aristotle has said, there would be nothing (of the sort) one in number, not even the one itself and being (tò on). He asks now whether being and the one—each of them without (also) being something different, that is, without having another underlying nature—are "beings" (ousiai) of the beings (ta onta). To ask this, however, is to ask whether the nature of being and the one—what "to be" (tò einai) is for the one and being—is itself the being (hē ousia). Or it is to ask whether one itself and being is something (ti), something whose "being" (ousia) is just that—the one and being—since there is nothing more universal to predicate (of it or them). The suggestion that this is the case, which Aristotle traces here to Plato as well as to the Pythagoreans (compare A6 987b22–24 in the light of 987a29–30), is paradoxical in holding that the "being" (ousia) of the beings (ta onta) is in its own right a being (ousia)—but compare D8!

The alternative approach is taken by the natural scientists, who like Empedocles lead their inquiry into more familiar ground and say what the one (or the one being) is. (Compare Z16 1040b19–21 and context.) And various suggestions were made on this score. But their different authors have in common the necessity they are under to make the one and being as numerous as the elements or principles that they identify as the source from which the beings (ta onta) have been generated and are. The reason is that they must make those principles account also for the oneness of each of the beings (compare 1001b6); and this is indeed the difficulty with their approach. But it is a difficulty that will have to be faced, if the position of their opponents should prove to be untenable.

Turning therefore to the examination of that position, Aristotle considers what would follow from its acceptance or rejection. If someone will not posit that the one and being is some being (ousia)—that is, if he will not posit that one itself and being itself is something (ti)—he can hardly posit that any of the other universals is, on the ground of its universality, something (ti) besides the so-called particulars. In addition, if the one is not a being (ousia), it is clear that number, too, would not exist as some nature separated (from or among) the (other) beings (ta onta). But, on the other hand, if being itself and one itself will be something (ti), there is this considerable perplexity: how will there be, besides them, anything different or how will the beings (ta onta) be more than one? The Parmenidean argument would necessarily follow, since what is different from being (tò on) is not. And there is the same perplexity for number and the one as for being. If one itself is something (ti)—since there will be, besides the one itself, no other one—it is impossible for number to be a being (ousia). But here there is difficulty both ways: for the reason already given, it is impossible for number to be a being (ousia) also in the case that the one is not a being (ousia).

Aristotle concludes the discussion and the chapter by taking up an objection of Zeno to the existence of the one itself. Although he suggests that Zeno (who held that being is magnitude and therefore bodily) pursued the question in a vulgar manner, he concedes that magnitude cannot be derived from the one itself or, more generally, from such principles as are alleged to account for number.

B5) It has become clear from B4 that number cannot be a being (ousia), whether or not the one itself is a being (ousia). Yet it appeared to be the case that, so long as being (tò on) is not something (ti), the so-called particulars (1001a23–24) can be, or the beings (ta onta) can be more than one. But now Aristotle says, taking up a related question, that if the numbers (and their kin) are not beings (ousiai)—as the argument of B4 as well as the additional considerations brought forward in the latter part of this chapter force us to conclude—what being (tò on) is escapes us, along with the "beings" (ousiai)—or the "being" (ousia)—of the beings (ta onta). Indeed, it becomes questionable whether one can properly speak of "being" (ousia) or being (on)—or, therefore, of beings (onta). It is to be noted here that Aristotle has as little use in this chapter as he had had in B4 for any "being" of the beings that is not itself some being (on ti; ousia tis) or, in other words, some "this" (tode ti).

In mentioning in B1 the question that he takes up here, he had listed (together with the numbers) the lengths, the figures and the points. Here he lists (together with them) the bodies, the planes and the points. And the difficulty that he points to can be provisionally said to be that of what (a) body is. (Compare A9 992a4–6, as well as On Generation and Corruption A5 320b23.) The question that he asks about the numbers and their kin had been included, at the end of B1, among those previously overlooked (consider 996a9 and following in the light of 995a24–27), although one could well say, on the basis of earlier discussions of Plato and the Pythagoreans, that it had already been considered. But the function that its consideration serves here, that is, the difficulty that this consideration of it is made to point to, is certainly new. The question is taken out of order—it is the first of the questions from the end of B1 to be considered (but compare pages 51–52 above)—in view of its connection with the perplexities that have immediately preceded it. In considering whether there is anything besides the particulars (as we were in one way or another called upon to do throughout our study of B4), we assumed and even took for granted that we knew them at least: as beings (onta) in the primary and least contestable sense of the term. That assumption is in need of questioning, however, and Aristotle has grasped the first opportunity available to him, after the completion of B4, to place it on the agenda for future scrutiny.

B6) The chapter begins in a manner reminiscent of that in which the second section of B4 (999b24–1000a4) had begun and, under the guise of a new question, it renews the consideration of the question to which the earlier passage was devoted. That question, in turn, had reminded us of a question that was mentioned in the latter part of B1 (996a9–10); and this is the question taken up explicitly in the last part of our chapter, where its treatment completes the delineation of a problem for scientific knowledge that had been raised not later than the first section of B4. That is, the last section of B6 (which is also the last of Beta) returns to the authentic question of the first section of B4 (see pages 48–49 above)—a question which, despite its importance for the argument of the Metaphysics as a whole, has been allowed since then to remain for the most part in the background—and sketches the beginning of an answer to it. And the opening section of the chapter, together with its predecessor (the second section of B4), forms part of the preparation required for the proper appreciation of that beginning.

The authentic question of the first section of B4, the problem raised there, is that of how it is possible—if there is not something besides the particulars and they are limitless (in multitude)—to get hold of scientific knowledge of those limitless (multitudes). The assumption underlying the question is that we become familiar with all things to the extent that there is something one and the same or that some universal is present to them (compare a2 994b20–23): what remained uncertain was whether a universal is to be understood as "something" one and the same, that is, as itself a particular. That assumption as to the condition for a scientific knowing of the beings, accompanied still by the uncertainty noted as to what precisely it calls for, retained its determinative role in the chapter's second section. Both sections can be said to have assumed further that the principles by which we are able to know the beings are those which are responsible for them (see B3 and pages 46–47 above; but compare also pages 43–44 as well as 47–48) and that the principles are beings themselves. The second section had asked, therefore, whether each of the principles is one only in kind (in other words, whether they are—those of each kind—unlimited in number, as they would have to be, if they are to constitute the elements of the particulars) or one numerically (as they would appear to have to be to make possible a scientific knowing of the beings). And it is this question, left unresolved (officially at least) in B4, to which Aristotle returns in the first section of our chapter.

He does so via a (more) general question not mentioned in B1, about which one might be perplexed: why must one even seek for beings such as "we" posit the forms (ideas) to be, besides those accessible to sense perception and the intermediates or mathematicals.

The reason given is that in the case of the latter, too, those that are alike in form (kind) are many (in number), so that their principles will be limited only in form (kind), and not in number. What Aristotle means here is not that the number of principles responsible for each of the beings accessible to sense perception is unlimited, but that—even if they should be, for each being, as limited as those of a spoken syllable—their number would, for the unlimited multitude of beings similar to that one in form (kind), be unlimited. The result is that, unless there are other beings such as some say the forms (ideas) are, there will be (for beings) no "being" (ousia), one in number as well as form (kind), nor will the principles of the beings (ta onta) be just so many in number, but only in form (kind). What those who speak of the forms (ideas) "wish" to say, then, and what it is necessary for them to say, is that each of the forms (ideas) is some being (ousia tis). But if "we" will posit that the forms (ideas) are and that the principles are one in number and not merely in form (kind), "we" have already said what impossibilities necessarily ensue.

The door that the second section of B4 had left open is thus definitively closed. And the problem that, as Aristotle had reiterated there, its closing would pose for a scientific knowing of the beings is thus again, or still, before us—now as an unavoidable one. Aristotle turns to it by raising a question that is fittingly placed last in Beta, although it had been mentioned at the end of B1 before several others, including an apparently closely related one which is taken up before it here (in the chapter's second section). The question that he raises in the last section is whether the principles are universals or what we call particulars. As the principles responsible for the beings, they are of course particulars. Though he does not say so, there can no longer be any doubt about this in view of what he does say now: that universals are not beings (ousiai). "None of the common (terms) designates some 'this' (tode ti) . . . but a being (hē ousia) is some 'this' (tode ti)." If universals (too) can be principles, one must say then that they are so in a new, as yet to be explained sense.

If however the principles are not universals, but on the level of the particularity (of the things), they will not be accessible to scientific knowledge, which is, in all cases, universal. The result is that, if there is to be scientific knowledge of the principles, there will be other principles prior to them—namely, those predicated universally. The "prior" principles, precisely as prior, are to be distinguished from the actual principles, those which bear responsibility for the coming into being of the beings and for their persistence in being. (Compare B4 1000b24–28 as well as 999b20–23.) They are principles in the new sense. What sense is that? And what is it that entitles them to be called principles of the *beings*?

The only hint in B6 of an answer to these questions, which are themselves new, is supplied by Aristotle in the chapter's brief central section, where he takes up a question that he describes there as closely related to "these": whether the elements *are* potentially or in some other manner. This could well appear to be a non-question: how can elements which are themselves merely potential bring about actual beings? Or, as Aristotle puts it, if the elements *are* merely potentially, it can be the case that none of the beings is. The reason is that merely potential elements may belong to what is not (as do other potential beings which, as such, can but have not yet come to be); but from *elements* which are not, no being can come to be. On the other hand, if the elements *are* in some manner other than merely potentially (as, indeed, they must be), there will be something else (ti allo) prior to the (actual) principles. For the potentiality (in one sense of the term) or, perhaps better, the possibility (for something to be) is prior to "that cause" (the elements which bring about its being). (See D12 1019b21–33 and compare the treatment of astronomy in B2: pages 43–44 above.)

G1) A philosophic science is a theoretical one of the truth; but we do not know the true without the cause (a1): truth (or nature) is being as caused or insofar as it is caused. The science that we seek is therefore a science concerned with causes and principles, indeed with the first or highest causes (A1–3, G1). But are those causes accessible to scientific knowledge (a1–2, B2–4 and 6)? Was it not doubts on that score that led Aristotle to refer to the philosophic science as one that we seek (A2, B1 and 2)? However that may be, the fourth book of the work as we have it (Gamma) begins with the assertion that there is some science that pursues theoretically being (tò on) as being (on) and what belongs to it as such. Is our seeking, then, at an end?

None of the other sciences is the same as this science of being as being. They all cut off some part of being and pursue theoretically what accrues to that part. This does not mean that they all restrict their investigations to some genus or class of the beings: by way of illustration here of sciences that pursue only a part of being, Aristotle refers to the mathematical sciences, and these can be said to investigate all of the beings—though only, for example, insofar as they are numerable. But none of these others is concerned universally (katholou) with being as being. Aristotle has been gradually unfolding the role that universals would necessarily play in a philosophic science, a role that is by no means either obvious or unproblematic (B2–4 and 6). But are the universals in question universals that pertain to being as being? What sort of universals would those be?

Since we are seeking the principles and the highest causes, it should be clear to us that they are (principles and causes) of some nature: "of itself" according to the ms. reading generally accepted, "of themselves" according to ms.Ab. And it is from this fact, apparently, that the conclusion is drawn here that we must grasp the first causes of being as being. Being, then, or rather being (tò on) as being (on) is apparently the nature that the principles and causes we are seeking are "of."

In what way are they "of" it? They cannot be causes of being in the sense of bearing responsibility for its coming into being as it is and for its persistence in being, even if one can speak of a coming-into-being of being: only something "beyond" being (Republic 509b6–10) could bear such responsibility. Nor can they be "of" being as its effects, as the effects of something besides themselves: they would not, in that case, be the first causes of being as being. It is tempting to regard them as the beings responsible for the coming into being and the persistence in being of all other beings, as in that sense the first causes of being. Aristotle accordingly raises the question whether those seeking the elements of the beings were seeking "these principles," that is, the principles under discussion here. But he answers it at once by saying that it would have been necessary then for the elements to be "of" being not incidentally but insofar as (the beings are) beings (the pl. "onta" as in mss.EJ)—by saying, in other words, that it would have been necessary that one be able to account on their basis for the beings, as beings. For as he had suggested in the last section of B4 (in connection with the closely related case of the oneness of each of the beings), this is something that, on the basis of the elements, one cannot do (see page 55 above). The causes of being in question then must be the determinations of being as being, in the sense that they express what it is (for anything) to be or what (its) being a being entails. And it is in this way, as its determinations, that the principles and the highest causes are "of" some nature, "of itself" and "of themselves": that is, as it appears, that they are "of" being as being.

But what can it mean to call being, or being as being, some nature? (Compare G3 1005a32–33.) To have a nature is to be some kind of being, and not another kind. It is to share (more or less) certain traits with other beings of the same kind, while differing, by virtue of these same traits, from others of another kind. In giving an account of the nature of beings of some kind, we bracket both the differences among them and what they have in common with beings of another kind, including the "to be" which they share with beings of all kinds (A9 990b34–991a2). To speak of the nature of some being is to speak then of a part of what it is. (Compare Physics B1 192b20–23 and 32–34.) And, as this already implies, its being—to disregard for now a usage that makes being (ousia) synonymous with nature (D4 1014b35 and following)—is all that it is. When we seek therefore to give an account of the being or "to be" that is common to all of the beings as beings, our efforts seem necessarily to founder on the rock of the diversity and even opposition in which the beings stand to one another, in which they stand to one another as beings. We seem to lack here the possibility of subordinating the diversity to a likeness on the level of (an all-inclusive) class or kind.

Or is that possibility implicit in the diversity itself? The diversity of the beings has as its presupposition what we have been taking for granted all along: that being is beings. This is indeed the root of the distinctiveness of beings, of the possibility and necessity of distinguishing them from one another. But this means that being is number, as the more subtle of Aristotle's predecessors had already concluded (B5 1002a8–12), and that the beings share as beings the fact of being numerable, together with everything that flows from that fact. The determinations of being as being will then be those which belong to beings as numerable.

But have we not already heard that to pursue being as the mathematical sciences do—which means, among other things, to investigate the beings insofar as they are numerable—is to pursue it only in part, to fail to pursue being as being? And this objection to them is consistent with what we have also seen: that the being of any being is nothing less than all that it is. We may recall in this connection that those who concluded that being is number were preceded by other thinkers who identified it with body (B5 1002a8–11). And while the case for the conclusion that being is number was bolstered, to say the least, by the discovery of the problematic character of that identification (B5 1001b29–1002a8), it may be wondered whether those who, in turning to number, abandoned it did not thereby lose sight of something that the earlier thinkers had grasped, however imperfectly. It is perhaps then also for this reason that Aristotle raises the question in our chapter of whether those seeking the (bodily) elements of the beings understood themselves to be seeking the principles of the beings as beings (compare B5 1002a10–11) and that, in adding that it is "for us, too" to grasp the first causes of being as being, he associates himself with their effort, in particular. In short, it seems to be necessary to make a new beginning with regard to being, if we are to learn what can reasonably be expected from a science of being as being.

G2) We have suggested that a science of being as being will be concerned with such causes or principles as are "of" being in the sense that they express what it is for anything to be or what its being a being entails. Is this one sense or two?

Insofar as the beings are beings, they are numerable: they are (severally, not collectively) numerable as beings; numerability is entailed by their being. But does it express for each being what it is for it to be? What we call a being we are aware of as some particular and, at the same time, as some particular that is. But we are aware of the "is" in such a way that it cannot be separated from the particular, as whose "is" we are somehow aware of it. And the formulation with which we have been wrestling already points, perhaps, in this direction. In "being as being" (on hēi on), the second "being" may refer to the being that is or to its "is"—which is to say that it refers at the same time to both. If the science of being as being is to concern itself then with more than what being a being entails, the possibility of its doing so will have first to be established. And it is more precisely for this reason that a new beginning with regard to being must now be made.

What do we have in mind in calling anything a being or saying of it that it is? Aristotle opens our chapter with this question insofar as it is raised by the fact that we apply the term to objects of a number of different sorts. He likens our use of "being" (tò on), in this respect, to our use of the terms "healthy" (tò hygieinon) and "medical" (tò iatrikon). In each of these cases, too, we apply the term in question to objects of a number of different sorts—but with a view to their relatedness to one (object) and to some one nature: health, in the case of "healthy," and (the art of) medicine in that of "medical." In the case of "being" (tò on), what we look to in calling anything a being or saying of it that it is—the one principle, as Aristotle now calls it—is beings (ousiai), in the sense of this term which is listed first in D8 (1017b10–14; compare also Z2 1028b8–13, H1 1042a6–11, and Categories 5 2a11–14). There is also this difference to be noted from the other cases. Whereas health, for example, is not called healthy, it is said of beings, just because (they are) beings (ousiai), that they are (they are called "onta"). Still, no light is cast on beings (ousiai) when, for this reason, it is said of them that they are. It is rather what we have in mind in saying of anything that it is, that is illuminated thereby. What we have in mind is "ousiai"—or what bears one of a number of relations to them. (Compare again A9 990b34–991a2; compare also 1003b26–29, as these lines are given in mss.EJ according to Jaeger and, for E, Christ.)

The science of being as being will concern itself then with its objects in their relatedness to "ousiai," for it is by virtue of that relatedness that they are, that we call them beings. But in any field the most authoritative knowledge is of what is first in the sense or senses that the others (with which the science is concerned) are dependent upon it and that they are said (to be what they are) on account of it. If, in the field that concerns us, this "first" is "ousia" (sing.), then it would be incumbent on the philosopher to have possession of the principles and the causes of the "ousiai" (pl.). In possessing those principles and causes, he would know the "ousiai"—and this knowledge would be the authoritative component of a science of being as being—but he would not know them as beings (onta), as things which are. It is rather of what is dependent upon them, of the others, that it is to an extent meaningful to say that they are beings: one designates them thus as such dependents. But as for the "ousiai" themselves, if we discount a principle whose validity (in the upward direction) we were compelled to question in the case to which it was applied (a1 993b24–27 and context), there is only habit to make the reference to the "ousiai" as "onta" appear meaningful to us (compare a3 994b32–995a6). In order to restore, therefore, the science of being as being to such life as it is capable of, Aristotle must have recourse after all to the numerability of (any) being as (a) being (1003b22 and following); and thus he has to accept the assimilation of philosophy to mathematics (1004a6–7) that he had excluded (G1) or objected to (A9 992a32–b1) earlier.

But if the "ousiai" cannot meaningfully be called beings, what can they be called or to what domain do they truly belong? According to a suggestion which Aristotle made in drawing the argument of Beta to a close, an "ousia" is "some this" (tode ti) (B6 1003a9; compare B5 1001b29–32). Now, as the grammatical form of the term already indicates, a "this" is not an object that we are aware of merely by having it "in mind" or even by seeing it: it stands before us in such a way that we must point to it. In other words, it belongs to the world of which we ourselves form an indispensable part, a world that we articulate, indeed, by means of our "critical" faculties of sense perception and intellectual perception (compare Posterior Analytics B19 99b35) but that those faculties only help to give us—a world, in short, that we could not reconstruct solely on the basis of what they provide. The domain, then, to which the "ousiai" belong or which they constitute, is the world as it is given to us in our most elementary and least contestable experience, in the experience that underlies and completes perception. And, since it is with "ousiai" above all that a philosophic science is concerned (1003b16–19 and 1004b8–10), we can understand, therefore, how Aristotle could say in his Ethics that it is from experience that we obtain the principles or starting points that such a science requires (Nicomachean Ethics Z8 1142a16–20).

There is however no reference to experience in our chapter, where Aristotle is at pains—if the development of a rhetorical argument can be said to have cost a master of rhetoric pains—to assign the theoretical pursuit of the "ousiai" and that of the predicates or contraries which have as their principle the one (or being and the one) to a single science (1004a31–34). A still higher point of the development is reached when the list of contraries, whose principles are now taken to be both multitude and the one, is expanded to include those, such as warm and cold or love and strife, to which "almost" all trace the "ousiai"; for this permits Aristotle, in concluding the argument as a whole, to convey the impression that the theoretical pursuit of the "ousiai" and what belongs to them is either identical to or a part of the theoretical pursuit of being as being and what belongs to it as being (1005a11–18). The earlier conclusion (1004a31–34), of which this is a more radical restatement, had referred to a passage "in the perplexities" where, however, a distinction was drawn that neither of the passages in Gamma makes mention of: it would have interfered with the argument now being made to do so (compare B1 995b18–27 and Ross ad loc.).

Something of the distance that lies between a philosophic science and "metaphysics"—or between the expectations that attend each of them—becomes visible in the pains that Aristotle is at here to bridge the gap between a science of the "ousiai" and a science of being as being. That is, it becomes visible to the extent that those pains become visible. But he makes them visible by exposing the seams, or the stages, of his argument.

G3) Aristotle turns here to a question that had truly been posed "in the perplexities" (compare G2 1004a31–34); and he does so without referring to the earlier treatment of it (B1 995b6–10, B2 996b26–997a15). As a result, the question is easily disposed of on the basis of the conclusion drawn in G2. It concerns the investigation of the principles that all use in demonstrating anything about any genus of beings (onta). Since these principles belong to all of the beings as beings (hēi onta), rather than to some (one) genus apart from the others, it is obvious that the theoretical pursuit of them belongs to the one who knows (or is familiar with) being as being. The only difficulty would seem to be posed by the fact that some of the natural scientists, too, undertake to say something about them: natural science is to be distinguished from the science of being as being. But since the latter is taken here, in accord with the conclusion drawn in G2, to be or to encompass a science of the "ousiai," the distinction must be based, in the context, on the fact or claim that nature is merely some one genus of being (tò on). Whereas the natural scientists are concerned indeed with the whole of nature and therewith, as they think, with what there is of being (tò on), he whose theoretical pursuit is universal (as to being) is said to be concerned also with "the first ousia" and (only thus) with "all of ousia" (compare A8 990a3–5 with 988b24–26 and 989b21–27, as well as E1 1026a23–32).—According to an apparently extraneous remark that Aristotle makes in this context by way of criticism of what "some" have undertaken to say about the manner in which the truth is to be accepted (as truth), we must come to scientific endeavor already knowing "the analytics": that is, the matters treated in the two works of that name, in which he explains the nature and basis of demonstration. But if we can know such matters before our seeking proper begins, it is difficult to see how the requisite knowledge of the principles of demonstration—of their identity as well as their truth—can be dependent upon a science of being as being. However that may be, Aristotle enters now into a lengthy discussion (extending to the end of G6) of the firmest of all of these principles, without having as yet deployed any such science.

He first tells us something about the principle and only then identifies it. The firmest principle will be that which it is impossible to be mistaken about: the source of any sure knowledge must itself be sure. And it will therefore be the one most known (or familiar), for it is about what they do not know (or are not familiar with) that all are deceived. Nor is it dependent upon a supposition (of something other than itself); for the principle which he who understands anything of the beings (ta onta) must possess, or what he who is to know (or become familiar with) anything must already know (or be familiar with), is not (known) by supposition (taking the reading of ms.Ab at 1005b16), that is, by the supposition of something other than itself. The principle or opinion (G6 1011b13) which, Aristotle asserts, fits the description that he has given is this: it is impossible that at the same time and in the same respect the same (thing) both belong and not belong to the same (thing).

In support of his assertion, he offers here the following reflection. It is impossible for anyone to <u>hold</u> the same (thing) to be and not be (or to belong to something and not belong to it). Some think that Heraclitus speaks along these lines; but it is not necessary that someone also hold (to be the case) what he says. And if it is inadmissible that contraries belong at the same time (and in the same respect) to the same (thing or person), as the principle identified as firmest is later said to entail (G6 1011b15–22); and the opinion expressed by one of a pair of contradictory assertions is contrary to the opinion expressed by the other; then it is manifest that it is impossible for the same person to <u>hold</u> at the same time the same (thing) to be and not be, for he who is mistaken about this would possess at the same time contrary opinions. (But it was a principle about which it is impossible to be mistaken that was said to be the firmest.) And therefore all who demonstrate anything rely on this opinion—which is by nature the principle also of all the other principles of demonstration—as the ultimate (or most fundamental) one.

In short: if the principle in question is true, it follows (through one or more steps) that one cannot fail to hold it; and since one cannot fail to hold it, it is the principle we seek. The quasi-circular character of the proceeding (compare G4 1006a3–5) is indicated also in this way. In our chapter, Aristotle establishes the impossibility of holding contradictory opinions by identifying them as contraries; whereas in the passage from G6, to which his argument tacitly appeals, he establishes the inadmissibility of contraries belonging at the same time to the same (thing or person) by showing that assertions to this effect are contradictory. But he does not even claim to be demonstrating here the truth of the principle he has called "firmest" but only to be indicating that it is one which we cannot fail to hold.

G4) Aristotle acknowledged in G3 that some think that Heraclitus says that the same (thing) is and is not. He responded there that it is not necessary that someone also hold (to be the case) what he says. But he now grants that there are some who not only say themselves that it is admissible for the same (thing) to be and not be but (say) that they also hold (or that it is admissible to hold) this to be so. And he grants further that this logos—that the same (thing) is and is not—is used by many of the natural scientists (and not merely pronounced by one or more of them). Moreover, his showing in G3 that the denial that this is possible is firmest of all the principles was based, as he says here, on the assumption of its impossibility. There are some therefore (not the natural scientists) who—ignorant as they are of what one must seek to demonstrate and what not, of the fact that it is impossible that there be a demonstration of everything—think fit to demand a demonstration of its impossibility. Although Aristotle regards a demonstration, strictly speaking, as unavailable in this case, he suggests that the impossibility in question may, under a certain condition, be demonstrated elenctically: through refuting the one who contests it. And in undertaking to provide such a demonstration, he perhaps intends to give some indication also of the basis on which he will respond later on to his fellow natural scientists.

The condition that must be fulfilled if there is to be an elenctic demonstration is that he who contests what is to be demonstrated in it grant its principle or starting point. The starting point that he must grant, not only here but "for all such cases," is not that something either is or is not: to ask this of him would probably be held to beg the question. It is rather that, in speaking, he signifies something to himself and to another. And this he must grant, Aristotle observes, if he would speak at all.

What has he granted, then, in granting it? What is clear in the first place is that a name (to begin with this primary element of speech) signifies that "this" (some "this") is or is not: "justice" signifies that there is (there where I point) justice; "injustice" that there is not. This much is signified by the use of the mere name; there is no need to add the "is" or "is not" (compare G2 1003b26–29). In addition, we will assume that the name—Aristotle supplies here his own example, "man"—signifies a "one" (the thing we are calling man) which is, at the same time, two: two-footed animal. In other words, in giving something (which may in fact not be one—reading "ouden" with the mss. at 1006b10) one name, we assign it to a class that we recognize it as belonging to; we say, in effect, that it is "one of those." And in doing so we depend on, we take our bearings by, certain traits (for example, self-movement or a particular form of it) that it shares with other members of the class, with other things of that kind. (Compare pages 62–63 above.) If we make that dependence explicit by naming, in turn, these traits, the preeminent among them, we give the definition (logos) of any member of the class, as such; and it becomes then possible to ask whether there are in fact any members of it, any things which fit the definition. But the name by itself already carries an implicit definition with it, just as its use by itself already amounts to an assertion that there is something of the kind or, as in the case of "injustice," that there is not. To signify, as we are assuming a name does, a "one" is then to signify of a particular thing that it has certain traits that make it a member of some class. And the name can do this because it signifies also, implicitly or explicitly, the definition of any member of the class (logos: the reading of ms.Ab at 1006b3; compare 1006b22–28, as well as G7 1012a23–24).

Now, if a name not only signifies something but signifies in the way indicated a "one," if "man" for example signifies a "one" in this way, it is inadmissible that what it signifies, "the being for man" or the definition of man, be "what it is for man not to be" or the definition of man's not-being. And from this it follows, according to Aristotle, that it cannot be the case that the same (thing) is and is not man. But if the question concerns the admissibility of the same (thing) at the same time being and not being, not the name "man"—for others may call "not man" him whom we call "man"—but the thing, as Aristotle himself stresses, why does the conclusion that he draws follow from the way in which we are assumed to use the name? The reason, which he is content to leave unexpressed, must be that the thing in question here is the thing as named, for it is the name that excludes, by its signifying, that which contradicts what it signifies. A being that we call man may, then, or may not fit the definition that is carried by the name; but it cannot at the same time be man (that is, a being bearing the name) and not be man.

This argument is the most rigorous of those offered by Aristotle in G4 on behalf of the principle that he has undertaken to demonstrate elenctically. This is no doubt why he placed it first, why he developed it at suitable length, and why he appended to it, in particular, the observation that those who say that the same thing is and is not do away with the "ousia" (of beings) and "the what it was (for them) to be" or (their) definition. He thereby indicates that, in demonstrating that it is impossible for the same thing to be and not be, he is defending the possession (by beings) of "ousiai" in this secondary sense that came to be rendered as "essence" (compare Categories 5 2a14–19, 2b29–37, 3b10–21) and therewith also such necessity as is connected with "essence" (G5 1010b23–30;

compare Parts of Animals A1 642a32–b2). More precisely, he indicates that, in demonstrating that impossibility as he was just now demonstrating it, he was defending the cause of "ousia" in this sense. This has implications for the way in which what is thus defended must be understood.

In other words, the beings which are suggested to have "ousiai" are (as the discussion of them here also confirms) beings or things such as that demonstration took them to be. (The clarity of this discussion is much impaired by the editors' acceptance at 1007a34 of the emendation "kath'ou" for the "katholou" of the mss. There must be a first universal if there is to be non-accidental predication, whether that universal by itself is the ultimate subject of predication or, as the substitution of "Socrates" for "man" at 1007b4–6 would tend to indicate, not. Compare Categories 5 2b37–3a6 with 3b10–18 and 2a34–b6.)

The last argument in the chapter is to the effect that even if all things are and are not as they are, there is in the nature of the beings (ta onta) a more and a less (in the approach of one particular to another or to a certain trait or character); and this (by itself) would make it possible for our thinking to mark out boundaries (among them). (Compare B4 999b20–23 and page 50 above.)

G5) Aristotle turns in this chapter to the natural scientists to whom he had referred at the beginning of G4, those who make use of the logos that the same (thing) is and is not. But he does so only after taking two preliminary steps. He first spells out and confirms the connection that he had alluded to, also in G4, between that logos and the logos of Protagoras according to which all things are truly as each of us opines them to be or as they appear to us to be: the two logoi stem from the same opinion or reflection and, as they entail one another, stand or fall together. The Protagorean logos is one way in which someone might understand his notorious thesis that "man is (the) measure of all things"—as it is put in the Theaetetus, "of the beings, that they are; of the non-beings, that they are not" (151e8–152a5)—though it is not the only way in which that thesis might be understood (I1 1053a35–b1, Laws

716c4–6). Aristotle does not mention the thesis here. (Compare pages 66 and 71–72 above.)

Instead he offers an observation—and this is the second of his preliminary steps—bearing on the manner in which arguments such as the one that he is about to take up or resume must be conducted. One must have regard to the differences among their addressees. Some, having fallen into perplexity, came to hold the opinion to be combated; and "the ignorance of these is easily cured." Others argue for the sake of argument. It is tempting to take Protagoras as representative of the latter class. He is a self-professed sophist (Protagoras 317b4 and context). And, of sophistry, Aristotle had remarked earlier in Gamma that, while it approaches philosophy in some respect, it is distinguished from philosophy by the choice of life of the sophists (G2 1004b17–26). Presumably this means that, even if the sophists see something of the difficulties which must be overcome on the path to a genuine science (B2 997b35–998a4), it is not for the sake of attaining the greatest possible clarity about the matter that they pursue them. But if Aristotle's addressees fall here, as he thus indicates, into the two classes of the sophists and the sophistically inclined, on the one hand, and the naively perplexed, on the other, they do not include the natural scientists with whose opinions he is now chiefly concerned and to whom his own arguments (as, for example, at 1009a36–38 and 1010a32–35) appear to be directed.

The reason may have to do with the fact that their opinions have a harsh consequence. They are bound to have a profoundly dispiriting effect on those endeavoring to philosophize—that is, on potential philosophers, who are likely, as such, to belong to the class of the naively perplexed. The effect does not extend, at any rate, to the natural scientists themselves who, having most of all seen the truth that admits of being seen, most of all seek it and love it. More precisely, the effect in question stems from their opinions when they are made manifest (in speech), as they are by some of those who hold them. (Consider the differences that Aristotle points to, in this regard, between Democritus, Homer, who is included here among the natural scientists, and Anaxagoras—reading "tinos" with the mss. at 1009b27—on the one hand, and Empedocles and Parmenides, on the other.) Aristotle himself mentions the opinions only to combat them. And, even in combating them, he imposes on his discussion the limitation that we are considering. He directs to the natural scientists or to their assertions arguments which are meant primarily for others and only indirectly or through this medium for them.

It is true that the scientists are occasionally included by Aristotle among the perplexed (1009a22–30). They might then appear to fall within rather than outside of the classification that he has given of his addressees. But, as is perhaps confirmed by the fact that some of those who argue for the sake of argument are also included here (G6 1011a3–4), perplexity is not necessarily naïve perplexity. Aristotle includes the natural scientists among the perplexed by way, let us say, of indicating that there is some foundation for their opinions.

They held, as indeed we have already heard, that the beings are only the sensibly perceived (1010a2–3; A8 990a3–5) and that it is inadmissible that what is not (or non-being) come to be (1009a25–26; A3 983b6–20). And, holding these views, they were troubled by the observation (1009a24) of contraries coming to be from the same (thing): the thing from which the contraries come must then already be, and in like manner, both of them. They were troubled also by the observation (1010a7) that all of perceptible nature is in motion (compare B4 999b1–5), for nothing is truly predicated of what is changing: what is in every respect and in every way changing, at any rate, does not admit true predication. (Yet only the professed followers of Heraclitus went so far as to think that one must refrain from speaking altogether.) Now, one cannot be troubled by such observations without granting some credence to the observations themselves, that is, to sense perception—however much there may be, in the sensibly perceived, of the nature of the undefined and of that of their being and not being as they are (1010a2–4; compare G4 1008b31–33).

Doubts were entertained, however, also on this score. It was thought by some, for example, that the same (thing) seems on tasting sweet to some, bitter to others. Somewhat more adequately, it was thought that what appears (through the senses) to many of the other animals are (traits) contrary to those that appear, about the same (things), to us (compare Statesman 272b1–c5); and that even what seems from sense perception (to be so) to each himself for himself is not always the same. In other words, the "perceptions" of the senses vary, not only in accord with changes in whatever gives rise to them, but also due to changes in the bodily condition of the "perceiver" (compare 1010b21–23). And this could appear to leave us with an unpalatable alternative: to regard all of the (contrary) sense appearances as true—if we insist on the identification of the beings with the sensibly perceived, as sensibly perceived—or to regard nothing as true, at least not in a way evident to us.

To the difficulty posed by the fact that contraries are observed to come from the same (thing), or to the inference drawn from this observation, Aristotle responds that "being is spoken of in two ways." Presumably he means as potential being and actual being: for he also says here that the same (thing) may at the same time be contraries potentially, but not actually, and that there is a manner in which it is admissible for something to come to be from what is not (or from non-being).—White, for example, may come to be in a surface which is potentially white but actually not white: thus white comes to be in it from what is not white (from its actual color), though not from what is not simply. (Compare G7 1011b29–1012a1, as well as Physics A8 191a23–b29.)—This solution of the difficulty is better than the second one that is offered here, according to Thomas (Commentary on Aristotle's Metaphysics, para. 668 on 1009a36–38). It is a good one not because it disposes of all questions that could be raised about the matter, but because it renders in the most adequate way what we observe, while remaining true to principles that we cannot help holding.

In response to the difficulty posed by the observation that all of perceptible nature is in motion, an observation that could seem to cast doubt also on the existence of any imperishable being (B4

999b4–5), Aristotle concedes here only that the place or portion of the perceptible whole, of the heaven, which is "around us" is subject to perishing and coming-to-be without let-up. He suggests, in other words, that the motion to which the other, the greater portion of the heaven is subject does not entail the perishability of it or its parts. Beyond that, he demands that the natural scientists be persuaded (to accept the validity) of that part of his response to the first difficulty which Thomas had judged the inferior one (compare 1010a32–35 with 1009a36–38). If we disregard, then, the admittedly disputable argument with which he opens his response (1010a15–23), what remains is a remark that complements well the last argument of G4. Quantitative change is not the same as (does not always amount to) qualitative change. And we know (or recognize) all things by their form, that is, by their preeminent traits or qualities.

He responds last to the doubts about the reliability of sense perception that he had spelled out in the topical center of the chapter. The first part of his response defends its reliability by recourse to the following points: (1) the distinction between sense perception, which is not false as to its own proper objects, and our receptivity (phantasia) to appearances (phainomena) more generally; (2) a demand that the superiority in truth, which our deeds show that we recognize, of what appears to us when we are healthy, strong and awake, and close to the appearances, over against what appears to us when we are in the opposite position or states, be acknowledged; and (3) the introduction of the notion of the authority of an opinion or perception. For just as the authority of the opinion of a doctor, as to whether or not one will get well, is superior to that of someone ignorant of the art (though it may not prove true in a given case), so the authority of a sense as to its own proper object is superior to its authority as to the proper object of another sense: sight is of more authority as to the color of food than as to its flavor (compare G6 1011a25–27). But in regard to its own proper object none of the senses ever says, of the same object at the same time, that it both is and is not as it is.

The question had been raised, however, whether it does not do this at different times, as the result of a change in the bodily condition of the perceiver that may or may not correspond to a change in what is to be perceived (1009b12–15 and context). Aristotle turns to this difficulty in the second part of his response. He does not have recourse here to what he has already demanded under (2) above. He says rather that, even at a different time, a sense did not dispute (with itself) about the "pathos," the experienced quality or trait, but only about that to which the quality has accrued. The same wine may seem at one time sweet, at another not sweet; but not "the sweet"—how it is, whenever it may be. It never yet changed, but (the sense) is always true in its regard. And whatever will be sweet is necessarily of this sort. Now, the necessity that whatever is to be sweet (or called by that name) be of a certain sort is a necessity connected with "ousia" in the sense of "essence." And Aristotle adds to this part of his response the observation that "all of these logoi" do away with necessity, just as they do away with the possession by anything of an "ousia" in this sense (compare G4 1007a20–21 and following).

He appends to the whole response a remark about the presupposition, as one might understand that presupposition, of all of the difficulties that he has been considering. If there is only what is sensibly perceived, nothing would be if animate (ensouled) beings, without which there would not be sense perception, are not. But, having come to this point, Aristotle checks himself. That there would be neither sensibly perceived (or perceptible) beings, nor perceptions of them, is perhaps true; for "this" (the antecedent is unclear) is a "pathos" of the perceiver. But that whatever they are which underlie and produce the perceptions should not be, even without sense perception, is impossible. For sense perception is not (perception) of itself, but there is besides the perception something different, which is necessarily prior to it.—By this remark, Aristotle indicates at the same time a certain agreement with the thesis, properly understood, that "man is (the) measure" and the limits to that agreement. For the impossibility or necessity in question here is not one dependent on the fact that there is man. (Compare Prior Analytics A13 32b4–10.)

G6) By the device of a summary sentence towards its end, bringing to a conclusion the treatment of the "firmest opinion" that began in G3, Aristotle makes clear that at least the greater portion of this brief chapter forms part of that treatment. What then is the function of the chapter within it? What bearing, that is, does the chapter have on the considerations to which we have been led by it thus far? We must try to answer this question on the basis of indications that are unusually terse and elliptical.

"There are some who are perplexed both among those who are persuaded of these things and among those who only say these logoi." So the chapter begins, with a division that reminds us of that between the naïve and the sophistically inclined made use of in G5. What perplexes them both concerns judgment. If, as we heard in G5, what appears to the healthy, for example, is superior in truth to what appears to the unhealthy, who judges as to who is healthy and, generally, as to who will judge correctly in each case? Now, when it is put in this way, the problem is rather easily disposed of; and those who are troubled on this score are easily persuaded of this. Aristotle must mean the naïve ones among the perplexed he had mentioned at the beginning of the chapter (compare also G5 1009a16–22 and G4 1006a5–11). But what then are the non-naïve among the perplexed troubled by? He does not tell us. Or, rather, he tells us only this much: that it is a problem, connected with judgment, which one is confronted with even if one has seen or, perhaps better, after one has seen that what we might call the naïve problem of judgment is easily disposed of.

The non-naïve among the perplexed are not persuaded of what they say: that all of what appears is true. Yet in seeking to be forced in argument to give up the contention, to be made to contradict themselves in the defense of it, they show that they think that it is, to some extent at least, defensible. They are not like those who say that what appears is true, on account of the causes (of this opinion) mentioned previously—that neither to all, nor even to oneself always, do the same things appear, but often contraries at the same time—and (who) on account of this (say also) that all things are alike false and true. They are not perplexed as to the contention that all of what appears is true, which they say merely for the sake of argument, but about something else that is in some way connected with it.

Aristotle suggests that the defense of the contention requires that they make all things relative to something or other (pros ti): if there are also some things that are of themselves (what they are), it would not be the case that all of what appears is true. The reason given is that whatever appears must appear to someone. What is of itself (what it is) would thus, in appearing, put itself into a relation to someone and, to that extent, appear as what it is not (relative to something); and not all appearances would be true. So far then as it appears, this is the case. But need it appear? And if the only things which are of themselves (what they are) do not in any way appear (to us), their existence (insofar as we can infer it) would suffice to refute, not the contention that all that appears is true, but its converse: that all that is true belongs to the realm of appearance, that is, to a realm lacking within itself sufficient warranty for the permanence of the stability it exhibits (compare pages 31–32 above). Could this be the thought that is troubling or perplexing the non-naïve? (At G5 1009b12–15, it was said to be because they hold understanding to be sense perception and the latter to be alteration that the natural scientists say that what appears by sense perception is necessarily true.) Is it in the end for the sake of exploring this thought that Aristotle suggests to them the experiment of doing more thoroughly what they were already on the way to doing in linking appearance with truth: of making all things relative?

He has in mind not merely the relativity to thought (opinion) and sense perception of their objects (as such objects) but also, or even in the first place, a relativity that supplies the deepest ground for the former and that consists in the mutual relations of the objects themselves. If the things or beings as we primarily know them, for example, are the things or beings as named (see pages 70–71 above), then each of them is fully what it is only together with others of its kind, only as a member of a class to which it belongs by virtue of traits that link it to them, while separating or distinguishing it from others of another kind. Or, as it is put more generally in the Sophist, difference (which means relation, 255d1, 6–7) is coextensive with being (258d7–e1, 259a4–6; compare 255c12–d1).

To all of this Aristotle makes the following objections. (1) If all things are relative to thought (opinion), there is nothing that has either come to be or that will be, unless someone has thought it in advance. We might reply that the thinking of what comes to be, as it comes to be, suffices for preserving the relativity in question. But this reply would require that we know what we do not know: that whenever there is coming-to-be, there is thought. (Compare Categories 7 7b15–8a12.) (2a) If man is man as (he is) thought, he will not be that which thinks but only the object of thought. But why should man not be thought as thinking, and why conversely should there not be in every thinking some awareness of itself, which is also to say, some objectivity? (Compare Nicomachean Ethics I9 1170a29–b1.) (2b) If each thing will be (what it is) in relation to that which thinks it, that which thinks will, in turn, be in relation to an unlimited number of kinds of things. But why should the microcosm (Physics Th2 252b24–28) not be in relation to an (in principle) unlimited number of kinds of things?—It remains true, however, as we could have been led to recall by Aristotle's first objection, that the thinking which is in a way responsible for all things is not responsible for itself. And its very existence, therefore, testifies to a potentiality of the perhaps limitless realm that transcends its grasp.

G7 & G8) The discussion of the so-called principle of contradiction has extended from the latter part of G3 to the end of G6, that is, to some seventeen pages of the Oxford text. The discussion of the so-called principle of excluded middle, the only other principle of demonstration considered in the portion of Gamma devoted to these principles (G3–8), is contained within the limits of G7, which takes up less than two pages of text. Yet it is only upon its completion that Aristotle ventures to say, at the beginning of G8, that "these things having been determined" the impossibility of what certain other assertions contend has become manifest. The assertions in question are those which contend univocally either that nothing is true or that all things are true.

So far as one can judge from the conclusions that he draws from the arguments deployed, again in G8, against them, he is concerned now more with the former of these assertions than the latter (see 1012b9–10 and 12–13; compare 1012b24–25 with 26–27; consider also 1012b2–4). Those who make this assertion say that nothing prevents it from being the case that all things are similar, in the way they are, to the way the diameter is commensurable (to the side of the square). Now, the diameter is such that it appears to be commensurable, that is, to be something that a geometer knows it cannot be (A2 983a12–21). The assertion with which Aristotle is concerned suggests, then, that all of being is like that. And by tying our two chapters together as he has done, he calls attention to the light that may be shed by the argument of G7 on this suggestion that has surfaced in G8.

According to G7, it is inadmissible that there be any "in-between" of contradictory assertions; rather a (predication) which is one, whatever it may be, must necessarily be either affirmed or denied of a (thing) which is one. Now, while the reach of this principle is understood to extend beyond speech to being (compare 1012a5–9), its evidence appears to lie chiefly in speech, whose character it is to affirm or deny (G4 1006a28–30), or in that silent speech, which is thought (1012a2–3; compare G8 1012b11–12 and Sophist 263e10–264a3). For the apparently different argument that appeals to what is involved in change tacitly identifies change, simply, with intelligible change (1011b29–1012a1; compare G5 1010a7–9 and 15–22). When Aristotle speaks of how those who have come to adopt the inadmissible opinion are to be approached in argument, he says therefore that one must begin from definition (1012a21–24; compare 1011b25, 1012a3 and 11, and also G8 1012b5–7). He prepared that remark by mentioning two errors by which, some by one, some by the other, the addressees (of the arguments to be made or which have already been made) were led to their opinion. For "it is needful to state not only the truth but also the cause of the error (falsehood); for this contributes to conviction"

(Nicomachean Ethics H14 1154a22–23). Yet the causes that he mentions clearly identify those led astray by them as belonging to the naïve among the perplexed. It is "all of these" then that are to be approached in the manner indicated.

Having made this clear, he turns abruptly, at the end of G7, to men of a different cast. "The logos of Heraclitus, asserting that all things are and are not, seems to make all things true; that of Anaxagoras, (asserting) that there is something in-between (what) contradictory assertions (assert), all things false." The Heraclitean logos contests, then, the principle of contradiction; the Anaxagorean logos, the principle of excluded middle. It is this logos that is said to make all things false. And it is the one whose content is indicated here: "for when (all things) are mixed, the mixture is neither good nor not good (compare 1011b32–33 on change), so that there is nothing true to say."

One may doubt that the logos of Heraclitus makes all things true. In the form in which it was alluded to in G5, it threatens to suggest rather that nothing is true (1010a7–15). And it is said at the beginning of G8 to assert that all things are true and all things are false. We can take this as an additional example of the latitude Aristotle avails himself of in rendering the positions of his predecessors (see page 29 above). It permits him here, at the beginning of G8, to indicate that the logos of Heraclitus is less fundamental than the Anaxagorean logos reported at the end of G7. (The impossibility of the logos of Heraclitus is said to rest on the impossibility of the two univocal assertions mentioned here; and the more plausible of these was said to be entailed by that Anaxagorean logos.) Or it permits him to indicate that it is less fundamental from the point of view of the implicit argument of these two chapters.

He begins his assault on the univocal assertions that are the explicit theme of the greater part of G8 again from definition or, more generally, from speech (1012b5–13). Additionally, he suggests that each of the two assertions refutes itself (1012b13–22). That, for example, which says that all things are false, makes itself false as well. But perhaps an adherent of Anaxagoras would allow that it is false to say that all things are false, since it would be truer to say that they are neither true nor not true (compare in G7 1012a6–7 with 27–28 and recall also 1012a31). Finally, he turns to another pair of univocal assertions, one of which (that all things are in motion, the rendering of the Heraclitean logos given in G5) entails (as Aristotle admits now) that nothing is true. In combating this new-old position, he says first that what it entails (that nothing is true, that all things then are false) has been shown to be impossible. This remark must refer to the arguments we have just considered. He then repeats, in abbreviated or expanded form, three of the four arguments he had used to combat the position in G5 (with 1012b28–29 compare 1010a15–22; with 1012b29–31 compare 1010a25–32 and 32–35). He omits the second of those earlier arguments (1010a22–25 and page 76 above). Those who assert that all things are like the diameter in its commensurability need not deny that things undergoing ceaseless quantitative change retain, for a time, a sameness of quality that allows us to recognize them by some form. Nor is the Anaxagorean logos on which their assertion may in the end rest incompatible, when that logos is properly understood (A8 989a30–b21 and page 24 above), with such an admission.

The thoughts conveyed by a written work are not limited to those expressly stated in it. They include those to which an attentive reader of it may be led. A writer who is a master both of understanding and of expression will have anticipated those thoughts, and he may even have provided deliberate pointers to them. In that case, we readers may hope, by paying due regard to such pointers, to discern the direction of the path that he has already traversed and even to move some of the way along it.

D1) Delta, which appears in a catalogue of Aristotle's works that does not list the Metaphysics (Diogenes Laertius E23) and may have existed also as a separate work, is thought to have been written before the other books of the Metaphysics (Ross Vol. I, pp. xiv and xxv). Some of the evidence brought forward in support of this conclusion might indeed be questioned. Of the two passages in other Aristotelian works that are suggested by Ross to refer back to Delta, one (On Generation and Corruption B10 336b29) could just as well refer to G2, E2, or Z1, while the other (Physics A8 191b27–29) is more likely to refer to G5 1009a30–36. But we need not contest the conclusion itself, since it can have no bearing on the only question that can be of serious concern in this connection. As Ross himself insists (p. xiv), "It is important to distinguish two questions which may be asked about the order of the books (of the Metaphysics). There is the question of the order in which they were written, and the question of the order in which they were delivered as lectures." Only the latter of these questions can concern us, the question whether (whenever it was written) Delta was intended to occupy the place in the work that it now occupies. And this question can be settled, to the extent that it can now be settled at all, only by showing either that it serves a function in that place or that it does not. But neither the one nor the other can be shown without a scrupulous examination of Delta itself; and this means an examination that is open to the possibility that it has such a function, that it is (where we now find it) in its proper place.

This possibility is thought to be excluded, however, by the fact that the first part of Kappa, which consists of repetitions of some of the contents of Beta, Gamma, and Epsilon, passes over Delta in silence. For this is thought to confirm the suspicion that Epsilon, and not Delta, was intended to follow Gamma (Ross Vol. I, pp. xvii-xviii). But to judge of whether Kappa does confirm this suspicion, one would have to know that the function that its repetitions serve would have been served also by the repetition of parts of Delta. Otherwise, the author of Kappa may have passed over Delta for the reason that he had no use for it, and not because he did not find it in the place where we do. And since the function of the repetitions in Kappa is something that, prior to our study of the book, we cannot know, we will take the provisional step of turning for guidance to Thomas, whose suggestion as to their function derives some support from a remark in Kappa (7 1064a36) which is not to be found in the passage being "repeated" (in this case, E1). Thomas suggests that "in order that a clearer understanding of the separate substances may be had, Aristotle first makes a summary of the points discussed both in this work and in the Physics which are useful for knowing the separate substances" (Commentary on Aristotle's Metaphysics, para. 2146). In accord, then, with this suggestion, we will assume provisionally that what has to be shown, if it is to be established that Delta is in its proper place, is not merely that it serves a function there but also that that function is sufficiently different from the one attributed by Thomas to Kappa as to render the contents of Delta unsuitable for inclusion among the repetitions of the later book.

Delta is devoted to explaining the ways in which certain terms are used or "said." Aristotle does not present in it his own views. He merely reports the usages in question. But the selection of the terms, the order in which they are considered and that in which the usages are in each case listed, the distinctions which are drawn among the usages, the examples illustrating them, and finally the comments and observations that are added from time to time—these are all his responsibility, with the result that his voice is hardly less audible here than it was in the first four books of the work. Now, even as he began to uncover in those books the foundations on which a genuine science would have to rest, he was pursuing the question of the very possibility of such a science. And therefore he exposed, with a ruthlessness that was tempered only by the how of his doing so, the most powerful objections that had been raised to its possibility, whether by its enemies or by its friends. This is the background, then, against which Delta must be read, if one is truly to determine whether or not it is in its proper place. And we will accordingly try to see what he may have wished to convey in it to a reader who has grasped something of the argument of the work thus far.

The science that we seek is one concerned with the cause or the "on account of which" (A1 981a24–b13) or with certain causes and principles (A1–2 982a1–6), namely, the first principles and causes (A2 982b7–10; compare A1 981b27–29, G1 1003a26–27, and A3 983a24–26). Why have two terms, "cause" and "principle," been used—synonymously (A3 983a26–b6, A5 986a13–15, B3 999a17–19) or nearly so (compare G2 1003b22–25)—where one term would apparently do? And the same question could be raised regarding "principle" and "element" (B1 995b27–29, B3 998a21–25, B4 999b31–33, and B6 1002b32–1003a1). Or, if it was necessary that two or even three terms be used, why has the necessity in question not been brought more fully to light?

The first term considered in Delta is "principle"; the second is "cause" (D2); and the third is "element" (D3).

"Principle" is used in six ways. In the second of these usages, it is that from which each thing would most finely come to be. Aristotle gives only one example: in learning, one must sometimes begin not from the principle of the thing (to be learned) and what is first (in that sense) but from that from which one would most easily learn it. In the sixth usage, on the other hand, it is (the) first from which the thing is known or knowable. This, too, is said to be a principle, indeed a principle of the thing, as for example their premises are principles of demonstrations (compare D2 1013b16–23). At this point, having completed his listing of the usages of "principle," Aristotle remarks that "the causes are said in an equal number of ways." But in the same breath he restricts the scope of the remark by what he adds in its support: "for all the causes are principles." The restriction is understandable in light of what he observes in the next place. It is "common to all of the principles to be the first from which (something) either is or comes to be or is known (recognized)." For, as this observation confirms, what he takes the usages of "principle" to suggest is that there is a sort of principle that makes something known or knowable, without bearing the first or fundamental responsibility for either its coming to be or its (persisting in) being. Did Aristotle himself accept that there are principles of this sort? And, if so, did he regard them as principles of the things?

These questions may be related to another, which he forces us to ask here by his next observation. Having just spoken of what all the principles have in common, he turns to a division among them: "but of these, some are internal (to the things of which they are principles), others external (to them)—wherefore (he continues) nature is a principle and also element and thought and choice and being (ousia) and 'the on account of which.'" The connection established by his "wherefore" instructs us to try to place the examples, whose enumeration it introduces, into one or the other of the classes distinguished in the clause that immediately precedes it. Nature, for instance, can be regarded as an internal principle of motion, as we have heard in the Physics (B1 192b20–23), and element likewise is internal. Thought and choice and "the on account of which" are just as clearly external (compare E1 1025b22–24 with 1013a10–14). But what about being (ousia) in the sense of essence? (Ousia differs from the other principles in this list also in lacking the definite article, an anomaly that Ross alone of the recent editors does not seek to remove.) Is being (ousia) a principle internal to that whose essence it is? In reflections that have taken their departure from rather different starting points and that have yet to be drawn together, Aristotle has begun to intimate that this is not an easy question to answer, either in the affirmative or in the negative (compare pages 20 and 43–44 above with 70–72).

D2) For his treatment of the ways in which "cause" is "said" Aristotle simply repeats, with what seem to be rather insignificant variations, a large portion of a chapter in the Physics (B3) in which he had already treated of this subject. But he does so without referring to the earlier work. He had referred to it, in all probability to the same chapter, in an earlier treatment of the ways in which "the causes" are "said" (A3 983a24–b1). For a more adequate consideration of the matter, he had referred the reader there to the Physics, and not to the partial repetition of the Physics chapter in question in D2. If this reference and non-reference are both meaningful, then, something must link A3 with Physics B3, while at the same time separating it from D2. And since D2 is but a repetition, with what we are assuming to be insignificant variations, of a portion of Physics B3, we are compelled, in our search for clues as to what may constitute the link, to look to those portions of the Physics chapter that have not been repeated in D2 but are lacking here.

It is the first part of Physics B3 (194b16–23), the introduction to the treatment of the causes repeated in D2, that is most helpful in this respect. The reason given there for turning to the question of the causes is that we do not think we know a thing until we grasp "the through which" (it is and comes to be) and that this is to grasp (its) first cause. And the conclusion is drawn that we must do this in regard to generation and corruption and all natural change (grasp their first cause), so that when we know their principles we may attempt to bring to or under them each of the things we seek (to know). No discernible distinction is made between "principle" and "cause"; and this is consistent with the assumption that to know a thing is to know its first cause.

Now in A3 the same reason is given for the need to grasp knowledge of the most basic causes: it is when we are familiar with (its) first cause that we say we know each thing. And there too "principle" and "cause" seem to be used without any distinction being made between them (983a29, b3–4).

We can speak then, in the case of A3 and Physics B3, of an orientation or outlook that they share. But this shared outlook cannot be attributed to D2, precisely because the introduction supplied by the Physics to the treatment of the causes borrowed by D2 is lacking or because the place of that introduction is taken here by the treatment of "principle" in D1. It is true that the assertion is made in D1 that "cause" and "principle" are used in an equal number of ways (that is, interchangeably). But a pointer to the untenability of that assertion is added at once. Above all, the question is very clearly raised of whether what bears the first or fundamental responsibility for a thing's being or coming to be is also the first from which the thing is known or knowable. And to raise this question is to point, at least, to the further questions that have to be raised if the answer to it should prove to be a negative one. What sort of principle, in that case, is it that makes a thing known or knowable and in what relation does that principle stand to the thing itself? These are all questions, then, with which we now approach the passage from the Physics. But to approach it with new questions and a new outlook is perhaps to see it differently than we did before, to be struck in it by what would not before have given us pause. And since the outlook presupposed in the Physics was presupposed still in A3 and even beyond (see page 58 above), our loss of confidence in it would be a small sign of the progress that our author expects and even demands that the reader make as he works his way through the text.

But does not Aristotle himself give authoritative sanction to the assimilation of principle to cause by endorsing the inclusion of the so-called formal cause among the causes, among what are said to bear the responsibility for things? In A3, it was indeed this cause, listed first there and called the being (ousia) and the "what it was (for a thing) to be," to which ultimate responsibility for things was ascribed (if it is "the ousia" and "the what it was to be" that "the logos" at 983a28 stands for or replaces). And the formal cause has a place also in Physics B3, and therefore in our chapter, where it is listed second, after the material cause. The material cause is called here the "from which" some thing comes to be, which remains internal (to what comes to be). In A3 it had been called more simply the matter and the substratum. There, too, it was obviously an internal cause or principle, but no statement was made to this effect. The formal cause is called in D2, as in Physics B3, the form (eidos) and the paradigm—which is then said to be the logos of "the what it was (for the thing) to be." The identification of the formal cause as a logos (the logos or account of the character of a thing) is clearer here than it was in A3, just as the silence as to whether it, too, is internal (to the thing) is louder.

Or is any possible doubt on this score put to rest by what Aristotle says when he repeats the list of what are said to be causes, by way of concluding the first half of the discussion? The relevant portion of the passage goes as follows: "The elements of syllables and the matter of implements (artifacts) and the fire and earth and all such (constituents) of bodies and the parts of a whole and the premises of a conclusion are causes as 'the from which'; but of these, some (are causes) as the substratum—for example, the parts—but the others (are causes) as 'the what it was to be'—(for example,) the whole and also the composition and the form (eidos)." The second of these clauses continues the thought as if Aristotle had said in the first that such instances of "the what it was to be" as were mentioned there belong among the constituents from (and of) which a thing is. Yet, while giving in this way the impression that he has said this, he has not said it in fact (compare D4 1015a6–7 and Physics B1 193b5–6). Caution requires us therefore to assume that the words ("but of these") with which the second clause begins refer to the items that were mentioned in the first, without regard as to whether they belong or do not belong to "the from which" of things. And the wording which requires of us this caution is an example of a caution of another kind, of the delicacy with which Aristotle is discussing here the questions that now concern us.

In the early part of our chapter, he distinguishes between a cause and the genera of that cause, applying the distinction explicitly to both the material cause and the formal cause. Later on, he extends this distinction to causes which are merely incidental (accidental). Toward the end of the chapter, he distinguishes more precisely between a cause (whether proper or incidental) that is a particular and its genus, without limiting the application of the distinction to one or more of the four sorts of causes he has listed in the chapter, but without applying it to any of them explicitly either. Is the formal cause, understood as it is here as the logos of "the what it was to be," ever a particular? In the last portion of the Physics chapter (195b21–30), which is not repeated here, he had made it clear that particular causes are those responsible for particular things and causes that are actual (at work) those responsible for actual things. The distinction between causes (whether proper or incidental) that are potential causes and those which are actual was introduced earlier, in the part of the Physics chapter that is repeated. At the end of this part, that is, at the end of our chapter, Aristotle makes use of both of these distinctions to remark that "the actual causes and the particular causes are and are not (cease to be) together with" their effects, but that this is not always the case with causes by (or in respect of) potentiality (or possibility). For a house may cease to be while its builder (who may someday build another house) still lives. Ross, who takes the "and" in "and the particular causes" to be "explicative" merely, protests that

Aristotle fails to mention (what his example after all confirms) that particulars can be potential as well as actual causes (see the note at 1014a20). But Aristotle may have had a reason for directing our attention more to non-particulars that are causes by potentiality. For it is insofar as it expresses what sort of thing whatever will be sweet must necessarily be, whenever it should be sweet (G5 1010b21–26), that "the sweet" does not simply cease to be when sweet things do. (It follows that Ross's suggestion that the "and" before "the particular causes" is explicative must be rejected.) On the other hand, one cannot say of "the sweet" what Aristotle says elsewhere, in another listing of the four sorts of causes, of those that he puts there in the place of the material cause: that by their very being they make necessary the being of the thing (Posterior Analytics B11 94a21–22; compare Physics B7 198a20–21). In accord with this, he does not speak here of what all the causes have in common, although he had said what all the principles have in common (D1 1013a17 and following) and he will say what all elements have in common (D3 1014b14–15).

D3) It seems to be the material cause which is at issue in the discussion of "element." In an earlier treatment of element in B3, it had been a question of whether to hold the genera to be (the) elements and principles (of things) or rather (the constituents) from which each thing is in the first place, (those constituents) remaining internal (to the thing). D3 is clear as to the fact that the genera can be called elements only metaphorically (compare pages 46 and 48 above). In the non-metaphoric sense, an element is said here to be the first constituent from which (a thing) is composed, (that constituent) remaining internal (to the thing), indivisible in respect of its form into (something of) a different form. What this means is explained via three examples, the same that had been used in B3 of the internal constituents of things, but treated somewhat differently here than they were in the earlier chapter.

The elements of a syllable, an articulated sound, to take the first of these examples, are the ultimate constituents into which it is divided, which are themselves no longer divided into other articulated sounds different in their form. Rather, if they should be divided, their parts are like them in form—as the part of water is water. Another example is afforded by what are said here to be the elements of demonstrations: the first demonstrations, which remain internal to many (other) demonstrations (that are based on them or presuppose them). Aristotle indicates that this example, the third, is of a sort that resembles, without being identical to, that of the first two. The first demonstrations, precisely as first, will be divisible into parts, their premises, which are not like them in form, since they are neither demonstrations themselves nor conclusions of demonstrations. (In B3 it was the conclusions of those primary demonstrations that were said to be elements; and the question of the division of elements was not raised—compare D2 1013b20–21.) The elements of bodies, on the other hand, the central example here, are the ultimate constituents into which bodies are divided, which are themselves no longer divided into others (or other bodies) differing in form. But this is merely what those who speak of elements of bodies say.

The source from which (some thing) first comes to be, which remains internal (to what comes to be), was included also among the principles discussed in D1. This in itself is not surprising, since "all the causes are (also) principles." The examples used to illustrate the principle, however, were a ship's keel, a house's foundation stone, and the heart or brain of animals or whatever else (belonging to them) happens to be taken to be of this sort. As the examples make clear, what was meant by the principle was the part from which production or growth begins, a part that retains a place, distinct from those of other parts, in the completed thing. In the case of animals, moreover, the part is a moving one (Physics B2 194a1–7) and, as such, at least a partial source of the motion responsible for their coming to be. But when Aristotle turned explicitly to the source of motion, which he included among the principles in D1 and the causes in D2, he referred to it as external (explicitly in D1, implicitly in D2): for example, the parents or the father of a child, rather than the seed (but compare D2 1013b23–25). And thus, in speaking in D2 of the material cause—which he called there, as we have seen, the "from which" some thing comes to be, which remains internal (to what comes to be), and also the substratum—he was silent as to any motion that might belong to it as such (but compare 1013b18–19, where fire and earth appear as examples of it: earth was absent from the original of D2 in the Physics). Similarly, his treatment of "element" here in D3 is silent as to the presence of motion in those bodies (like fire and earth) which are taken to be the elements of the others and which, according to what we have heard in the Physics (B1 192b8–23), do contain an internal principle of motion.

If, then, Aristotle has turned to "element" at a point in the argument of the work at which a somewhat sharpened appreciation of the formal cause, and therefore also of its limits, has made a reconsideration of the material cause desirable, what contribution has the discussion of "element" made to such a reconsideration? Perhaps this. In raising more questions than it has answered, it has given indication of the difficulty of the task.

D4) If nature is the same as truth, being as caused or insofar as it is caused (pages 31 and 60 above), it makes sense that the chapter on the usages of "nature" should follow those devoted to the problem of the causes. Moreover, what is caused is limited, but perhaps also secured, by its cause or causes. And the chapter on "necessary" follows immediately upon that on "nature." But as we partially saw (pages 31–32) the conclusion that truth or nature is being as caused is not free from difficulty. It is more in keeping with caution therefore to note, and it may also be more useful to note, that in the Physics, where much of what Aristotle reports about "nature" is already to be found, the treatment of nature (B1) preceded, rather than following, that of the causes (B3). For this difference in placement, whether or not it affects the content of the treatment of nature in D4, is bound to affect how we read that content.

"Nature" is said here, first, to be used for the coming-to-be of what grows: as if, Aristotle adds, "phusis" were derived from "phuō" (to grow).—This usage is mentioned in passing in Physics B1 (193b12–13).—It is said next to be used for that from which what grows first grows, which remains internal to (a part of) what grows. This is close to the usage (the third) ascribed in D1 to "principle" that was understood in such a way as to include also the parts from which the production of artifacts begins. As we may gather from a remark later on in our chapter, a nature can be ascribed only metaphorically to artifacts. Thirdly, it is said here to be used for the source due to which its first motion is present in each of the natural beings as such. (The class of natural beings is larger than that of growing things but of course includes them: Physics B1 192b8–15.)—It is with this understanding of nature that the treatment in Physics B1 begins.—And by introducing, after the mention of this third usage, an excursus on growth that might more appropriately have come after the two usages mentioned before it, Aristotle distances the three usages of "nature" with which he has begun from the two with which he will conclude his account.

In the first place was the coming-to-be of growing things: not the part from which they first grow, nor any cause of the growth. Nature was taken—here against the Physics (B1 192b35–193a1)—to be just the growth or motion itself or the way of being of natural beings (of a certain sort). From this beginning, he proceeded to the first growing part, the part that preeminently exhibits the motion in question; and, from this part and its motion, to the source or cause of the motion (in it and other natural beings). Does his proceeding so—to the starting point of the treatment in the Physics—amount to an ascent? From a phenomenon, in this case motion of a certain sort, one ascends presumably to its preconditions, here what exhibits the motion (Physics G1 200b32–33), and then to its source or cause. But if there cannot have been a beginning to motion tout court (Physics Th1 250b11–15 and following), must not motion of some sort be as primary or elemental as any cause that might be alleged for it? It is the same with particular things whose definition includes motion and which are no longer seen therefore as what they are, if one abstracts them from the motion (Physics B2 193b35–194a7): one cannot account for their motion by tracing it to them in that abstracted state (compare On the Soul B1 412a27–28 and b10–11 with b25–27).

Fourthly, "nature" is said to be used for the "first from which" any of the natural beings either is or comes to be: a "from which" that is in itself "lacking arrangement" (the arrangement or form of the thing which comes to be from it) but that is at the same time unchangeable, or at any rate unchanged (by receiving that arrangement) from its own power (dunamis)—which is as much as to say, from its own way of being or form. This is a very precise formulation of how the material cause is generally understood (A3 983b6–18).—And the second understanding of nature taken up in Physics B1 identifies it with this cause.—The material cause has a claim to the title of "nature" insofar as it is responsible for the being or coming to be of the natural beings (see also Physics B1 193a9–11). If the first examples then (both here and in the Physics) are of the matter of artifacts, which is "said" to be their nature, this is because in the case of some artifacts, like copper and wood implements, we can see a matter that retains its own power or form, while receiving the form of the artifact. And it is in this manner that "they say" the elements are (the) nature also of the natural beings: some speaking in this connection of fire, others of earth, of air, of water, or of something else of this sort, some speaking of some of these (as elements), some of all of them. But is what we see in the being and coming to be of some artifacts ever seen to be the case in natural beings?

Any "matter" that is identifiable will have its own form. That is, it will be some thing in its own right and not simply the matter out of which some other thing is or comes to be. As a thing in its own right, moreover, it will have also its own matter, which will in turn have its, and so on until a first matter is reached—if it is reached, if there is such a matter (compare 1015a7–10, as well as Physics B1 193a17–21, with Th7 1049a18–27). It is assumed in the passage that poses this question (Th7) that a first matter would be identifiable, as fire for example; but there is a division among the textual authorities (at 1049a27) as to whether it would also be "some this." That is, there is division as to whether it is, as identifiable, a thing in its own right, as we have assumed any identifiable matter must be. For if we stick to this assumption, as we are inclined to do, we must conclude that a truly first matter would have to be unidentifiable. And if we identify it accordingly only as "matter," we can hardly say more of it than that it is the surplus, over and above the sensible/intelligible form, that belongs to any "this" as a constituent of the world of our experience (see page 66 above). In particular, we have no basis for ascribing to it a permanence that the things of our experience lack themselves (compare Physics B1 193a23–28 with pages 12–13 above).

This is perhaps why "nature" is used, as Aristotle says in the fifth place, for the being (ousia), in the sense of essence, of the natural beings.—This usage is the third and last taken up in Physics B1.—It is perhaps also for this reason that Aristotle himself, "from what has been said," calls this being (ousia) the first nature and this usage of the term the authoritative one (compare Physics B1 193b6–7). And Empedocles, who in lines of verse (Diels/Kranz B.8) that Aristotle quotes here in partial and altered form denies that "nature" is properly used in this way, does so apparently on the ground that the constitutive "mixture(s)" of all mortal things are as fleeting as they are: "nor is there any end to wretched death." In our consideration of the chapter on cause (D2), we came across a way in which Aristotle was able to contest this and to suggest, rather, of the form or the shape or the being (ousia) of the natural beings—what he also calls here (in D4) the end of their coming-to-be and which he says is "somehow" internal to them either potentially or in (their) completion—that it does not simply cease to be when they do (page 91 above).

To be responsible for the coming to be and the (persisting in) being of the other natural beings, the bodies that have been called elements would have to be in motion, as indeed according to the Physics they tend to be. Yet Aristotle is as silent in this chapter as he has been in the two preceding ones as to any motion belonging to them, or to the material cause, as such. He thus leaves himself with no alternative to asserting that the principle or beginning of the motion belonging to natural beings is their being (ousia). But it is one thing to say that the definition of those beings, and therewith the being (ousia) that the definition is or renders (compare D2

1013a26–27 as well as pages 20–21 above), includes motion. It is quite another to trace responsibility for the motion to that being (ousia).

D5) From "nature" he turns, as we have seen, to "necessary." Of what does not admit of being otherwise than as it is, "we say" (compare D4 1014b33) that it is necessary that it be in that way. And all other things (said to be or to make necessary) are "somehow" called necessary by reference to this usage of the term. Among other necessary or necessitating things, Aristotle mentions constraint, when it renders inadmissible that some thing move or rest in accord with (its) impulse. He does not mention the impulse itself, which would govern movement and rest in the absence of such constraint. Elsewhere he had spoken of a twofold necessity: "the one in accord with nature and the impulse (of the being in question), the other through constraint, counter to the impulse—just as a stone moves both upwards and downwards from necessity, but not on account of the same necessity" (Posterior Analytics B11 94b37–95a3). He evidently did not wish to speak of nature in connection with necessity as it is understood here. (Compare Physics B9 200a30–32 and pages 95–96 above.)

He mentions in the last place the conclusions of demonstration, which are necessary if it is not possible for the first premises of the syllogism to be otherwise than as they are. In this context he adds the remark that, while for some things there is a cause, different (from themselves), of their being necessary, for others there is none, but things different (from them) are of necessity, on account of them. "So that," he continues, "the first and authoritatively necessary is the simple (tò haploun)" which, since it does not admit of being in more ways than one, does not admit of being otherwise than as it is. It follows that, "if there are some permanent and motionless beings, there is nothing constraining or counter to nature for them."

D6) In reading this chapter on "one" (and therewith also on "the many" 1017a3–6, 1016b9–11), with its share of greater as well as lesser difficulties, we must be careful not to miss the woods for the trees. There is no "one" itself (compare not only B4 but also G2): to be (a) one is—Aristotle does not appeal at this point to how the term is used or "said"—to be (the) principle for some number (of things). For the first measure (of them) is (their) principle and the first (thing) by which we know or become familiar with (them) is the first measure of each genus. For each (genus), then, (the) principle of the knowable is "the one" (for it). But then "the one is not the same (thing) in all the genera." (1016b17–21) It follows also that "the one" is not to be identified with "the simple" referred to at the end of D5 (compare also L7 1072a30–34). It is rather, in the preeminent case, the things or beings (ousiai) themselves (1016b1–3; compare 1016b21–23)—whose very names signify not only what, but also that they are and that they are each one (pages 70–71 and 63–64 above). But if it is wrong, therefore, to attempt to trace the oneness of each of the beings to a "one" other than the being itself (page 56 above), the question must still be raised of where in it its oneness resides or of what, in or about it, confers on it that oneness. And this question, which is the same as that of what renders it a—that is, one—being, supplies the underlying theme of our chapter.

The chapter opens by distinguishing what is said to be one with respect to (some) accident (that accrues to it) from what is said, with respect to itself, to be one. An example, if not the simplest example, of the former is that the musical (individual named) Coriscus (is said to be) one with Coriscus. Is it the part of a philosopher, Aristotle had asked in G2 (1004b1–3), to investigate whether (for example) Socrates and Socrates sitting are the same (thing)? We may now be in a better position than we were then (1004b5–10) to grasp the significance of such an investigation. For if "the one" is none other than the things or beings themselves, which as particulars can never be free of accidents (like those designated by "musical" and "sitting"), the accidents of each of them must belong, it would seem, to its oneness. Yet, as the distinction with which the chapter opens implies, the oneness of a particular being with its accidents is not its oneness with respect to itself, its proper oneness or what we are now attempting to understand. Aristotle also suggests in this context that the accidental (one) might be spoken of, in the same way, of a genus and some (one) of the universal names: that, for example, "man" and "musical man" (might be said to be) the same (thing). And the question would then arise of whether this is because (the name) "musical" accrues to "man," (which) is "one ousia," or because both ("man" as well as "musical") accrue to some particular like Coriscus. But in the latter case, "man" would presumably belong to him as (the) genus and "in the ousia" but "musical" as a state or quality "of the ousia," that is, of Coriscus himself. Did the first "ousia" refer to Coriscus himself or to his "essence"? Or is the authentic ousia not captured by this distinction? Since "Coriscus" is the name of a man, the authentic ousia is the particular (in this case, Coriscus) insofar as it is a member of some genus or class.

Having treated in this way of accidental oneness, the chapter moves on to the oneness of things with respect to themselves. There appear to be two manners in which things are said to be one with respect to themselves (1015b36 and 1016a17; compare 1016a24, 32). But the second of these—which finds their oneness to consist in their having a substratum of the same form, so far as sense perception can discern, or in their belonging to one genus, or in their "what it was to be" having the same definition—is so far from making them one in number that it presupposes rather that they are many in this respect. This appears to push the whole responsibility for making a thing one in number back onto the first of the manners in which things are said to be one with respect to themselves: by virtue of being continuous bodies (or magnitudes). Yet when Aristotle speaks, immediately after his survey of these manners, of the things that are preeminently one, he assigns the determination of their oneness to an act of intellectual (not sense) perception that discerns in the first place their "what it was to be." And to discern, of some thing, its "what it was to be" is to see it together with other things, which share with it that "what it was to be," or to see it as a member of a class (compare Categories 5 3b10–18). And therefore, in speaking explicitly towards the end of the chapter of what is numerically one, Aristotle assigns responsibility for such oneness not to mere continuity but to a oneness of matter, by which he means, as he makes clear in the context, informed matter (1016b31–36; compare 1016b11–17).

D7) From "one" (hen) he turns to "being" (tò on). As should no longer surprise us, especially after D6, it is not in fact a question of "the" being (as in B4 or G1) but of what, in any way, can be said to be. It is noteworthy, therefore, that the things (ousiai) are not included among the classes of beings (onta), although in loose but habitual usage they are called "beings" (G2 1003b6). They are indeed alluded to, as what entitles the accidents accruing to them to be said to be, and alluded to as beings; but they are not included in their own right among the listed classes. And, in accord with this, when Aristotle is compelled at the end of the chapter to mention them—for they, too, are said to be by way of potentiality, that is, to be in or to be that from which they may come to be—he must add them explicitly to a consideration that has hitherto applied the distinction between potentiality and actuality/completion only to "those (beings) that have been mentioned" in the chapter (compare 1017b6 with 1017a35–b2). It is true that the following chapter (D8) is devoted to "ousia" (in its various usages); but this fact does not make the omission of the things (ousiai) from a chapter devoted to listing the classes of beings (onta) any the less noteworthy. And in seeking an explanation for it, we may have to have recourse therefore to the indications as to the relation of the things to being and the beings that we glimpsed in G2 or to the interpretation that we ventured of those indications (pages 64–66 above). But if the omission of the things from the listing of D7 must be explained in this way, their omission would serve as a confirmation of the soundness of that interpretation as well as a reminder of it. And the reminder is a timely one insofar as the understanding of being conveyed by the interpretation is to be modified here or made more precise.

The modification is in a way prepared by the distinction with which the chapter opens between what is said to be by way of accident and what is said to be of itself, the same distinction, in the same words, that had been made for a different purpose in D6 with regard to "one." Accidental being is then explained as we have seen. The being of an accident is traced to its belonging to what is called here, loosely, a "being" (on) and is in fact a thing (ousia), not identified as such (compare D6 1015b20–22). This is consistent with the understanding of what makes a being a being conveyed in the pages already referred to (64–66), so long as one adds that what is here said only of accidents applies also to what belongs to a thing as the thing that it is. But which, then, are the beings said here to be "of themselves"? They are, according to what Aristotle suggests, the forms of predication, the so-called "categories," or rather the predications themselves that are made in those "categories." (Most but by no means all of these are of accidents.) Being or to be (tò einai) is said by him to signify the same as each of these predications. And this is as much as to say that each of them, without requiring the addition of an "is," by itself signifies being. There is no difference between "man is walking" and "man walks."

Now just here, where we are apt to be misled by a somewhat specious similarity to a passage in G2 (1003b26–30), as well as by an understanding of the "categories" which takes them to include "ousia," we must be careful not to misconstrue Aristotle's suggestion and thus perhaps miss the difficulty that it confronts us with. The so-called "first ousiai" or what we have been calling the "things," which are neither said of any substratum nor are they in a substratum (Categories 5 2a11–14), are precisely what the "categories," as the forms or classes of predications, cannot include (3a 36–37). And therefore the listing, in the work of that name, which includes "ousia" (that is, even "first ousia") is described as a listing, not of "categories," but of the various ways in which something is said without being combined with something else (Categories 4 1b25–28; compare 5 2a11–14). Here in D7 on the other hand (as also in E2 1026a35–b1 and Topics A9 103b20–23), where Aristotle speaks of the forms of predication, "ousia" is replaced by "what (it) is," by kind or definition—not things, but what numbers of them share. But the difficulty with which his suggestion confronts us does not lie in its exclusion of the things from what are said "of themselves" to be, an exclusion that we have already taken account of. It lies rather in the attribution, to whatever can be predicated of the things, of a being that belongs to the predicated beings "of themselves" and not insofar as they are dependent on the things (compare G2 1003b5–10). How is the independence of these beings, as beings, from the things to be reconciled with their dependence, as beings, on them, a dependence that has just (so far as accidental being is concerned) been reaffirmed? Or how is their quasi-independence as beings to be understood?

Perhaps we can begin to understand it by starting from the fact that what they are dependent on are the things (ousiai)—these and not some further, in itself unidentifiable substratum. For they are already parts of the things, not something that emerges merely as an after-product or by-product of them. This is so to a considerable extent even of the accidents, as Aristotle has just reminded us in D6, but still more of the beings which belong to the things as the things that they are, or which delimit and define them (compare D8 1017b17–21 as well as B5 1001b32–1002a12). More precisely, the latter are what belong to them as their essence or form, once their generation has been completed (D4 1015a10–11). Yet that generation remains the generation of the things, rather than of those aspects of them which constitute their form. One might even say that the forms are not generated or that there is no genesis of them (Z8 1033b5–8)—which does not mean that they always are (Z15 1039b20–26, H5 1044b21–22). It means rather that they cannot be adequately accounted for by recourse to the process of generation (of the things) to which they owe their being, for there are necessities/impossibilities connected with the formal aspects of things that cannot be traced to their generation (if they are the result of growth) or to their making (if they were made). The maker of the square-shaped thing did not make the incommensurability of the diagonal with its side. And something more or less similar to this would have to be said with regard to the accidents. Thus the beings with which we are now concerned—those said to be, or to be also, "of themselves"—remain dependent, as beings, upon the things of which they are the parts or relations. But, precisely as those parts or relations, as giving expression to what and how the things are, they set limits to them which cannot be explained as derivative from that dependence. (See pages 71–72 and 99 above.)

From the beings said to be by way of accident and those said to be of themselves—better: from the beings that may be said to be either by virtue of accruing to or belonging to the things or of themselves, Aristotle turns to being as what is true. In this usage of "to be" and "is," as "the emphatic position" (Ross ad loc.) of the "is" indicates, there is an affirmation of the correctness of a prior predication (which may remain unspoken), of a pre-existing awareness. In other words, the thing said to be what it is said or thought to be is seen also as an object of that pre-existing awareness, as is the "what." In the being ascribed here to the "what" its being the object, that it is, of our awareness is then tacitly included. There is no reason to suppose that the beings belonging to this class are any others than those belonging to the class or classes treated before it.

The beings that have been mentioned in the chapter are said to be, even when they belong only potentially, and not actually or in their completion, to the things to which they are attributed. Aristotle does not criticize this usage as a loose one: as objects of our awareness, the things are also what they may (but also may not) become. But by reserving for another occasion a treatment of the question of when such potentiality is present and when it is not yet present, he indicates that there must be some substantial ground for it.

D8) What is called "ousia" according to the usage which is mentioned first are the simple bodies like earth and fire and water and as many (others) as are of this sort and, generally, bodies and the living and "daimonic" (divine or heavenly) things, and their parts, that have come together from bodies. All of these are called "ousia" because they are not predicated of a substratum; rather "the others" (are predicated) of them. On a more precise rendering of them (Z16 1040b5–10), the ousiai of this class are just the things. But there is another manner in which "ousia" is used.—

There are altogether just these two manners (1017b14–15 and 23).—Called "ousia" in this second manner are [a] whatever, internal to such (ousiai) as are not predicated of a substratum, should be a cause of their being: like the soul, Aristotle adds, for a living thing; [b] as many parts as are internal to such (ousiai as are not predicated of a substratum) and delimit (each of them) and signify (it) as "some this": parts which, should they be taken away, the whole (thing) is, as some people say or think, taken away; and [c] "the what it was to be," whose logos is a definition (of each thing of which it is "the what it was to be"): this, too, is called an "ousia" of each. As for [c], nothing is said as to its being a cause of any thing (or of the being of any thing) whose "what it was to be" it is. (Compare Z10 1035b14–16.)

It thus turns out, according to Aristotle, that "the ousia" is used either of the ultimate substratum, which is no longer predicated of another, or of whatever, being "some this," should be also separable; and here he adds, apparently on his own authority, that the shape and the form of each (thing) is of this latter sort. Now the juxtaposition of "the ultimate substratum, which is no longer predicated of another," with "the shape and the form of each (thing)" could tempt us to identify that substratum with "matter." But this is merely a summarizing statement, and nothing in the chapter thus summarized has pointed to "matter." The only ousiai said to serve as substrata were those mentioned first, and of them it was said more than once that they are not predicated of a (further, more ultimate) substratum. So we must take Aristotle's summation to mean rather that "the ultimate substratum" (too) is, in each case, "some this" (compare 1017b17–18) and separable. What distinguishes it then from what is called "ousia" according to the other usage is that the latter, whether regarded as an internal cause of the being of some thing or its delimiting parts or its "what it was to be," <u>is</u> predicated of a substratum, namely, of the thing in question. As for the claim that, as the shape and the form of each thing, "the ousia" in this sense is not only "some this" but also separable (from the thing)—as it must be, if it is a cause of the being of the thing, that is, of the thing (B3 999a17–19)—Aristotle's view of the matter must be gathered from the argument of the Metaphysics as a whole, or from the progression of that argument.

D9 & D10) Here Aristotle treats of what are said to be the same or different (hetera), therefore also of what are said to have a difference (diaphora), and of what are said to be like or unlike (D9); of what are said to be opposed in various ways, contraries especially, and of what are said to be different or the same in form (D10). He will treat in D11 of what are said to be prior or posterior. The same and different, like and unlike, and contrariety, as well as prior and posterior, had been singled out for mention, from among all of the distinctions that dialecticians attempt to investigate in their own way, in B1 (995b20–25; compare Topics A1–2). Aristotle had, in effect, asked there whether the theoretical pursuit of all such distinctions is a concern also of the science that is being sought in and through the Metaphysics. In doing so, he made clear that this is a different question from the one that he had asked immediately before it as to whether the theoretical pursuit of what accrue of themselves to the things (ousiai) is of concern to that science along with, what is certainly of concern to it, the theoretical pursuit of the things (B1 995b18–20: on the meaning and import of this question, see pages 100–103 above). But he failed in the context to clarify the relation of the same, different, like, unlike, contrariety, and prior and posterior and the others—not to mention what accrue of themselves to them (B1 995b25–27)—to what accrue of themselves to the things. And this enabled him then to appeal in G2 to the earlier passage, even as he was in the process of assimilating to one another the classes that he had there, apparently, set apart (1004a31–b4 and page 66 above; compare also 1004b17–26 and context, the reference to the dialecticians, with the reference to them in B1 995b23–24 and context). That is, he assimilates in G2 the class consisting of what belongs to the things (ousiai), including what belongs to them as the things that they are, to that consisting of the same and different and their kin, taken as the class of what belongs to being (on) as being or to being and the one (1003b33–1004a2, 1005a11–18). But this was just the question that we were left with in B1 and that we are now, in the wake of the treatment of the one and of being and of ousia in D6–D8, compelled by D9 and D10 to come back to: is this the way in which what accrue of themselves to the things (ousiai) must be approached, if they are to be understood?

The same and different and their kin are indeed fundamental distinctions in the sense that, without them, we would be unable to articulate our world (see page 79 above). It is tempting, therefore, to attribute to them such primacy, expressed in G2 as a primacy in being, as would make them responsible not just for the possibility of articulation but for the articulation itself, for the shape that the world in fact assumes for a sufficiently thoughtful human being. And if this is a temptation that G2 came close to succumbing to (see, for example, 1003b33–1004a2 together with 1004b27–1005a5), it makes sense that the effort made there to endow the distinctions that are also their own theme with the weight that is presumably conferred on them by a closeness to the one and to being is appealed to by both of our chapters (1018a4–9 and 35–38). Yet each of them, and still more both taken together, supplies evidence of the fluidity, not to say confusion, that attaints even or precisely the first of these distinctions when they are abstracted from their uses in the articulation of the world given to us in experience and are left so-to-speak to themselves. And this tends to confirm what we may already have come to suspect: that the beings which belong more immediately to the things, which are expressed in the forms of predication, and which as we saw in D7 cannot be understood from below (that is, by starting from the things, taken somehow in abstraction from the beings that belong to them), can as little be understood from above, by starting from the most general of distinctions, taken as the fundamental distinctions of being as being.

D11) As has already been noted, this chapter on what are said to be prior or posterior shares with its two predecessors their link to B1 (995b22) and G2 (1005a16).

Some of what are said to be prior (to what they are being compared with by the use of this term) are said to be so as the closer to some principle, which is defined either simply and according to nature or in some more or less arbitrary way (compare D1 1012b34–1013a4)—"as if there is in each genus something (that is) first and (its) principle" (compare G2 1004a25–31). In regard to place, for example, there are some (places) defined according to nature: for example, the middle and the extreme (parts of the world); while, in regard to time, there is "the now" which is used as a principle and first. In regard to motion, what was first to move (something) is—this, too—some principle simply. In regard to power, the choice of the more powerful, which governs another's movement or nonmovement, is a principle insofar as choice itself is a principle (Nicomachean Ethics Z2 1139b4–5). Aristotle could have appealed to the allegedly natural right of the stronger (Laws 690b4–8) if he had wished, in this case, too, to speak of what is simply or according to nature a principle. Similarly, in regard to order, he speaks here only of something defined as first, whose definition governs the arrangement (of the other members of the class). (Compare the treatment of this sort of priority in Categories 12 14a35–b3.)

In another manner—the second of three treated here in which what are said to be prior are said to be so (compare 1018b29–30 and 1019a1–3 with 1018b37–38)—what is prior according to knowledge (is said to be prior) "as if (it is) also prior simply" (compare D17 1022a9–10). What is said in this "other" manner to be prior is thus distinguished by Aristotle from what were said to be prior in the manner discussed before it, as well as from what are said to be prior in the manner discussed after it.

Since knowledge is acquired by reason (logos) and by sense perception, what is said to be prior according to knowledge will vary accordingly. For reason, the universals are prior; for sense perception, the particulars. (That is, knowledge combines in some way awareness of particulars with awareness of universals.) For reason, that which accrues is prior to the whole (the thing to which it accrues)—for example, "music" is prior to "musical human being"—for the logos is not whole without (its) part. What, then, for sense perception corresponds to this priority of the part for reason? Since it is not admissible for music (the part) to be, if there is not someone musical (the whole), we might expect that it is the whole (the thing) that is prior for sense perception. But Aristotle does not say so (or give any other answer to our question). What he indicates by his silence is perhaps this: the wholes (the things) are not grasped by sense perception, nor by reason—either by itself or in combination with sense perception—though, so far as they are grasped at all, they are of course not grasped without these (compare page 66 above). And they are prior, therefore, not according to knowledge but in some still more fundamental manner.

In that manner, discussed by Aristotle in the third place, what admit of being without others that do not admit of being without them (are said to be) prior in nature and ousia. What we have seen before about the relation of the beings that accrue to them to the ousiai or things (pages 100–103 above) may have prepared us to some extent for considering ousia (together with nature) as the standard for the most fundamental priority (1019a11–12). But the superiority of the ousiai or things was not understood hitherto as a superiority in being, strictly speaking (see pages 64–66 above as well as Physics Th7 260b17–19; compare the remark of Alfarabi quoted by Shuki B. Abed in Aristotelian Logic and the Arabic Language in Alfarabi p. 123: that from the point of view of natural science as distinct from logic, "the existence of a thing is nothing other than the thing itself"). And here Aristotle speaks of the priority of the ousiai or things as resting on the admissibility of their being (tò einai) without others. But the reason is perhaps suggested by what he adds at once: "but since 'to be' (is said) in many ways, first the substratum is prior, and therefore ousia is prior [compare D8]; then, what (are prior) in potentiality and in actuality/completion (are prior) in other way(s)." Now, what are prior in actuality/completion would be, in the preeminent case, just the ousiai or things. The addition amounts therefore to an admonition not to lose sight of potentiality—and in particular, as the sequel confirms, such potentiality as lies in the fact that the wholes or ousiai are potentially their matter or those of their parts that will be (and will be without them) when they themselves are dissolved. What Aristotle points to, in saying of the ousiai or things that they admit of being (without others), is then nothing so much as their perishability, the perishability of the naturally prior. But it is not for this reason, or not for it alone, that they are not said to be prior also according to knowledge.

D12) The naturally prior are the wholes or ousiai. They admit of being without the actual (separate) existence of their matter or parts, an existence that presupposes their own dissolution. They are thus prior in actuality/completion to such parts or matter; but these are potentially prior to them. The parts or matter will exist when they are no more. This potential genesis or coming to be of their parts or matter is, then, at the same time their own potential perishing or ceasing to be, a potentiality which belongs to them as the actual/completed things that they are. But the potentiality in question, as any potentiality (dunamis), belongs to them not severally or separately but insofar as they are affected by, and affect in turn, other things. This appears to be the principal result (1020a4–6) of the chapter on potentiality or power/capacity (dunamis) that Aristotle appends to his treatment of what are said to be prior or posterior. And it raises the question of whether the naturally prior should not, rather than the things, be said to be the complex of them in their mutual relations (or what we today are accustomed to call nature). This, in turn, could point to the further question of whether we might find in that complex itself the permanence that we are unable, apparently, to find in the things (but compare pages 53–54 above).

The "dunamis" of some thing is its power/capacity to initiate movement or change in another (or in itself as another) or its power/capacity to suffer movement or change at the initiative of another (or of itself as another). For we say, in virtue of the "dunamis" by which it suffers what it suffers, that it is capable (dunaton) of suffering; but sometimes we say this only when the change in question is for the better. It is understandable therefore that, additionally, the states (hexeis) in virtue of which things do not suffer change for the worse, or do not easily do so, are called "dunameis" (pl.); for detrimental change, up to and including perishing altogether, is undergone not from being capable but from not being capable and lacking something. Yet even what is (in the process of) perishing is, it seems, capable (dunaton) of perishing; or it would not have perished, if it was incapable (adunaton) of doing so or, as one could also render "adunaton" here, if this were impossible for it.

In the latter part of the chapter, Aristotle turns explicitly to this other manner of rendering both "dunaton" and "adunaton": as "possible" and "impossible." Impossible is that whose contrary is not only true but of necessity true: what is impossible, is not only false but of necessity false. The possible corresponding to it is then that whose contrary is not of necessity true. But this may be either something whose contrary is necessarily false, that is, something which is itself necessarily true (for the necessary, too, must be possible [On Interpretation 13]); or what is in fact true; or what admits of being true.—The diagonal of the square, whose commensurability with the side is of necessity false, is the sole example offered by Aristotle for what is "adunaton" in this manner.

D13) Each of the next three chapters is devoted to one of the "categories" (forms or classes of predications), in which the beings that define and delimit the things, or more generally that accrue to them, are to be found (D7 1017a22–30, Topics A9 103b20–27). The particular theme of each of them is treated also, and at greater length, in the Categories. But just as much of what is said there is not repeated here, so some of what Aristotle says here is lacking there. Presumably, he is here most concerned to bring out what must be taken into account in understanding the basis for a philosophic science, which will be, as is becoming ever more clear, a science of the ousiai or things.

That it is "just so much" (poson) is said of what is divisible into constituents, each of which tends naturally to be "some one" and "some this." In the case of magnitudes—as well as that of multitudes consisting of anything other than monads or points—each of these constituents will in turn be something that can be said to be "just so much." But will it also, will every magnitude in other words, be necessarily "some one" and "some this"? Unless we are meant to accept that even a line, for example, is an ousia (1020a20 and Ross ad loc.), it seems unlikely that this is Aristotle's suggestion here. One might wonder rather about its converse: whether everything of which one can say that it is "some this" or a thing, together with each of its parts (in the sense of part called to our attention in D11), is not "just so much" or of some magnitude.—Among what are said to be "just so much" by virtue of belonging to some thing that is "just so much," is "music" (1020a26–28; compare D11 1018b34–37).—Motion (and therefore also time) is said to be "just so much" by virtue of the divisibility of that of which the motion is a "pathos" (of what suffers the motion). By this Aristotle means, however, not the thing that is in motion but the magnitude along which it moves, that is, the magnitude against which the "so much" of the motion can be measured. He thus allows to the motion, here as in D4 (pages 94 and 96 above), some independence of the thing in motion, considered in abstraction from its motion.

D14) In one manner, what is said to be "tò poion" (just the sort something is) is the difference (diaphora) of or within the ousia. For example, man is an animal "of just some sort" because he is a two-footed animal, whereas horse is a four-footed one. "Tò poion" (one should retain the article with the mss.) is thus more obviously a qualification of something than "poson" was, which could be taken to be the thing (of some magnitude) itself. But of what is it a qualification? "Two-footed" is a qualification of animal and therefore of man. But according to the Categories—the chapter on ousia (5), not that on quality (poiotēs), which treats "tò poion" without taking notice of questions like this (8)—even man, along with animal, is a qualification in turn of something else: of "some this," which is "of just some sort" because it is animal and man (3b10–23). At this point, however, the question arises of whether we know the "this" in question, except insofar as it is animal and man (see, even as to sense perception, the enigmatic remark of Posterior Analytics B19 100a16–b1 and compare page 72 above). But, in knowing it as animal and man, do we know it as the thing or whole as which it is given to us? (See page 108 above.)

"This, then, is one manner in which quality (hē poiotēs) is said: (a) difference of (an) ousia"—Aristotle first repeats himself. He does so apparently in order to distinguish this manner from another one, which affects the mathematicals as well as whatever else there may be that lacks motion. As for the mathematicals, "of just some sort" in this other manner are the numbers: for example, among the non-primes, those which are the product of two factors ("plane" numbers) or those which are the product of three ("solid" numbers). And, to speak generally, quality is said in this other manner to be "what, besides 'the just so much' (tò poson), is present in the ousia; for (the) ousia of each (is) that (which it is) once: for example, (the ousia) of the six (monads) is not what (they are) two times (of) or three times (of)"—in other words, it is not their factors—"but what (they are) once; for (the) six (are) once six."

A difficulty has been felt to lie here in the fact that Aristotle insists that the ousia of each of these numbers is what they are once, immediately after pointing to the complexity within the ousia of each. Indeed, he justifies his pointing to that complexity by this insistence: they would not be the distinct numbers that they are, if they were not also complex. Moreover, their oneness is the oneness of that complexity, of the manyness consisting in that complexity. It can therefore, and it must, be understood as such. Here the many are truly one, and the one many (Philebus 14c1–10, 15d4–8). But does the same hold also for such ones as man (compare D18 1022a33–35, as well as Sophist 251a5–b8)? Do we, in their case, have an equally clear grasp of a whole that comprehends their manyness?

Aristotle might seem to suggest as much by withdrawing his suggestion that the manner in which quality is spoken of in the case of numbers is distinct from the first manner that he mentioned (1020b13–17). But why, then, did he introduce it as a distinct one? According to his new suggestion as to the second of the two manners in which "tò poion" would be spoken of, it is the "pathē" (qualities/sufferings) of the ousiai that are in motion (the things) which supply the counterpart to "the difference of or within the ousia"—those "pathē" in accord with whose changes the bodies (themselves) are said to undergo alteration—or it is the "pathē" of the (bodies) in motion, insofar as they are in motion, and the differences (diaphorai) of or among those motions.

D 15) The distinction between the mathematicals (numbers, in particular) or what is without motion and the things in motion, a distinction which has its place in the consideration that D14 led up to, is carried over to this chapter on what are said to be "toward something" (pros ti). Some of these are said to be "toward something" in that they are said, precisely as what they are, to be "of another" (1021a26–29; compare Categories 7 8a28–35). But others, among which are what is known (or knowable), thought (or thinkable), and perceived by the senses (or perceptible), are said to be "toward something" in that another is said (to be) toward them (1021a29–b3). In his treatment in the Categories of what are said to be "toward something," Aristotle insists, in such cases, too, on a reciprocity in these relations that extends even to a convertibility of terms (7 6b28–7b14). Dropping or modifying that insistence here (compare, with 6b34–36, 1021a31–b3), he stresses rather the dependence, for example, of what is thought (or thinkable) on the thinking of it. Would he then maintain here, as he maintains in Categories 7 (7b33–35), that it is admissible for much of what is known or knowable (epistēta) to be, in the absence of an animal capable of, or possessing, knowledge or science (epistēmē)?

Aristotle easily establishes in this chapter a clear connection between "the one" and "the equal, like, and the same" (compare G2 1003b33–36, 1004a9–10 and 16–19) by using categories as middle terms (1021a8–14; compare pages 105–106 above).

D16) The theme of this chapter—complete/perfect (teleion)—falls within the bounds of the theoretical program proposed in G2, as do the themes of D25, D26 and D28 (1005a5–18; as for that of D17, compare 1004b32 and context). The themes of D19,

D20, D21 and D23, on the other hand, belong to the categories, either as one of them (D23) or as subdivisions of another (D19–D21).

If one approaches the chapter in the expectation or hope of finding in the "teleion" a standard of completion or perfection that, as independent of and above the things, they can be measured or judged by (compare D18 1022–a14–16), one is bound to be disappointed. Offered here, for taking one's bearings in this respect, are only the thing itself (understood as consisting of parts that may or may not all be present in it), its virtue (the form of virtue proper to it as the sort of thing that it is), and its end (telos). And if the last of these is not to be understood to be its perishing or death (teleutē), it must be understood as its (proper) "for the sake of which" (compare Physics B2 194a28–33), that is, as something which may well turn out to be, again, the thing itself and which, in any case, the "teleion" does not determine. The guidance that we can reasonably expect with regard to completion or perfection comes then in each case less from the "teleion" than from the thing—which means from its genus (1021b15, 33), if we know it insofar as it is a member of a class.

D17) There is an obvious kinship between the theme of this chapter—limit—and that of D16. For example, the end (telos) of each thing is said to be its limit. The end is understood here primarily as the goal of its motion and therefore also as its "for the sake of which" (Ross's punctuation rather than Jaeger's). Less clear is whether "the for the sake of which" is understood to be the same as the ousia of each, "the what it was for each to be." But it is at any rate the latter which is the limit—in the sense of principle—for the knowledge (of each): "and, if of the knowledge, then of the thing." The reference the chapter makes to the usages of "principle" and therewith to D1 points to the qualification which this assertion requires (page 86—compare also 107 and 111—above)—valid as it may be, without qualification, for the thing as member of a class (compare pages 70–72 and 99 with 112 above).

D18) The first theme of this chapter is "that by which." For instance, the form and the ousia of each thing (or attribute) is said to be that by which the thing is of a certain sort (or has the attribute). But the first, as matter or proximate substratum, in which (the attribute) naturally tends to come to be is also said to be that by which (a thing has the attribute). And the expression is used in several other ways as well.

Since "that by which" is said in many ways, it is necessary that "by itself," the other theme of the chapter, be said in many ways, too. However that may be, the usages of "by itself" to some extent correspond to those of "that by which." First mentioned is "the what it was to be for each." This is what each by itself is said to be. But the example here is "Kallias" (a particular man): "the what it was to be for Kallias." Do particular things have, as particulars, a "what it was to be," that is, a definition? (Compare Thomas, Commentary on Aristotle's Metaphysics, para. 1054.) In the central place is the additional suggestion that a thing is said by itself to be what it, or some part of it, is the first recipient of. For example, man by himself is alive; for the soul, which is some part of man, is the first (recipient) in which life (or living) is.

This remark is an improvement on what was said about soul in D8 (1017b14–16). But, insofar as it identifies the matter or substratum (the condition, in other words) of soul with soul, it falls short of the authoritative statements of Z10 (1035b14–16) and On the Soul B1 (412b10–11). Yet even or precisely those statements—according to which soul is "the what it was to be" for a certain sort of body—could in one respect tend to mislead us. They could tend to make us forgetful of the fact that every actual soul is a particular soul, the soul of a particular. Was it to remind us of this fact that Aristotle spoke in this context of "the what it was to be for Kallias"?

If every actual soul is a particular one, a knowledge which sees, as such, the particular always as a member of some class remains nevertheless tied to the sheer particularity of its possessor or possessors. And one might consider in this light the enigmatic suggestion with which the chapter ends (as given in Jaeger and Christ, without the emendation of Ross).

D19–D21) The order (or ordering) of what has parts, with respect to (their) place or (their) power or (their) form, is said to be (its) disposition (or disposing). A disposition by which the disposed is either well or badly disposed is said to be (its) state: order as such need not be good or bad order. (Compare D22 1023a5–7.)

The "in-between" of what is had and the one who has it—as making (poiēsis) is in between whenever something is making, something being made—is also said to be a state or, to translate less freely, a having (hexis). The "in-between" in question is like some being-at-work (energeia) of what has and is had; motion is of this sort; a state or having in this sense cannot itself be had. (Compare pages 110 bottom-111 top above.)

Quality/suffering (pathos) has already been treated in Delta, in the discussion (D14) of "just the sort something is" (tò poion) or quality (poiotēs). There, as here, its connection with alteration and motion is stressed.—In none of these chapters does Aristotle appear to take his bearings by the treatment of their themes in Categories 8.

D22) "Deprivation" (sterēsis) is used if something which naturally tends to be had is not had, most strictly when it is not had by that whose nature it is to have it, when and under the conditions that it naturally has it. Additionally the taking away of anything due to constraint is called "deprivation": the aforementioned cases need not, then, be due to constraint. They may have to be traced, no less than nature itself (the natural order), to natural causes.

D23) "To have" (or hold) is used in many ways. In the first of these to be mentioned, it is applied to the leading (of something) in accord with the nature or the impulse of what leads—and not, as the examples make clear, of what is led. Additionally, as is mentioned somewhat later on, when something is hindered from moving or acting in accord with its impulse, it is said to be held by that which is hindering it: as columns (are said to hold) the weights lying on them (which they hinder from falling) and as the poets make Atlas hold the heaven—as if (by its own impulse) it would fall onto the earth, as some of the natural scientists say as well.

One of the manuscripts (Ab) adds here, in illustration of what the latter say, a line from Hesiod (Theogony 517): "Atlas holds the wide heaven by strong necessity." If one accepts the addition as genuine, as perhaps one should, one would have to conclude that Aristotle considered Hesiod to be one of the natural scientists and that he regarded it as possible that a natural scientist might choose, on occasion, to speak as a theologian (compare B4 1000a9 and A4 984b27–28).

D24) The theme of this chapter on how "to be from something" is said shows up here without the warrant of a connection with G2 or the Categories. (As to the theme of D22, see G2 1004a10–16 as well as Categories 10.)—In one usage of the expression, the "from which" is said to be so as (the) matter (of things); in another one, as the first moving principle (the origin of the motion in question). In another one, (it is) from the composite of (or from) the matter and the shape (that things are said to be), as (for example) the parts from the whole and the stones from the house. In explanation, apparently, of this usage, Aristotle says that the shape (morphē) is (an) end (telos), but complete/perfect (teleion) is what has (the) end. (Compare pages 107–108 above.) There is also a usage in which the form (eidos) is said to be from the matter of the form, as from its part; for "man" is from "two-footed" in another way than the composite ousia is from the perceptible matter.—In reviewing this presumably complete enumeration, we are bound to be struck by the fact that the form or shape itself is not said to be the "from which" of anything.

In its concluding portion, the chapter turns to an alleged usage of a very different sort. What comes after something in time is said to be from it: for example, night (is said to be) from day and a storm from fair weather. In some of these cases, like those just mentioned, there is change "into one another" (in other words, day in turn follows night and fair weather a storm); in others, there is only a succession in time: for example, when a sailing was from or after the equinox. The mention of the equinox in connection with a division between recurring and non-recurring change could remind one of the question in this regard that Aristotle posed in the last chapter of On Generation and Corruption (B11 337a34–b13), a question to which he gave there an inconclusive answer.

D25) Aristotle is, in this chapter on how "part" is used, as little of a mind as he was in its predecessor to deny that things are composed of their form and what has the form (whether or not they can also be divided into these components) or to deny that the form is in the matter. (Compare pages 86–87 and 89–90 above.) Yet the parts of the form, which is apparently a whole, appear to be indistinguishable from those of the logos that makes clear (as to) each thing (what it is). (Consider the "carelessness" that Ross complains of, Vol. I, p. 340 top, as well as the similar anomaly in D28 that he alludes to in his note to 1024b4.)

D26 & D27) The first of these chapters is on how "whole" is used; the second is on the use of a term that is applied only to wholes, to wholes which are magnitudes. The first speaks also of the universal as a sort of whole: it makes the many that are embraced by it one by being predicated of each of them (so that) each is one or all are one severally. (Compare D6 and pages 99–100 above; D26 refers explicitly to the earlier chapter a bit further on.) This is one of the ways in which the form was perhaps suggested in D25 to be a whole (1023b17–19 and 24–25): what is called there "the form without the 'just so much'" is just the genus or class. As for the other way in which the form was suggested to be a whole, most explicitly in D25 (1023b19–20 and 22–24) but also in D24 (1023a35–b2), it appears to find no particular echo in this pair of chapters. (Compare page 112 above.)

D28) In the last of this series of chapters, which began (in D24) with the tacit admission that the form (eidos), its paramount theme throughout, is not the "from which" of anything, Aristotle turns to the usages of "genus." The first to be mentioned is "the continuous generation (of things) having the same form: for example, it is said 'for as long as the genus of human beings may be'" (compare

Prior Analytics A13 32b8–9). Since nothing comes from the form, it cannot guarantee the persistence in being of the class of those who have it. Nor can it have been responsible for the emergence of the class. The first human progenitor of a particular tribe of human beings is described later on in the chapter as their first mover (which is) "like in form." And in a further reference to the first mentioned usage, Aristotle goes so far as to speak of continuous generation "of the same form" (compare pages 102–103 above).

D29 & D30) A remark that Aristotle finds cause to make at the end of D28 gives expression to a thought to which we were led by his discussion in D9 and D10 (compare page 106 bot. with 1024b12–16). It concerns the categories, about which we have heard quite a lot in the intervening chapters. D29 and D30, on the other hand, are about "the false" (and, therewith, the true) and "accident" respectively. (For the relation of these themes to the theme of the categories, see D7.) These facts are insufficient as a basis for establishing the order of the second part of Delta (D9–D30), but they are noteworthy as indicators of the presence of order, of an argument, even here.

The final chapter, on "accident" (sumbebēkos), by distinguishing the usage of the term treated here as the primary one from another, in which it is used for attributes that belong to a thing by itself although they are not in its definition, provides an opportunity for Aristotle to remark that it is inadmissible for accidents proper to be everlasting. The chapter on "the false" closes with a critique of the defense that Socrates makes in the Lesser Hippias of the willingness on occasion to lie. Aristotle spells out his disagreement with Plato or his Socrates in such a way as to allow the reader to see that it falls short of being complete.

In one of the ways in which "the false" is applied to a thing (as distinct from a logos), it is said of something that is but tends naturally to appear (phainesthai) either as not of the sort that it is or as what it is not. For example, shadow drawing and dreams are false in these ways; for they are something but not that, the appearance or imagination of which, they are responsible for.

"Phantasia," the term translated here as "appearance or imagination," can mean either or perhaps also both together: that is, it is perhaps best taken in this context as imagination together with its object. But, in taking it in this way, we should keep in mind that, if there is a "false phantasia" (1025a6), there must also be a true one. In the case of the latter, what is responsible for the "phantasia" will appear in or to it as what (and as of the sort that) it is. Or, as one can also say, it will be what (and of the sort that) it appears to be. But what appears, in the most important case, in this way are just the things: "phantasia is not the same as sense perception" (G5 1010b3; compare pages 66, 108, and 111 above). And the things will thus be responsible for the "phantasia" in question or for its objects in no other way than, according to Aristotle, health makes health or wisdom makes happiness (Nicomachean Ethics Z12 1144a3–5): by being those objects.

E1) As we have tried to show, Delta is rich in questions bearing on the desideratum of a philosophic science: on the availability of a sufficient basis for it; on the character of the science possible on such basis as may be available. The preparation for the appreciation of those questions was laid in the argument of the work hitherto or by what we ventured to call the progression of the argument (page 105—compare pages 85 and 89—above). There is no reason to suppose that its progress, carried forward in Delta itself, should have come to an end there.

The first chapter of Gamma had begun by asserting that there is some science that pursues theoretically being (tò on) as being (on) and what belongs to it as such. That chapter had accordingly gone on to observe that none of the so-called "partial" sciences investigates being as being universally (1003a22–25). The counterpart at the beginning of the first chapter of Epsilon, to the assertion with which Gamma begins, is a reminder of the task of a philosophic science. And in this connection the observation is made that "all" sciences fail to concern themselves with being (on) simply and as being (on). Our chapter does identify, later on, a science that would pursue theoretically being as being, what it is and what belongs to it as being. That science is theology; and it is the first of the sciences by virtue of the exalted status of the primary object or objects of its knowing—what is permanent and without motion and separate or separable (from perceptible being)—and universal insofar as it is first. But there will be that science only if its primary objects are, something which is left entirely open here (1026a10–13 and 29–32, as well as E2 1027a17–19; compare Z2 1028b27–32 and Z17 1041a6–9, as well as Z16 1040b26–1041a3). And only in that case will there be a science that pursues theoretically (also) being as being; for the alternative of a first philosophy that is universal in the manner of a certain unnamed mathematical discipline (1026a23–27) has been silently rejected along the way. The true alternative to theology is physics (natural science), whose objects are neither separable nor without motion (1025b18–21, b26–28, b34–1026a3, a13–14, reading here "achorista" with the mss.): if there is no different ousia, alongside of or beyond the naturally constituted ones, physics would be the first science (1026a27–29).

This would not necessarily rule out all scientific consideration of being as such (G3 1005a31–33), but it would render questionable any unqualified censure of the sciences for failing to concern themselves with being simply and as being. To the observation that the sciences do fail to make this their concern, our chapter appends a twofold criticism of them: "nor do they make any argument (logos) for the 'what (it) is' (of the genus with which they are concerned) . . . ; nor, likewise, do they argue (legein) at all as to whether that genus is or is not. . . ." By appending the criticism to the observation, the text appears to suggest that there is a connection between the facts to which they refer. Is the failure or even inability of the sciences to establish by argument the existence and character of their objects to be traced to their failure to make being simply and as being their concern? Or is it not rather the other way around: that such clarity as we have about the objects of our concern, which are also the objects of the sciences, is the only genuine access to "being" that we have? (Compare pages 64–66 above.) We might also note here that the sciences admittedly do make clear the character of their objects (1025b10–16)—in the manner in which it is possible for them to do so (Posterior Analytics A9 76a16–18 [compare B7 92b12–15], A10 76a31–36, B8 93b15–B9 93b28, A18, B19 99b15–19 and b34–100b5, B13 97b31–32)—and that the instruction offered in our chapter on how definitions in physics need to be made makes no mention of "being." To this last point, however, the objection might reasonably be made that a comprehensive reflection on the beings, which divides them somewhat tentatively into three classes, underlies the instruction and that a reflection of another sort on being takes up the remaining chapters of Epsilon, to say nothing for now of the books which follow it.

E2 & E3) The first of these chapters begins with a reminder of the fourfold division of being—or of what is "simply" so-called, as it is said here (compare E1 1025b9)—that had been given in D7. The threefold division of E1 served to distinguish the objects of physics (inseparable [from perceptible being] but not without motion) from those of some mathematical disciplines (without motion but perhaps not separable but as if in matter) and from those of theology (separate [or separable] and without motion). In what relation to that threefold division does this new/old fourfold one stand? —Immediately after reminding us of it, the chapter embarks upon a lengthy discussion of one of its members, a discussion that continues to the end of E3. Accidental being had been treated perfunctorily in D7 (and somewhat less so in D30); why is it necessary to treat it at length in the present context (compare E4 1027b33–1028a4)? —Each of these questions may prove to point to a third one, in connection with which they would ultimately have to be understood. Given that a first science, even if it should be physics rather than theology, cannot dispense entirely with reflection on being, what is the necessary scientific purpose which is served by the minimum of such reflection that is possible and indispensable?

In order to make a start toward answering this question, we might return to the fact that the identification of theology as the science that would pursue theoretically being as being was accompanied by the silent rejection of a universal science (of being simply and as being): in other words, that identification amounted to a denial of the possibility of such a science. The knowledge of being to be expected from theology itself cannot have been understood then to be such as the rejected science might have been expected to provide. It must have been understood rather to be derivative in some way from theology's knowledge of what we called earlier its primary objects. Now those objects are or include the permanent causes of the highest of the manifest beings (E1 1026a15–18); and to know their permanent causes is to know the limits of the changes to which those beings—and, to that extent, being or beings altogether—are subject. But the limits, or the permanent necessities to which beings as beings are subject, are what any science must seek to know if it is to become worthy of the name. If it is not theology, then, but physics which is the first science, its very possibility as a science will depend upon the finding of a path—other than the one to which theology would have been able to lay claim—to such an understanding of necessity as is sufficient for a genuine science to rest on (compare E2 1027a17–19 with 1026b27–29 and E1 1026a10–18). And since the necessity or necessities in question will be those which limit the beings, it would not be unreasonable to call any reflection that should enable us to grasp them a reflection on being. Indeed, it may not be going too far to suggest that those who raised the question of "being" (Z1 1028b2–4) did so from the beginning in search of the foundation that science requires.

In introducing the discussion of accidental being, Aristotle indicates that its purpose is to show that there is no theoretical pursuit (possible) in regard to the accidental. This enables him to return to the subject of science at the end of E2; but in the meantime, in repeating the introduction, he has relegated the purpose thus indicated to second place: on account of what there is no science of the accidental will "perhaps" be clear "at the same time" from a discussion which, to the extent that the accidental admits of being discussed, will treat of its nature and of the cause on account of which it is.

The most difficult and also the most important challenge with which the discussion confronts the reader is that of following the author's use in it of the term "of (or by) necessity." He appears to bring accidental being to light against a background of necessity and regularity: that is, by contrasting the accidental with those among the beings which are always in the same way, because they are that way "of (or by) necessity," and those among them which are, not indeed "of (or by) necessity" nor always in the same way, but for the most part (E2 1026b27–33 and 1027a15–17: for the way in which the latter passage must be translated, a matter of some importance, one should consult Smyth's grammar, paras. 2761 and 2942). On closer inspection, it becomes clear that the existence of the accidental is dependent only on that of beings which are in the same way for the most part (E2 1027a8–11); and Aristotle finally admits as much, by raising the question whether or not there is any "always" belonging to the beings—whether or not any of them are permanent—without at the same time calling into question the existence of the accidental (E2 1027a17–19 and following). The accidental, then, is a correlate of what is for the most part: if the one is, the other will be; and if one is not, neither will the other be. And as for the "always," if it does not belong to any of the beings—if none of them are permanent—there could appear to be no necessity among them either (E2 1026b27–29 and 1027a8–9). When Aristotle says therefore—in the same context in which he has first indicated that what the accidental presupposes is the existence of what is for the most part rather than of what is always (E2 1027a8–11)—that, if the accidental will not be, "everything will be of (or by) necessity" (E2 1027a12–13), it is all too easy for the reader to draw the conclusion that he means that everything would then be always in the same way. This is not what he means, however, as it is the chief burden of E3, where the crucial remark is in effect repeated (1027a29–31), to show. The necessity that he has in mind is neither determinative (only) for some permanent being, nor is it understood to be derivative from such being. It is the necessity that there be for everything which is coming to be and perishing some (sufficient) cause (1027a31–32)—a necessity from which accidental being is exempt only insofar as it does not, as what it is, come to be (compare D30 1025a28–29, reading "hēi" twice in a28 with ms.Ab).

From this we can see the significance of a correct rendering of E2 1027a15–16: one must take this as one's principle (or starting point), the question "whether there is nothing that is either always or for the most part. . . ." Aristotle can conceive, at least, of such a state of affairs (compare On the Heaven G2 301a4–11); and what he suggests by referring to it as and where he does is that the necessity now in question would, as we must assume, hold even there. Finally, it is in this context (that is, on this basis) that he now allows that there may be science of what is only for the most part (E2 1027a20–21; contrast Nicomachean Ethics Z3 1139b18–24).

In concluding our consideration of E1–3, whose importance for the architecture of the Metaphysics as a whole can hardly be overestimated, we note only that the injunction with which E3 ends (1027b14–16) tacitly withdraws a suggestion as to the cause of the accidental that was ventured in E2 (1027a13–15; compare 1027a26–28).

E4) According to the sentence with which this last chapter of Epsilon begins, consideration of accidental being can now be let go, since the determination (of such being) that has been given (in E2–3) is sufficient; but the consideration of it is let go again, for a different reason, later on in the chapter, where accidental being is put in the company of being as truth (1027b33–1028a3). And the latter is admittedly still in need of examination (1027b28–29; as to accidental being itself, see the end of E3). In partial justification of the postponement of that examination, Aristotle says here that being as truth is a different being than those which are authoritatively beings: pronounced as it is, prior to the examination in question, this judgment would seem to be premature. And it is in fact revised later on (Th10 1051b1–2: Ross wishes to excise the offending words from the text or to remove them to a place where they can do no harm). The revision is made in the wake of a consideration of potential being; and it is noteworthy that potential being is deliberately passed over without mention in our chapter (the author refers at 1028a1–2 to "the (one) remaining genus of being"), though just as deliberately pointed to by the reminder (of the fourfold division of being of D7) with which the chapter ends. To his credit, Christ alone, among the recent editors, does not seek to excise that reminder from the text.

Z1) By what we regarded, in imitating it, as an almost unavoidable looseness of speech, ousiai were referred to in Epsilon as beings (E1 1025b18–21; consider also 1026a27–32). In Zeta, however, that loose usage is made official policy. By the addition of "kai tode ti" (Z1 1028a11–12) to the "ti esti" which had stood alone (at D7 1017a25) in the passage referred to here, what was there the first of the categories is reinterpreted to accommodate it. (Consider in this connection the ambiguity, as to what precisely are included among the antecedents of "tōn houtō kategoroumenōn" at 1028a13, introduced by the preceding "men . . . de" as well as that due to "allōn" at 1028a33–34 [Smyth para. 1272]; and compare pages 100–101 above.) But this permits Aristotle to take up the question "which is the ousia?" (Z1 1028b4) or "which are (the) ousiai?" (Z2 1028b28) under the rubric of a reflection on being (Z1 1028b2–7). Now, the question left open in Epsilon (E1 1026a10–11, 27–28, and 29; E2 1027a15–16 and 17–19) and that on whose answer the determination of whether physics or theology is the first science was said there to depend (E1 1026a27–32), is the question as to which the authentic ousiai are. It is true that the consideration of this question is dropped in Zeta almost as soon as the question is taken up; or, rather, its consideration is postponed so that a different, if closely related question—what is ousia?—can be taken up first (Z2 end). But the postponement is necessary, if an obstacle to our discovering which the authentic ousiai are that is posed by an ambiguity in our understanding of the term is to be removed.

The ambiguity in question is one that has been called to our attention on more than one occasion and that we have even discussed (see, for example, pages 71–72 and 99, as well as 103–104, above), without however having been compelled to face it squarely or, therefore, definitively to remove it. How, then, is the consideration of it prepared in Zeta itself?

According to the lines from the beginning of this first chapter that we have already touched on, the same predication that signifies what (a thing) is (ti esti) signifies also, or in so doing, some "this" (kai tode ti). (1028a11–12) Is it the "what" that is the "this" in question? Or is it not, rather, the thing of which the "what" is predicated? But is predicating its "what," saying what it is, that which signifies a thing also as some "this," that is, as a thing (and not merely the thing that it is)? (Compare pages 99–100 above.)—Although all predications in the categories are predications of being, (the) first of these beings is "the what (it) is" (tò ti esti), which signifies the ousia; for, whenever we say of a "this" (merely that it is) "of some sort," we call it good or noble . . . , but whenever (we say) what it is . . . , (we call it) man or god; and the others are called beings by virtue of being the "how much," for example, or the "of what sort" or the "what (it) suffers" of the being (that is) in that way. (1028a13–20) The being that is "in that way" is, presumably, the ousia that is signified by "the what (it) is." But is that ousia, for example, "man"? Is it not, rather, the "this" that is called man? But, in that case, it is by calling a "this" man, for example, that one signifies it as the ousia that it is.—Someone might even be perplexed, therefore, as to whether such terms as "walking" and "enjoying health" signify in each case a being; for nothing so-called is either of a nature (to be) of itself or able to be separated from the ousia (of which it is predicated); but rather "that which (is) walking" and "that which (is) enjoying health" are perhaps among the beings: these are more apparently beings because there is for each of them some definite (defined or delimited) substratum, which appears in such a predication, namely the ousia and the particular. (1028a20–28; compare D7 1017a22–30) Since it is, in each case, clearly a question of a single substratum, what "the ousia" and "the particular" of this formulation refer to must be the same: that is, it is the particular that is the ousia. But it (the particular) would not be that ousia, and perhaps not even, strictly speaking, a particular, a "this," if it were not also delimited or defined by being put into a class such as "man."

On this basis—on the basis of the foregoing considerations—Aristotle draws the conclusion at which the chapter has been aiming: it is clear, then, that it is on account of this (the ousia) that each of those, too, is (the predications in the categories, or in the other categories), so that the ousia would be that which is, in the first place, and . . . that which is, simply. (1028a29–31; compare G2 1003a33–b10 and b16–19) There is no mention either here or at the beginning of the chapter of being, in any sense other than that signified by the categories (the predications made in them) together with, or expanded to include, ousia. And this silence, for which E4 has in a way prepared us, is consistent with what we have seen by looking at the broader context in Zeta: that the focal point of Aristotle's attention here is not being—giving a precise account of it—but ousia. On the other hand, as he suggests at the end of our chapter, to treat of ousia is to treat of what those who speak of being (and who divide over whether it is one or more than one, limited or unlimited in number) have been searching for and have been perplexed about all along.

Finally, as to his contention, in the intervening passage, to the effect that ousia is first in every way: in logos, in knowledge, and in time—what he says in elaboration or justification of it confirms that he understands by ousia here the particular, taken as a member of a class. It is the particular, and not its "what" or class character, that can be said to be (in more than one way) separable (1028a33–34; contrast E1 1025b27–28 and 1026a13–14, according to the mss., as well as H1 1042a28–31); and it is again the particular, taken as we have said that it is, that <u>has</u> a logos. On the other hand, a particular is known, to the extent that it is known, through knowledge of its "what," of its class or class character (1028a36–b2; compare pages 107 and 111 above).

Z2) The question that Z1 has shown again to be paramount and the one to which Aristotle therefore turned at the chapter's end is the question "which" (tis) is the (authentic) ousia or, to put it in the language that he inherited, "which" (ti) is the being that is in that way. Was this question not answered by him, in the course of the chapter, even before he set himself the task, at its end, of pursuing it theoretically? (Compare 1028a16–18 with B4 999b1–5 and pages 50 and 52–53 above.)

However that may be, he begins this new chapter by saying what "we say" (in answer to it): that the animals and the plants, and their parts, are ousiai, as well as the natural bodies, like fire and water and earth and each (of the bodies) of this sort, and what are either parts of them or from them, whether (from) parts or all (of them), like the heaven (compare Physics Th2 252b27) with its parts, stars and moon and sun. Though the expression of it is insufficiently precise (compare Z16 beginning, as well as page 103 above), this suggestion is nevertheless a formidable one due to the ground on which it rests: the manifestness of bodies (in which it locates ousia or does so in the first place). (Compare B5 as well as pages 56–57 and 62–63 above.) Aristotle pauses, therefore, just here to put the question, as one requiring investigation, "whether these alone are ousiai, or also others; or some of these, or also (some) of (the) others; or none of these, but some different ones" (1028b13–15).

Now, if "these alone" are ousiai, as the natural scientists contend (A8 990a3–5 together with G3 1005a31–33), physics would be the first of the sciences (E1 1026a27–29). And this may be the reason why, from early on, there were thinkers who adopted a different view (Plato <u>Sophist</u> 246b6–8 and context; compare A8 989b21–33 together with A5 beginning). Aristotle mentions Plato and Speusippus (who succeeded Plato as head of the Academy) in connection with efforts to "extend" the ousiai (1028b24) to include, besides the perceptible (beings or things), beings that are permanent (1028b19; compare B4 999b4–5) or to find, among the principles of the ousiai, a principle peculiar to soul (1028b22–24; compare Plato <u>Laws</u> 892a2–7). These are the only thinkers whom he mentions by name, although he makes it clear that they were not alone in their resistance to limiting the ousiai to the perceptibles. And, whatever may have been his reason for calling our attention especially to them, his doing so strengthens our impression that the alternatives to the scientific view that he mentions here are all ones (or, at the minimum, akin to ones) that he has already considered (A5–6 and 8–9, B2 and 4–5) and even dismissed. All the more remarkable is the fact that he offers in the chapter no suggestion of his own as to any ousia besides the perceptible ousiai. The question in that regard requiring investigation concerns then what has been finely or not finely said by these others (1028b27–28). Or as he also puts it, more broadly, here (the questions are) "which are ousiai; and whether there are or are not some besides the perceptible ones; and (as to) these (the perceptible ousiai), how they are; and whether there is, besides the perceptible ones, some separable (or separate) ousia—and on account of what and how—or (there is) none" (1028b28–31). This is obviously a repetition, a sharpening, of the earlier formulation that we quoted (1028b13–15); and here the status of the perceptible bodies as ousiai is no longer in question.

Z3) It is at this point—that is, at the end of Z2—that Aristotle suggests that the task of giving an answer, if only in outline, to the question "what" ousia is (ti esti) be taken up "first." The investigation that is postponed for this purpose, whether for a shorter or a longer period—in other words, the investigation to which it is suggested to be a necessary preliminary—is that concerning in the first place the assertions of the thinkers introduced or re-introduced in the latter part of Z2: in particular, the assertion that there is, besides the perceptible ousiai, an ousia that is separable or separate (see Z17 1041a6–9). Those who have recourse to such an ousia are guided in doing so by some notion of what an ousia is. And the task that Aristotle now turns to, beginning with our chapter, amounts to a first step on the way to clarity about that notion and its adequacy.

As the words with which the chapter begins could serve to remind us, however, it is a task that he has taken up once before in the work (compare D8 beginning). And that earlier effort culminated in the assertion, made there apparently on Aristotle's own authority, that the shape and the form of each (thing) is an ousia of such a sort as to be "some this" that is also separable (1017b24–

26). Now to say the least, this assertion is not altogether dissimilar to those that he has just now distanced himself from and called into question. If it, too, then must be considered to have been placed under scrutiny here, the judgment to be rendered on it will depend upon whether the account of ousia, of what it is, given in the earlier passage is, tacitly or explicitly, reaffirmed in this later one, rather than being modified by it or corrected. We will assume throughout, in comparing the two accounts, that whatever is not so modified here retains the validity that it had there.

The accounts (that in D8 and that in Z3, which we will treat for now by itself, although it is, strictly speaking, only the introduction to the account in Zeta) clearly have much in common. Each speaks of what are "called" ousiai: that is, they both purport to take their bearings by usages of the term that are not necessarily Aristotle's own. (Compare page 85 above.) Each mentions, as the later statement acknowledges that it does, four such usages. According to the earlier statement, the usages that it mentions fall into two groups or classes: there are "two manners" of using the term (1017b23; compare b14–15). The classes consist on the one hand of "the ultimate substratum" and, on the other, of the three other usages. The four usages mentioned in the later statement can also be said to fall into these classes—the one consisting of what it calls "the first substratum," the other of the other three usages—but little attention is drawn here to the fact. This is hardly noteworthy in itself, but it may go together with a further difference. While the earlier statement recognizes no disparity in rank between the "two manners" (of using the term) that it speaks of, this later one accords an unambiguous preference to the substratum. It is the first (or ultimate) substratum—that of which the others are predicated, while it is no longer predicated of another (1028b36–37; compare 1017b13–14 and 23–24)—which especially seems or is thought to be ousia.

Consistent with this difference is a change by the later statement in the other usages that it mentions. The earlier one mentioned first in this connection what is internal to such ousiai as are not predicated of a substratum and is a cause of their being; second, those internal parts which (merely) delimit such ousiai and signify (each of) them as "some this"; and third, "the what it was to be," whose logos is a definition of each (of the things) of which it is called (the) ousia. The order appears to be a descending one. Of "the what it was to be," which was put last, it was said neither that it is internal to the ousiai not predicated of a substratum nor that (as internal to them, at any rate) it is a cause of their being or what signifies (each of) them as "some this." (Compare pages 87 and 126–127 above.) One is free to doubt, therefore, whether what Aristotle said in summary characterization of the class of ousiai to which it belongs can properly be applied to "the what it was to be." It is of what is an internal cause of the ousiai not predicated of a substratum, rather, if not also of their delimiting parts, that one can perhaps say that it (too) is "some this" that is also separable, an ousia of the sort that the shape and the form of each (thing) was there said to be. Yet, of these three "other" usages of ousia mentioned in the earlier statement, only the third, "the what it was to be," is retained in this later one, where it is put first in a new group of three, ahead of the universal and the genus.

But what then becomes here of the claim of the shape and the form to be ousia? Does that, too, disappear, along with the usage or usages of the term with which it was associated in the earlier statement and which the later one has not retained? Apparently not, as we see by considering a last difference between the two statements. In the earlier one the substratum, even or precisely the ultimate substratum, was taken to be the bodies (or better, the things). But the later statement (that is, Z3) withholds judgment as to which of three alternatives that it introduces—one of them, the shape (1029a3) or the form (1029a5–6)—is the first substratum. And so, in this way or on this basis, a new basis, it too entertains a claim on the part of the shape and the form to be ousia, indeed, the ousia. As for the old basis, it was as we can see now the opinion that there is such an ousia as is the ousia <u>of</u> something (1017b22–23 and 25–26): namely, of a substratum that, as "ultimate" or "first," is never itself of anything (1017b13–14, 15–16 and 23–24; 1028b36–37). The old basis is still visible in the later statement, which says of each of the three other usages, but evidently not of the substratum, that (what it refers to) seems or is thought to be (the) ousia of each (thing) (1028b34–36); but this remark serves now only to prepare the decided preference that is accorded, immediately thereafter, to the substratum (1028b36–1029a2). As the question now stands, then, "the shape and the form" may well vindicate its claim to be ousia, and such ousia as is separable and (at the same time) "some this" (1029a27–30); but it must do so by proving to be the first or ultimate substratum.

Is it that substratum? Aristotle appears to be inclined to allow that it might be—if the form is prior to and more of a being (mallon on) than the matter and, for the same reason, than the (composite) of both. And the anticipation of this result appears to strengthen in him the opinion that an account has now been given, if only in outline, of whatever it is that ousia is: that it is what is not (said or predicated) of a substratum but that of which the others are (said or predicated). But at the very moment that he comes to this point he takes a step back. "It must not (be put) only in this way, for (it is) not sufficient; for just this (is what is) unclear and, in addition, the matter (then) becomes ousia" (1029a9–10).

What is the "just this" (auto touto) which is said here to be unclear? According to Ross (ad loc.), it is the immediately preceding statement, which (after all) answers the question of what ousia is (only) in outline. But what that statement asserts—that ousia is the substratum—would not by itself entail that matter become ousia, as D8 shows very well (see pages 103–104 above). The "just this" which is unclear must be, then, not the statement itself but what appeared to move Aristotle to make it: the anticipation that form will prove, on the ground of its presumed priority to both matter and the composite, to be the first or ultimate substratum. For "form" is a correlative term (compare 1029a4–5), and one might well suppose that what it is correlative to must be matter. Any recognition, in that case, of a claim of form to be the substratum would entail recognition of an accompanying claim to that effect on the part of matter. (See 1029a23–24, a remark that presupposes the identification of ousia with form.)

The reason for which Aristotle is reluctant to grant this recognition to matter is indicated in the lines that follow his step back. To be a substratum (that of which predications can be made), matter would have to be something, "ti" (1029a18 and 21). But this is precisely what, as matter, it cannot be (1029a20 and 24). In his note to 1029a27, Ross puts it very well, when he says that "the effort to find the truest reality in that of which attributes are predicated has left us with that of which nothing can be predicated." All that he seems to miss is the fact that the author has indicated as much. As for our suggestion that the notion of form as first or ultimate substratum is what Aristotle finds here to be unclear—he admits towards the end of the chapter that ousia, understood as such a form, is "most difficult of access" (aporōtatē) and for that very reason in need of investigation (1029a32–33 and context). He proposes, therefore, that we search (for it) first in those of the perceptible ousiai which are agreed (that is, also by him: see page 103 above) to be ousiai. And with this proposal the chapter ends. The lines which the recent editors (and translators) add here (1029b3–12), taking them from the place, after the first sentence of Z4 (1029b1–3), where they are found in all of the manuscripts and where they serve a necessary function, must accordingly be disregarded so that they can be considered where they belong.

Z4) Z3 has thus led up to a proposal with which it also closes: that ousia, understood as a form that is the first or ultimate substratum, be searched for first in the perceptible ousiai that are agreed to be ousiai. Z4 then opens with the proposal that our theoretical pursuit be of or about "the what it was to be" which, as it also reminds us, was one of the understandings of ousia mentioned "in (the) beginning." How are we to take this development?

The beginning referred to is the beginning of the attempt to answer in outline the question "what" ousia is (Z3 1028b33–37; compare Z2 1028b31–32). By referring to it here as the "beginning" (that is, the beginning of what we are still now doing), Aristotle indicates that we are still in the grip of this preliminary task. By reminding us, at the same time, of the distinction made in that beginning among the ways in which ousia was said there to be understood, he cautions against any premature identification of "the what it was to be" with form (compare Frede and Patzig Vol.II, p.57). The understanding of ousia as "the what it was to be" was among those distinguished from the understanding of it as the substratum; while form was introduced in the context as preeminent among the candidates to be the substratum (Z3 1028b37–1029a7). When Aristotle himself, later on in Zeta (Z7 1032b1–2, Z10 1035b32), identifies "the what it was to be" with form—or, rather, form with "the what it was to be"—he takes a step that calls therefore for interpretation, an interpretation that will have to take into account the distinction (between the two terms) that he has reminded us of, as well as the intervening discussion (of one of them) that we are about to consider. All of this means, however, that the opening of Z4 effects a change in the course of the argument from that signaled by the close of Z3, and an abrupt change, at that. And, as abrupt, the change is in need of the justification supplied by the lines which follow immediately upon that opening (1029b3–12), when they are read in their proper place.

Aristotle avails himself in them of the flexibility of a term (metabainein) that can mean either to change course or to advance. It is conducive to the task (ergon), he begins, to change one's course so that it is to (or towards) what is more knowable (or familiar). For learning comes about for all in this way: through what are by nature less knowable, to what are knowable more. And this is the task . . . : from (or of) what are more knowable to oneself, to make knowable to oneself what are by nature knowable. For what are for each of us knowable and first, often are barely knowable and have little or nothing of being (tò on); but, nevertheless, from what are badly known but known to oneself, one must endeavor to know what are wholly known (or knowable), advancing through these themselves (that is, through what one already knows somehow or other).—We must turn, then, Aristotle says here in justification of the step that he has already taken, to what is known to us, however badly or barely, and advance through it, through its progressive clarification and refinement, to the wholly or naturally known (or knowable). That to which we must turn, to which we have already turned, is ousia as "the what it was to be." That to the knowledge of which we must advance is presumably, or for all that we know now, ousia as a form that is the first or ultimate substratum.

But is ousia as "the what it was to be" already known or familiar to us, as Aristotle thus suggests here that it is? And, if so, where within the familiar lies the darkness that is cause or effect of the fact that we know even or precisely the familiar only badly or barely? For, as it seems, it is that very darkness, insofar as it leads us into perplexity in its regard, which may lead us also towards some clarity.

According to a remark in the earlier treatment of ousia (D8 1017b21–22), "the what it was to be" is that whose logos is (a) definition. A definition of what? Presumably, of each of the things, for "the what it was to be" is said there to be called the ousia of "each" (1017b22–23; compare Z3 1028b34–35). The logos that defines the things is then the logos of "the what it was to be"; or what their definition renders, what it expresses in speech, is just that: "the what it was to be" for them. "The what it was to be" is that, in things, which exactly corresponds to their definition.

But in Z4 Aristotle goes further: "the what it was to be," what (each) is said (to be) by (or of) itself, is each (reading "hekaston" at 1029b14, with the manuscripts). Now, if by "each" is meant "each particular thing," as the illustrative use that is made here of the singular "you" would tend to suggest as well, "the what it was to be," as each of these particulars, is surely ousia, since among the particulars, as perceptibles (B4 999b1–2), are the least contestable ousiai (Z3 1029a33–34, together with Z2 1028b8–13 and 28–31 and H1 1042a6–11). (We are still, to repeat, in the grip of the task of finding out "what" ousia is and therefore here, in particular, of determining whether "the what it was to be" is ousia.) And the question will then be only what constitutes for each thing "the what it was to be" or by what formula it is to be expressed.

It is Aristotle's consideration of this question, apparently, that makes it necessary for him to turn his attention to "composites" and, "since there are composites also in the categories (or the other categories)," to ask whether there is "for these, too" (the composites in the categories?) a "what it was to be." Two divisions or distinctions appear to be at work here: that between ousia or "some this" and the predications in the categories (compare 1030a18–20), and that between "some first" (being) and one that can be said only by predicating "what is other of another" (compare 1030a10–11). Do these distinctions coincide, as Aristotle gives the impression here of assuming that they do? Or do they not coincide, as he perhaps in fact means to indicate? The deciphering of the exceptionally difficult text that we have reached (Z4–6) may well depend on the answer to that question.

His investigation of the question that he has explicitly raised—whether there is for composites, too, or for composites in the categories, a "what it was to be"—proceeds via a consideration of the example, "white man." And the reason that he offers for his apparent inability to find, for such composites as are represented by "white man," a "what it was to be" is that the latter is "some just what," a term (hoper ti) that he uses to signify a species of a genus (Prior Analytics A39 49b3–8); and that whenever what is other is predicated of another there is no "just what." That is, predications in the categories are made of a substratum (1029b23–25) and a substratum that is other or different from what is predicated of it, as man (and even surface) is different from white (Posterior Analytics A22 83a24–32). And this means that the substratum, in this case a man, can cease to be what is predicated of it, in the manner that "white" is predicated of it, without ceasing to be simply; whereas it cannot cease to be "just what" it is, "man" or "animal," without ceasing to be simply (Posterior Analytics A33 89a33–b6). To this extent, "man" and even "animal" can be said not to be predicated of a substratum that is different or even other than itself (compare Categories 5 3b18–21). Or, as Aristotle perhaps also suggests here, a "just what" is the "just what" of "some this," but a "this" belongs only to ousiai.

But will not every ousia be, precisely insofar as it is "some this," that is, a particular (B6 1003a5–9), in the manner that a white man is? (Compare page 98 above.) An ousia will not be, then, not in every respect, either "just what" it is or—if "the what it was to be" is "some just what"—its "what it was to be"; and the latter in turn will not be each of the things or, for that reason at least, itself an ousia, as they or some of them are agreed to be. Or are we forgetting here ousia as "the shape and the form," which is "some this" that is also separable (D8 1017b24–26)? In concluding this portion of the argument, Aristotle does not speak of form (eidos) but rather of species (eidē): "the what it was to be" will belong, then, to nothing which is not a species of a genus, but only to these (1030a11–13).

In the build-up to this conclusion, he had said that there is a "what it was to be" of that, or rather of those, whose logos is a definition (1030a6–7). And rather than say what we did—that the things will not be, in every respect, "just what" they are or, therefore, their "what it was to be" (and vice versa)—he is inclined to deny of the composites and therewith of the things in particular, or of everything other than the species, that they have either a definition or a "what it was to be" (1030a14–17). He concedes at once that this goes too far; but in allowing to the others, as he does in the balance of the chapter, a definition and a "what it was to be" of some sort, he continues to insist that, in their strictest sense, the latter belong exclusively to what he calls here ousia or ousiai (1030b4–7, 1030a17–23 and 29–31). But which ousiai are these? The species? (Compare again B6 1003a5–9 as well as Categories 5 2a11–19 and 3b10–18.) Or does Aristotle mean only to point to the fact that the authentic definition of an ousia is not that which describes it in its particularity (1030a14–16), but that which gives the species or class and the class character? This would correspond to our practice of defining something by putting it into its class and identifying the class; but it entails the disproportion between an ousia and its "what it was to be" that we have mentioned. (Compare 1029b13–14, as the manuscripts have it, with the first sentence and the last sentence of Z6.)

Z5) As this chapter repeats and reaffirms the conclusion of its predecessor as to a definition and a "what it was to be" for composites or its dilemma in that regard (1030b26–28, 1031a7–14), the task of the reader is to discern what it is meant to add to the earlier discussion. It purports to concern itself with two perplexities that allegedly come to sight on the basis of that discussion. Its consideration of the first of these calls our attention to a class or subclass of composites that had not been singled out for special notice in Z4; and it is to composites of this class that the conclusion or the dilemma of Z4 is applied in Z5 or for them in particular that it is now reaffirmed. The composites in question are signified by terms like "male" or "female" that could appear to signify merely an attribute (which, as such, would require a substratum of some sort) but that in fact signify also the substratum of the supposed attribute or rather the class of that substratum: "animal," in this case. The clarification of "female" will require, therefore, the clarification of "animal"; and yet the definition or "the what it was to be" which Z4 would allow to "animal" or, at any rate, to one of its species (1030a11–17) will not, as we were led there to see, be just what "female" is, to say nothing of any particular female.

The description that Aristotle gives of the composites with which he is now concerned (1030b23–26) is equivalent to that which he gave in the Posterior Analytics of one of the two classes of "per se" attributes that he identified there (A4 73a37–b3); and he does speak of them as (such) attributes ("pathos" at 1030b24 and 31). But that he has something more or different in mind now is suggested by his exclusion of "white" from the terms that he is considering (on the ground that it admits of clarification without "man") although it, too, as he had noted in passing in Z4, is a "per se" attribute (of "surface") of the same class (1029b16–18; compare D18 1022a14–19). It is suggested most strongly by the attention that he pays in discussing these composites, both in his treatment of the first perplexity and, still more, in his treatment of the second, to "snub" (which cannot be clarified without recourse to the "nose" that it already is). For "snub" had been used by him in E1 to represent the class of all natural (beings) in a discussion of the manner in which definition and "the what it was to be" belong to them (1025b28–1026a5); and, included among the natural (beings), are the least contestable ousiai (compare 1025b34–1026a3 with Z16 1040b5–10). He knew, then, that in speaking, here too, of "snub" he could not help reminding some of his readers of those ousiai in particular.

What he says of "snub" in his treatment of the second perplexity is that to say "snub nose," if one can say it at all, is to say the same thing twice. For a snub nose would be, not simply a concave nose—as it would be if "concave" (which signifies merely an attribute) and "snub" were equivalent terms—but a concave nose nose. And "on this account," he continues, "it (would be) absurd for 'the what it was to be' to belong to such things: otherwise (the addition of noses) will go on without limit, for in a nose (which is) a snub nose, there will be yet another one." If "snub" can be adequately rendered by "concave nose," as has been all but admitted, it is difficult to see how or why the assignment of a "what it was to be" to snub should lead to a limitless repetition. Or could Aristotle have had in mind here the assignment of an ousia, such as "the what it was to be" is supposed to be, to what is already an ousia, and agreed to be so (a proceeding that can be likened to that of assigning a substratum to what is already a substratum, and indeed the ultimate one)? (Compare pages 103–104 and 95–96, as well as 132–133, above.) For if, to be what it is, the first ousia is in need of a second one, why should the second not be in need of a third, and so on without limit? (Compare Z6 1031b28–30 and 1032a2–4.) And, as it seems to me, these questions can be regarded as improper ones only by someone who has failed to notice that Aristotle has pointed (in Z1 and D6) to an alternative account of how an ousia comes to be what it is and who, in addition, would refuse to consider the suggestion that, in his innermost thought, Aristotle may not have been so devout an Aristotelian as some of his followers were and are.

Z6) The chapter begins by putting explicitly into question the very assertion with which the consideration in Z4–6 of "the what it was to be" may be said to have begun: that "the what it was to be" is "each" (Z4 1029b13–14, reading "hekaston" with the manuscripts). The investigation of the question whether "the what it was to be" is the same as or different from "each" is, furthermore, now said outright to be conducive to the investigation "about ousia" (compare page 136 above). That is, it is said to be conducive to the task of answering the question "what" ousia is. For it is that task—itself preliminary to the investigation as to which are (the) ousiai, that is, as to whether there are any besides the perceptible ousiai (Z2 1028b27–31)—whose pursuit has brought us to the consideration of the claim of "the what it was to be" to be ousia (Z2 1028b31–32, Z3 1028b33–36, Z4 1029b1–3). And this claim has come to sight as resting on the presumed identity of "the what it was to be" and each particular thing. As Aristotle puts the case for some such identity here: "each seems (or is thought) to be not other than the ousia of itself, and 'the what it was to be' is said to be the ousia of each." But where is that "each" for which this contention would be valid?

In the course of addressing this question, Aristotle comes to consider those ousiai—"if there are any"—which no different ousiai or different natures are prior to: such as, he adds, some say the ideas are. Here, apparently, one should expect to find that each is the same as its "what it was to be," and vice versa. For if they are different—if, for example, the (being) for being (on) is different from being (tò on)—then "there will be other ousiai and natures and ideas, besides the ones spoken of and prior (to them), and those (others will be) ousiai, if 'the what it was to be' is ousia." (I have translated Jaeger's text, without his addition of "mallon" at 1031b2, and thus preserved the more difficult manuscript reading, which retains the second "kai" in that line.)

These lines convey a thought of fundamental importance, not about the "ideas"—which, as Ross implies in his note on the passage, were not of serious interest to Aristotle (Posterior Analytics A22 83a32–34)—nor about any other idea-like ousiai, but rather about the perceptible ousiai that we all know and can agree to be ousiai. It is that, even if these ousiai are not the same as their "what it was to be," as we have come to see that they cannot be, we need not concede that there are any ousiai prior to them, unless (the condition expressed in the "if" clause) "the what it was to be" is ousia. But the only ground that has thus far come to sight for regarding "the what it was to be" as ousia is the supposition that it is, or is the same as, each particular ousia. And this, finally, is what is at issue in the chapter and what we are supposing now not to be true. The thought that Aristotle conveys then, in the lines which we are considering, is that, if it is not true that the particular ousiai are the same as their "what it was to be," there will not be other ousiai that are prior to them. They would remain, at least so far as the present discussion is concerned, the only ousiai, just as they are the only or ultimate substratum.

He puts the matter also in this way. If they are "loosed from one another," the ousiai and their "what it was to be" (pl.), the latter will not be beings ("onta" which is equivalent in the context to "ousiai"). It is true that he says at the same time—he is purporting to show the necessity (1031a29 as well as b11 and 22) that some ousia be the same as its "what it was to be"—that (if they are "loosed from one another") the former will not be known. "For there is knowledge of each whenever we know 'the what it was for it to be'." There will, then, be knowledge of each; but that knowledge will not be, what Aristotle has already indicated in many places and in many ways that it cannot be, complete. (One might consider also the repetition of this part of the argument at 1031b20–28.)

At the end of the chapter, he speaks of the sameness of Socrates and (the) "being" for Socrates. The latter, like "the what it was to be for Kallias" which he had spoken of in D18 (1022a26–27), is obviously not a "what it was to be" such as those that we have been considering throughout Z4–6. But it is perhaps what permits him to conclude the chapter and the section with the remark that what has been said is how "the what it was to be" is the same, as well as how it is not the same, as "each." Both in Z4 (1029b20 and 25–26) and in Z5 (1031a12), he had spoken of a logos <u>of</u> "the what it was to be." Toward the end of Z6, he asks "what prevents . . . some (things) from being simply (their) 'what it was to be,' if 'the what it was to be' is really ousia." And in that case, he adds, "the logos of them, too, (will be) the same" (1031b32–1032a1). This is the only mention in Z6 of a logos of "the what it was to be": there will be such a logos if "the what it was to be" is identical with some (beings) or if it is itself an ousia.

Z7) "Of what are coming to be, some come to be by nature, some by art, some from the spontaneity (of what is coming to be)." In this introduction of the theme of Z7–9, we appear to be confronted with another abrupt change of direction in the argument. But by declining to apologize for taking now the course that he pursues here (compare Z4 beginning), Aristotle indicates that the abruptness of this change of direction is more apparent than real. Among what come to be by nature are the things, like a man or a plant, that "we say are" or that "are" most of all ousiai (Z7 1032a18–19, Z8 1034a3–4 referring back to 1033b32). And those readers who have been impressed by the difficulties that were shown in Z4–6 to attend the claim of "the what it was to be" to the status of ousia cannot find it altogether surprising that Aristotle turns or returns here to the least contestable ousiai. But why does he take up in particular their coming-to-be (along with that of others)?

The claim of "the what it was to be" to the status of ousia was pursued (in Z4–6) by way of preparation for considering the claim of form to be ousia; and the claim of form had been suggested (in Z3) to rest on its claim to be a (or the) substratum. It was reasonable to assume, therefore, that the examination of "the what it was to be" was intended to bring us closer, somehow, to that notion "most difficult of access" of form as substratum. But "the what it was to be," which had been introduced (in Z3) as something distinct from the substratum, seems to have maintained the same distance from it through the course of Z4–6 (one might compare, in this connection, Z6 1031b15–18 with Z4 1030a11–14). And this does not prevent Aristotle from declaring, upon their completion, that he means by form "the what it was to be of each" (Z7 1032b1–2). Does this suffice then—especially for those readers who have drawn from the examination of "the what it was to be" in Z4–6 the negative conclusion as to its own claim (to be ousia) that seems to be warranted and despite what he adds here in Z7 as to form (that he means by it also "the first ousia")—for disposing of form's claim to be ousia?

There remains this difficulty. Form could seem to be what, along with matter, "always" must be present in advance, if there is to be a coming-to-be (Z9 1034b10–13: it is true that an alternative reading, that of ms.Ab, which replaces "always" with "if," would change the complexion of the remark; but compare Z8 1033b8–9). And this would seem to make form a part of the substratum, broadly understood, that must underlie any coming-to-be (Z8 1033a31–34 and b12–13). It is in coming-to-be, then, that a basis could seem to come to sight for identifying form with (a part of) the substratum, and therewith also for regarding it as ousia. And it is coming-to-be, then, that must now be taken up and examined. As for the attention which is devoted in this examination to the coming-to-be of the natural things, in particular, this is presumably due to the fact that, as they most of all are ousiai, it was in their case most of all that some such role for form (as we have been speaking of) was searched for (Z8 1034a3–4 and context). Aristotle had himself suggested (at the end of Z3) that we search (for form as substratum) in those of the perceptible ousiai that are agreed to be ousiai—only to drop the suggestion at once (at the beginning of Z4). He can be said to return to it now. The intervening chapters (Z4–6) thus come to sight as an attempt by him to indicate in advance of the search what a sober understanding of form, called there "the what it was to be," would take it to be.

According to the general statement at the beginning of Z7, which introduces the new theme, all things (panta) coming to be, come to be "by something" and "from something" and (come to be) "something": that is, (each comes to be) "this" or "just so much" or "of just some sort" or "somewhere." The natural comings-to-be are of those things whose coming-to-be is from nature: "the from which," what we call "matter"; "the by which," some (one) of the natural beings; "the something," a man or a plant or another one of the things that we say are, most of all, ousiai.

Here Aristotle interrupts his account of natural coming-to-be to say that all things (hapanta) that are coming to be, whether by nature or by art, have matter. For it is possible for each of them both to be—it is, after all, once it has come to be—and not to be. And this—the possibility for it not to be, or not to be how it is—is, for each, its matter (dropping the "in" before "each" at 1032a22 with Christ and ms.E). In other words, what are most of all ousiai are perishable. Moreover, matter in this strictest sense is a possibility of these ousiai (and others) rather than something within them. (Compare On Generation and Corruption A3 318a9–10 with a13–27.)

Resuming the account of natural coming-to-be, after this digression on matter, and repeating the last part of what he has already said about it, Aristotle says first that the "from which" is nature. He refrains from adding that we call this nature "matter." On the other hand, he speaks now of form, or at least he refers to it, in replacing the "something" (that what is coming to be comes to be) with "that in virtue of which" (it is what it has come to be). He says that this, too, is nature, for what is coming to be, for example a plant or an animal, has a nature. Ross, who refers us here to D18 beginning, comments in part as follows (*ad loc.*): "that which a thing becomes is identified with the form which it acquires and *in virtue of which* it is what it is after the change." As this would seem to imply, the form is present only after the change, that is, upon its completion. But Aristotle speaks here lastly also of the "by which" and identifies it now with "the nature called after the form, the (nature) like in form." It is like in form, presumably, to the nature of what is coming to be, since he adds that this (generative) nature is "in another: for (a) man generates (another) man." Still, the relation of the nature (called after the form) and form is not so clear in this case as was the relation of "that in virtue of which" to the nature that it was said to be.

That there is a role for form to play in coming-to-be itself is, however, clear in the case of coming-to-be by art. And this is perhaps why Aristotle turns now from comings-to-be on account of nature to the others, which are called "makings," and to that making in particular which is from art. It is in this context, at any rate, that he explains what he means by form. But this is to say that, in turning his attention now to art, he is likely to have kept one eye still on nature and the problem of nature. An additional pointer to this effect may be provided by the way in which he now amends the classification with which he had opened the chapter (see page 143 above). There spontaneous coming-to-be was one of three classes, along with coming-to-be by nature and that by art. Here the classes are reduced to two, the class of natural comings-to-be and the class of makings (to which makings from art belong), and spontaneity is no more than another way in which some—both of what are made and of what come to be from nature—come to be. The two remaining classes are thus drawn together by the fact that spontaneous coming-to-be occurs within the domain presided over by each of them; and they are at the same time rendered comparable or commensurable in this, too: that the comings-to-be proper to them must distinguish themselves, each in its own way, from the spontaneity that is their partial shadow. As Aristotle observes in the course of this transition (from nature to art) with regard to the things coming to be from nature, for example, there are some that come to be, the same ones, both from a seed and without a seed (1032a30–32). He will say later on that the seed is what has the form potentially (Z9 1034a33–b1): that is, it has the potential to bring it about that the form, of what comes to be through the motion due to the seed (Z9 1034b4–6), is present to that (completed) thing.

The form that plays a role, indeed a defining role (1032a32–b1), in making from art is "the form in the soul" (of the artisan). To speak of (a) form in the soul—to say, in effect, that form is such that it may be in the soul—is already to say something significant about it. But Aristotle also says here that he means by form "the what it was to be of each" and the (or its) first ousia. The relationship of form to the "each," of which it is "the what it was to be" or the ousia, is then clarified by what he hastens to add: that it is in a manner the same form that is of contraries, for the ousia of a privation is the ousia opposed (to it). Health, for example, is in a manner the ousia of illness, since it is by (reference to) the absence of health (that is, to health) that illness is clarified (the reading of mss.EJ at 1032b4–5, adopted by Christ as well as by Frede and Patzig). Now, the health that is at the same time the form of both health and illness is "the logos in the soul" (compare D25 and page 118 above) and (therewith also the principle of) the knowledge (possessed by the physician). It would follow that to speak of this form as being "in the soul"—or as having a logos—is to say the same thing twice. A few lines later on, Aristotle draws a distinction between health (or the house) without matter and health (or the house) that has matter; and in this context he calls "the what it was to be" "ousia without matter." This could seem to imply that what has come to be (in this case health or a house) is the ousia (in question) with matter. But would this be consistent with what he has already indicated in the chapter either about matter (compare page 145 with pages 95–96 above) or about form?

The role played by form in the making of something from art is described here by Aristotle with very great precision. He brings to light, for example, that what must be present in the mind of a physician is not merely the form of health but that of each of the states which intervene between the health to be produced and the first action that a physician can take to begin the motion that goes through those states to health (compare 1032b17–21 with b6–9). But it thus comes to light also that only the motion that begins with the action of the physician—and not the thinking that precedes the action and that takes its bearings by those forms—is (properly) called "making" (1032b9–10 and 15–17). From this we can understand why form is both identified with the principle (or beginning) of the change (1032b16 and 21–23) and, then again, distinguished from it (1032b24–26). And it is from the same point that the possibility (in some cases, like that of health) of spontaneous production can be understood, as Aristotle indicates here in passing (1032b21–30).

Whether the making is spontaneous or from art—indeed, this applies "as is said" (by the philosophers) to coming-to-be, simply or as such—it would be impossible (for anything) to come to be, if there were nothing present in advance. And it is manifest that "of (or by) necessity" (see pages 123–125 above) some part will be present, for the matter is a part: it is present in (the something that comes to be) and it is (itself) what comes to be (that something).—"Matter" is used here in a sense other than the strictest one. For example, the matter which is the substratum for the coming-to-be of health is said in this vicinity to be a man (1033a8–10), which is to say that the matter which must be present in advance of any coming-to-be is already itself a thing. In the course of the appendix (to the main body of the chapter) in which he makes this remark, Aristotle shows that what the matter comes to be is sometimes a modification of the thing that it already is (as when a man becomes healthy) and sometimes a new thing altogether (as when stones become a house). Even in cases of the latter sort, as he discusses them here, the matter remains identifiable as what it was before it became the new thing (which can be described, therefore, by reference to it: a stone house); or, as he has already suggested, the matter remains present "in" the new thing. However that may be, the necessity that he has insisted upon with regard to coming-to-be as such is the necessity that some thing be present in advance of it, not that the thing in question, the matter, remain identifiable (as what it was) throughout and even after the change. And he had referred earlier in the chapter to coming-to-be from a seed, an example that figures also in the parallel discussion of coming-to-be in the Physics (A7 190b1–5; compare 190a13–18).—After making it clear that the matter must be present in advance of any coming-to-be, Aristotle asks whether anything of what is in the logos (the logos of the something that the matter will become) must be present in advance, as well. His somewhat elliptical response suggests that an affirmative answer is possible, for the reason that the matter, too, can be said to be in the logos of that something.

Z8) In discussing Z7 we were compelled to use "matter" in two different ways. It came to sight as signifying on the one hand the possibility of ousiai not to be or not to be how they are (1032a18–22) and, on the other hand, what must be present in advance, if coming-to-be is not to be impossible (1032b30–1033a5). The two meanings of the term may be said, however, to converge on or in the notion of "privation," which was also developed there (see, especially, 1033a8–16). That is, the matter which must be present in advance of any coming-to-be as its substratum and which, as we saw, is itself an ousia, a thing of a certain kind or form, has (as such) matter in the sense of the possibility not to be what or how it is: it could not, otherwise, be the substratum for any change. But this possibility of any ousia not to be what or how it is, is not unlimited for it—it cannot become just anything, but only that whose form it is already fitted, fitted by what it already is, to receive. And it is its fitness to receive, under the appropriate conditions, a form which it does not now have that Aristotle calls the "privation" belonging to the ousia in question. In the notion of "privation" we find combined, then, those of "the matter" that an ousia already is and of "the matter" that is its possibility not to be what or how that matter is.—Aristotle reminds us of this notion of "privation" at the beginning of Z8 (compare 1033a25–27 with Z7 1033a19–22).

The principal task of the first half of the chapter is, as it appears, to show the following: "neither does the form—or whatever one ought to call the shape in the perceptible (thing)—come to be, nor is there a coming-to-be of it, nor (does) 'the what it was to be' (come to be), for this is what comes to be in another either by art or by nature or power" (1033b5–8). In the repetition (of this statement), according to which what has been shown is that "what is spoken of as (or called) form or ousia (compare 1034a4) does not come to be," Aristotle adds that it has been shown also that in the case of everything coming to be (the reading of Alexander, adopted by Christ and Jaeger) matter is in (what is undergoing the change) (1033b16–19). In a remark that intervenes between the two statements, he had said that "it will always have to be (the case) that the thing coming to be (undergoing the change) is divisible and (that there) is on the one hand 'this,' on the other 'that': I mean that (there is) on the one hand matter, on the other form" (1033b12–13). He adds now to what he has already added (to the first statement) in the repetition—namely, that there is matter in everything coming to be (undergoing change)—a partial repetition of the intervening remark: "and there is on the one hand 'this,' on the other 'that'" (1033b19). The "this" and the "that" or the matter and the form that must be present to every thing coming to be belong, then, both of them, to the matter: that is, to the thing that is undergoing the change (compare 1033a31–32 as well as Z7 1033a8–10). They are, namely, the form that it has, as the thing that it already is, and the matter that is the possibility for it not to be that thing or, more generally, not to be what or how it is. And this means that the question of the role, in coming-to-be, of the form which will be present to what is coming to be, when it has come to be, the form of which it has been said here that it does not itself come to be (compare pages 102–103 above), has not yet been answered.

And that is perhaps why Aristotle asks now whether there is "some sphere besides these"—besides spheres such as the bronze one he has been speaking of—"or a house besides the bricks"—besides such houses as are made of bricks or other materials. He responds to his own question with a further question: if this were the case, would there be a coming-to-be of any "this" (such as a sphere of bronze or a house of bricks), that is, any coming-to-be at all? (For the interpretation, see B4 1001a29–b1 and b3–6, in the light of a19–24.) He concludes that terms like "sphere" and "house" signify rather "just the sort" of thing some thing is (compare Categories 5 3b10–18). In other words, what they signify is not a "this" or delimited (as a true "this" would be). The same conclusion applies of course to "man" and "animal" and even to "bronze sphere" when it is used, not to point to "this one here," but generally. And he draws the further conclusion, which also completes the argument, that "the causality of (or due to) the forms" is of no use with regard to comings-to-be and ousiai (that is, with regard to their comings-to-be), nor would the forms, by (or of) themselves, be ousiai—on account of these things at least: that is, on account of forming any part of the substratum required for any coming-to-be (compare page 144 above).

By substituting in the midst of the sentence expressing it "the forms (eidē) as some speak (of them), if there are some besides the particular (things)" for "the causality of the forms (eidē)," Aristotle makes it possible, for readers who are so inclined, to suppose that his conclusion is directed against the ideas rather than the forms as he understands them (1033b26–29). But in the remaining lines of the chapter he contrives to use twice the phrase, one or the same "in form (eidos)" (1033b31–32 and 1034a8): form, in other words, is what two or more members of the same class share; it is, as shared by them, their logos, one can say (see pages 20 and 147 above). And he thus indicates that it is form in this sense that he has had in mind all along.—In attributing to him the conclusion that we have regarding the causality of the forms, we could seem to have overlooked the influence which they exert in natural generation as the forms of the ousiai that generate others, which will be like those ousiai in form or kind. Aristotle does speak of the generation of the natural ousiai in this last part of the chapter. But he does so only in order to make it clear that there is no need to ascribe causality in such generation, even or precisely for the coming-to-be, in the matter, of the form of the ousia being generated, to anything other than the ousia that in fact generates it: in the case of a man, for example, another man (1033b29–1034a5). And this is not to mention, what he also points out here, that the offspring is not in every case like in form to the ousia that has generated it. Nor is it to speak of the problem of spontaneous generation, to which he returns in the course of his treatment of spontaneity in Z9. (Compare Z9 1034a33–b6 with Z7 1032a28–32.)

Z9) This chapter has been subjected to much tampering with by the editors: one must persist, against them, in keeping to the received text if one is to see what Aristotle is pointing to here, that is, what the chapter is meant to add to the argument of the section which it concludes (Z7–9). For example, at 1034a23–24 the form (eidos) "house" is called a "homonymous part" of <u>the</u> house (that is, the house one can live in). At 1034a26–30 it is said of the heat in or due to motion (compare Z7 1032b25–26), which makes in turn the heat in the body that is perhaps either health itself or a part of health, that it "is said" to make health because "that which heat follows and accrues to makes health." It is the latter, in other words, whatever it may be, that in fact makes health. We should note also, in connection with the first of these observations, that the term "homonymous," which Aristotle seems to have reserved for use in this chapter (compare Z8 1033b29–32), where he uses it three times (1034a22, 23 and b1), may itself be used homonymously here. For it is used to signify, of an ousia that furnishes the seed in natural generation, that it is the same in form or kind as the ousia whose coming-to-be results from the motion due to the seed (1034a22–23 and b1). But its stricter use is that spelled out by Aristotle in the first lines of the Categories: "Called homonymous (pl.) are those of which only a name (is) common, while the logos corresponding to the name (is) different: for example, the man and that which is drawn (are each) an 'animal'."

After treating in the greater part of the chapter of spontaneity, and making there the attempt or the appearance of an attempt to confront the obstacle that spontaneity poses to the ascription of a causal role in coming-to-be to form or to ousia in the sense of form (1034a21 and following), Aristotle turns back in its last part to the theme or thesis of the first half of Z8 (page 149 above). He wishes to point out now or to add that the argument, which makes it clear, with regard to the ousia, that the form does not come to be, applies also to the "just so much," the "of just some sort," and the predications in the other categories (compare Z7 1032a14–15 on the "something" that whatever is coming to be comes to be). Just as the ousia comes to be, but not its "what" or form—the form, too, as we have seen, being called ousia—neither do the forms expressing "of what sort" or "how much" some thing is, and so forth, come to be. "But from these things is to be gathered what is peculiar to the ousia: that a different ousia, actually existing, which makes (what is made) is necessarily present in advance: for example, if an animal is coming to be, an animal; but (it is) not necessary that an 'of just some sort' or a 'just so much' (be actually present in advance of their coming to be where they do) but only potentially."

This enigmatic remark, which concludes the chapter and the section, is perhaps somewhat playful. In the case of any making or generating, the ousia responsible for it will have some "what"—its form or ousia—and be also "of some sort (or sorts)" and "just so much" as it is. But these predications, by which we know it or which express what is intelligible in or of it, need not correspond to or express that in it which makes or generates what it does. We might recall here what was said earlier in the chapter as to the heat which is merely "said" to make health, as well as what was intimated in Z7 regarding the relation of form to the generative nature that is called after it (1032a24–25 and pages 144–145 above). We know then, of what makes or generates, that it is an ousia and therefore, potentially at least, knowable as "what" or "of what sort" or "how much" it is; but we need not know the relation of what is expressed in any of these predications to that in the ousia which makes or generates. And we cannot say, therefore, of the ousia responsible for some thing coming to be "of just some sort" or "just so much," that it must be, insofar as it is responsible for them, such as they are. But we can say this, Aristotle seems to suggest here, of what is responsible for the thing's "what"—that it must be such as that "what" is—since it, too, is an ousia (if a different one, actually existing). It and the "what" (the form, as ousia) are homonymous, in other words. (Compare A6 987b7–10, retaining "synonymous" as providing the appropriate contrast to "homonymous," which must be retained as well, with Categories 1 1a1–12.)

Z10) The common theme of the three chapters that follow those which are devoted to coming-to-be, the coming-to-be of the natural things above all, is definition. There is a perplexity in regard to definitions—it is, again, above all with the natural things that the author is concerned, with their definitions—a perplexity whose consideration is conducive to the discussion of ousia (Z12 1037b9–14; compare Z11 1037a18–20). And this leads him to disclose now what he did not disclose regarding definition in his Analytics (Z12 1037b8–9). But to consider definition is to consider again form, or to continue the consideration of it: definition is of the universal and the form, at the same time that it is the definition of the thing (Z11 1036a26–31; compare Z10 1035a7–9 and b1–3, as well as Z15 1040a8–14). And therefore it is only upon the completion of this new section (Z10–12) that Aristotle will pronounce the verdict on form as substratum (and therewith ousia) that we have been anticipating (compare Z13 1038b1–6 with Z3 1029a1–7 and 26–33). For all of our efforts hitherto and for all of his efforts to guide our way, are we not still in search of the requisite clarity as to what form is?

Each of the chapters of which the section is composed begins with the mention of a perplexity (1034b22, 1036a26, 1037b9) having to do, in one way or another, with definition. The last of these perplexities concerns the oneness of that whose logos is a definition; and the second concerns what are and are not its parts: the parts of that which definition is of. Only the first perplexity—but in this it sets the tone for the whole section—concerns the relation of the logos that a definition is to the thing (pragma) of which it is the definition (Z10 1034b21 and 22; compare Z11 1036a30–31). Since every logos has parts, and the relation of the part of the logos to the part of the thing is like that of the logos to the thing, there is already perplexity as to whether or not the logos of the parts need be present in the logos of the whole.

Before taking up the perplexity for discussion, Aristotle mentions "in addition" a difficulty due to the alleged priority of the parts to the whole (compare D11 1018b34–37). In spelling it out, he points to cases where the part does not figure in the logos of the whole—rather, the reverse is the case—and he refers in passing to priority in logos and priority in being, that is, to the distinction between them (compare D11 1019a1–4 and 11–12).

The perplexity to be discussed first is then whether or not the logos of the parts needs to be present in the logos of the whole. In introducing it, Aristotle had referred to cases that appear to support, some of them one answer to the question, others the answer opposed to it; and he had adduced examples, one each, for the two sorts of cases (1034b24–28). Entering now upon the discussion, he first attempts to dispose of the perplexity, and to explain the conflicting examples (1035a9–14), by taking it into account that "part" is used in many ways (1034b32; compare D25). In fact, he is interested only in what "the ousia" (that is, the thing) is from as its parts—and, at the moment, only in one particular understanding of those parts. "If there is on the one hand matter, on the other form, and again (what is) from them; and (if) both the matter and the form and what (is) from them (are each) ousia; there is a way in which the matter is said to be (a) part of something and a way in which (it is) not (said to be a part), but rather what the logos of the form is from (are said to be parts)." We will disregard for now the apparent assimilation (repeated at 1035a10–11) of the parts of the form to the parts of its logos (compare D25 1023b22–24 and page 118 above with Frede and Patzig Vol. II, pp. 173–174), in order to ask the question left unsettled by the formulation we have quoted: of what are the parts of the form (or of its logos) said, in the absence of the matter, to be parts?

The answer is not so ready to hand as it might be thought to be, for one calls the statue also (what one would call it) as (a) form. And, more generally, one should call each (thing) its form and in accord with its having form (compare D25 1023b19–20), but one should never call (the thing) the material (component) by itself (1035a7–9). Is it the form, then, that is most truly the thing? Yet in the repetition (1035b1–3), Aristotle admits that it is only homonymously that the particular circle and the circle said simply (in other words, the universal) are both called circles—"on account of there not being a name proper to the particulars." In the interval, he had said that even if it is into bones and sinews and flesh that a man (upon his death) is decomposed, he is not for this reason from these, as if they were parts of his ousia, but (from them only) as matter. They are parts of the composite whole but no longer (parts) of the form and of what the logos is of, on which account they are not in the logoi (that is, the definitions) either. Moreover such (things) as are combinations of form and matter perish (are decomposed) into their material parts; but such as are not combined with matter but are without matter, like (the reading of mss.EJ and the original reading of ms.Ab) logoi of the form only, do not perish, either not at all or, at any rate, not in this way. Yet "Kallias perishes (is decomposed) into flesh and bones."

"Though the truth," Aristotle says immediately after the repetition we have called attention to, "has been spoken even now (or especially now), let us take up again (what we have been treating) and speak still more plainly" (1035b3–4). In other words, he makes a new beginning. He first repeats what he had said with regard to the priority of parts to whole (and vice versa), in introducing the perplexity to which the chapter is devoted (compare 1035b4–14 with 1034b28–32). Though it is longer and somewhat more explicit than the original, the restatement is incomplete: it is silent about priority in being as distinct from priority in logos (compare 1035b23–24). And in this way it reaches the conclusion that, whereas parts (which are) as matter—the parts into which, as into its matter, (what is decomposed) is decomposed—(are) posterior, parts (which are) as of the logos and of the ousia according to the logos (are), all or some (of them), prior. The term "whole" appears in the restatement only in connection with an example that is offered of the former sort of relation: a finger is defined by (reference to) "the whole" of which it is a certain part, namely, "man." Yet a thread is thereby held out to us that may help us to find our way in the somewhat intricate passage that comes next (1035b14–31).

For, as we learn here, "man" and "horse" and the others that in this way (rest), as universals, upon the particulars, are not ousia; but each is a sort of composite whole from (or of) the relevant logos and the relevant matter taken universally. The particular, on the other hand, is—like "Socrates"—from the ultimate matter (in other words, from the actual matter, which as such is of course particular: compare Z8 1034a5–8). The whole, then, to which a finger is posterior is a particular man. For, as Aristotle indicates now (thus reinstating the distinction that he had temporarily dropped), in separation from some such particular it cannot be, even: a dead finger is only homonymously a finger. Yet this leaves still unclear the answer to the question which Aristotle begins at least to confront in the passage that we are considering: what then of the logos or the ousia according to the logos, in the case in point?

What he says in this connection is that the soul of the animals—for it is this that is (the) ousia of what is ensouled—is the ousia according to the logos and the form as well as "the what it was to be" for the relevant sort of body. The reason that he gives is that, if the part of such a body, each part, is to be properly defined, it will be defined by reference to its work (ergon) and the work will not be present without sense perception. A dead finger, in other words, is not truly a finger. Thus their soul is (the) ousia of the animals (including man, of course); and the animals, in turn, are not indeed bodies but ensouled bodies. But this means that the soul is conceived here not as something that is or can be brought to bodies (which lack it) but rather as what is already present to some of them: their way of being as the sort of bodies that they are. (See On the Soul B1 412b10–26.) "So that," he continues, "the parts of this (ousia or soul) are prior, either all or some (of them), to the animal (as a) composite whole—as is likewise so on the level of the particular." Since the composite whole from (or of) the logos and the matter taken universally is not (an) ousia, it is only the latter level that can concern us here. "But the body and its parts are posterior to this ousia; and what is decomposed into these (bodily parts) as into (its) matter is not the ousia but the composite whole." Presumably the composite whole in question is the particular one. And "while these (bodily parts) are in one way prior to the composite whole (which is decomposed into them: see D11 1019a6–14) and in another way not (prior), for they are not able to be, even, (as what they are) when separated (from it), . . . some (of them) are simultaneous: such as (are) authoritative and the first (thing) in which the logos and the ousia (is), like heart or brain, perhaps" (compare D18 1022a29–32). Thus the body and its parts are posterior to the ousia that the soul is; and the parts of the body are posterior also, as the parts they are, to the particular composite whole—which is, in fact, the ensouled body itself; but some of them are simultaneous. To what? Perhaps, again, merely to the ensouled body of which they are the parts; but one cannot say that Aristotle has gone out of his way here to be clear.

What however he has done is to point to the fundamental question regarding form as ousia, while indicating at the same time what is at stake in its resolution. (Compare On the Soul A1 403a3–28.)

There is a part in the case both of the form—by "the form" Aristotle means "the what it was to be" (compare Z7 1032b1–2)—and of the composite whole, the one from (or of) the form and the matter itself (that is, the actual matter); but only the parts of the form are parts of the logos, and the logos is of the universal. As for the composite whole—he confirms that he means by this here the particular whole(s)—of these there is not a definition, but they are known, to the extent that they are known, with (or by means of) intellectual perception and/or sense perception. "But they are always spoken of and known by the universal logos." There is, then, a definition of them, without which they would not be known as the particulars that they are or even as particulars (see D6 and Z1); but it is not proper to any one of them. It remains the case that they are knowable only in part; and, among the reasons for this, the one that Aristotle mentions here is their perishability. What must be said then of the universals, which rest (as we put it earlier) upon the particulars?

Aristotle claims now to have disposed of what concerns whole and part and what concerns the prior and the posterior, as well (1036a12–13). But he adds a note as to how it is necessary to counter the inquiry, whenever someone asks whether it is, for example, the animal (presumably, the particular animal) that is prior, or the parts into which it is decomposed and from (or of) which it is. One must counter that (the answer) is not simple (1036a16); one must not (in responding to the question) speak simply (1036a23). Moreover, the answer will depend on that to a further question: is the soul too an animal or ensouled, is each the soul of each, or is the soul not an animal but different? (Compare 1036a1–2 with a16–19.) Aristotle does not say that this question, too, should be answered (compare Z11 1037a7–10).

Z11) There thus proved to be an impediment to Aristotle's speaking as he wished to speak in the latter half of Z10: "still more plainly." And the same impediment makes its weight felt in Z11, even though the argument comes perhaps closer here than ever before to clearing away a confusion which the impediment requires it, finally, to leave in place and even to continue to foster. In the circumstances, we should not be surprised that the discussion pursues a somewhat circuitous course.

Z10 had distinguished again and again between parts of the composite whole (of the form taken together with the matter), whether understood as a universal or as a particular (1035b18–20 and 27–30), and parts of the form alone. And it had done so as if the distinction was an obvious one or, at any rate, unproblematic. But Z11 opens with the observation that there is plausible ground for perplexity as to where such a line is to be drawn. In spelling this out it identifies, as we have been led to expect, such parts as are parts merely of what is taken together (with the matter) as material parts. What is the correlate of form, if not matter (see page 133 above)? And it assumes accordingly that form is what is able to be separated from the material parts or what becomes visible (to the mind's eye) when they are taken away in thought. But it then comes upon cases where this separation is difficult to effect. For example, "the form of man appears always in flesh and bones and (other) such parts; are these, too, then parts of the form and the logos?"

In their attempts to deny that they are parts of the form (1036b5–11), some had gone so far as to lead all things up (or back) to numbers (as to their forms). Aristotle pauses here to give a brief sketch of their assertions and of some of the difficulties into which they were led—at the conclusion of which he remarks that the cause responsible for there being some perplexity regarding what (pl.) concern definitions has been stated (1036b21–22). This is the only occasion in Z10–12, so far as I have observed, that he makes a remark of this kind (compare Z2 1028b30 as well as Z16 1040b30–32). And, for his own part, he draws the conclusion that it is idle labor (periergon) to lead all things up (or back) in this way and to take away their matter, for some "perhaps" are "this in this" or "these in such a state." And it is particularly inappropriate in the case of "animal," where this leads away from what is true and produces the opinion that "man" admits of being without such parts as have been mentioned, parts which must be present moreover in a certain state. But what, then, is the form of man?

It can no longer be held to be what becomes visible (to the mind's eye) when the material parts are taken away in thought. When that is done, "man" ceases to be visible. (This follows also from the identification of the form of man with his soul and of the latter with "the what it was to be" for a certain sort of body: compare Z10 1035b14–16.) We must take then a step back. If the form cannot be what becomes visible or intelligible when the material parts of the ousia we are concerned with are taken away, perhaps it is what is visible or intelligible in or of that ousia as it is, material parts and all. This would not mean that the form itself has matter, as Aristotle will soon again insist that it does not (1037a1–2: the inclusion of the words omitted by Frede and Patzig, on the authority chiefly of mss.EJ, need not be insisted upon, so long as the equivalence of form and the "what it was to be." is kept in mind). Both sense perception and intellectual perception, insofar as it follows in the wake of sense perception (Z10 1036a9–12), are of material things, without being themselves material—whatever may be the case with their substrata. But it would mean that the form could not be a particular (as the words that Frede and Patzig omit at 1037a1–2 acknowledge that it is not). As what is perceptible in or of the particulars—perceptible to the senses alone or together with the intellect—form would have to comply with the requirements of perception; and perception is not completed before what is grasped by it is grasped as a universal (Posterior Analytics B19 100a16–b1; compare Z10 1036a5–8, taking note of the revision effected by the repetition of "gnōrizontai"). And we would then be forced to conclude that the authentic correlate of form, as the universal that it is, is not matter but the particular or, rather, the particulars.

In explicit answer to the question as to the form of man, Aristotle says now that it is clear that the soul is the first ousia, (that) the body is matter, and "man" or "animal" is what is from both as

(a) universal. He leaves it open, however, here as well (compare 1037a7–10 with Z10 1036a16–17 and 24) whether the soul too (that is, the ousia or form) can be identified with "Socrates" (a particular man). If not, (it will be) "like the universal and the particular" (retaining "te" at 1037a10 with all of the manuscripts).—Shortly afterwards, among questions that he says are to be investigated "later" he mentions that which he will in fact take up in Z12. As he puts it here, it is the question what it is due to that definition is one logos: for it is clear that the thing (pragma) is one, but not by what it is one, since it has parts (the parts mentioned in or constituting the definition). At the beginning of Z12, where he no longer speaks of the thing (compare 1038a19–20), he asks what it is due to that that which definition is of is one. Is it the new understanding of form which is approached in Z11 that makes it necessary to raise this question? If so, what we learn from the treatment of the question in Z12 may help us to see better what precisely the new understanding takes form to be.—Aristotle closes Z11 with a summary statement (of a portion of the argument of Zeta) that betrays no awareness whatsoever of the development in the argument of the work to which the body of the chapter was devoted. (See particularly, in this regard, 1037a24–27 and 29–30.) Still, he indicates something by it. The summary covers that portion of Zeta in which "the what it was to be" is the primary theme. That is, it reaches back to the beginning of Z4. The summary statement with which Z13 begins, on the other hand, reaches back to the beginning of Z3, that is, to a chapter devoted to laying bare the claim of form to the status of ousia. The summary in Z13 thus amounts to a declaration that the examination of that claim has achieved a certain completion, a declaration that (to judge from the summary in Z11) could not have been made at the end of the earlier chapter. And this suggests that the chapter which separates the two statements has added something to an examination that would have been incomplete without it.

Z12) Aristotle asks here, as we have seen, what it is due to that that which definition is of is one. More precisely, he asks what it is due to that that whose logos is a definition is one. Now, that whose logos is a definition could be taken to be "the what it was to be" itself (D8 1017b21–23 and pages 135–136 above; but compare page 143 top). Or it can be taken to be that which has a "what it was to be": for example, a species of a genus (Z4 1030a6–7 and 11–12, as well as pages 137–138 above). And it seems to be from this latter sense that Aristotle begins here. In no case is that whose logos is a definition to be taken to be the thing (pragma), although the definition is a definition or logos of the thing (1038a19–20; Z11 1036a30–31; compare Z10 1036a2–8 and page 158 above). That is, it is not a particular but rather, in the example that he uses here, "man."

The oneness of "man" is in question and is so, apparently, because he is defined as the "two-footed animal." "Let this be (for present purposes) his logos." To what is it due that this is one rather than many: animal and two-footed? The relation of genus (animal) to differentia (two-footed) does not seem to be the same as that of a substratum to an attribute that is present to or in the substratum. And even if the relation were the same, this would not explain oneness in a case (such as "man" could prove to be) where the differentiae themselves are many: footed, two-footed, wingless. To what is it due that these are one rather than many? (Compare D6 1015b16–22 with Posterior Analytics B6 92a29–33.) Yet, as components in the definition, there is need that they be one, for the definition is some one logos and (it is) of an ousia; so that there is need that it be a logos of some "one" (namely, the ousia), for "as we say" the ousia, too, signifies some "one" and some "this." Now, the only "one" that is some "this" and that the ousia can signify as such, is the thing: for example, a particular man. (Compare Z8 1033b19–24 with Z10 1036a2–8 and see pages 150 and 158 above.) But in order to do this, the ousia itself—Aristotle now suggests—must be some "one." In the case in point, this would mean that "man" must be one. But his very logos proclaims him to be not one but (at least) two.

It is not enough, then, to say or to suggest, as Aristotle has come close to suggesting in Z11, that a form is related to the particulars which are its correlates as their universal. One must also account for its manner of being as that universal, such that it can confer on the particulars the meaning that it does confer on them by signifying each as some "one" and some "this."—The remainder of the chapter is taken up by a discussion of definitions by divisions. Aristotle claims neither that these are the only sort of definitions (1037b27–29) nor that his treatment of them here is exhaustive (1038a34–35). Presumably he turns to them out of concern with the problem that the first part of the chapter was devoted to spelling out and carries his treatment far enough to indicate the relevance of an investigation of them to that problem.

A definition of this sort contains nothing but the genus said (to be) first and the differentiae. The other genera are that first genus together with the differentiae that are taken with it. For example, if the first genus is "animal," the next could be "two-footed animal" and the next again "wingless two-footed animal" and so on, whether it is one differentia constituting, together with the genus, the (subordinate) genus or more than one. But if the genus simply is not, besides its species—Aristotle allows himself here to express the thought only in this conditional form, although it is in fact the pivot on which the discussion turns. For it amounts to the suggestion that the genus is not a "one" but rather many. And what holds for a genus must hold also for its species—for example, "man"—which are indistinguishable from the "other" (that is, the subordinate) genera. This is the core of the problem of the oneness of "man" as it is considered here.

Having reached this point, and with a view to what has just been suggested about the genus—that it is either not at all, besides the species, or is merely the matter out of which they are made by the differentiae—Aristotle says that definition is the logos from the differentiae. But he adds at once that each differentia (in the definition) needs to be divided by the differentia that belongs to it as the differentia that it is: for example, "footed" needs to be divided by a differentia that indicates a kind of foot, rather than by "winged" or "wingless." "And one always wishes to go forward in this way until (one) comes to the (differentiae which are) without (further) differentiae; and there will then be as many species . . . as there are these (last) differentiae. . . ." But if there are at that point many species, as Aristotle says that there are, then each of them must be itself a "one"—as he does not indeed say (compare On the Parts of Animals A3 643b33–34) but clearly implies, not only by what he does say but by the context in which he says it. What is it then, as best exemplified in this perhaps never-to-be-carried-through division by differentiae of differentiae (1038a12–14; compare On the Parts of Animals A2–3), that makes each of the species a "one" to the extent that it is one?

Since each species is many, it can be one only as the particulars that it is or consists of are, together, one. But they are one by the oneness of the look with which they are regarded, a look that sees in each something that is the same or similar to what it sees at the same time in the others. The species is indeed the group comprising the particulars, but the group is nothing but the particulars themselves, taken together and held together by the look in question. And it is the oneness of this look which is sharpened, to the limits of the possible, by the division by differentiae of differentiae. Aristotle concludes, therefore, that the last differentia will be the ousia of the thing—by which he means its eidos, its form or species—as well as the definition of it (1038a19–20 with 25–26). The identification of ousia in this sense with a logos has been prepared by the light that the argument of the chapter has cast upon form.

Z13) In this next set of chapters (Z13–16), Aristotle argues that no universal can be an ousia and that an ousia cannot be composed of ousiai (Z13 1038b8–9 and 1039a3–4; Z16 1041a3–5). That a universal cannot be an ousia does not mean, however, that form cannot be a universal, as we have been led to suspect at least that it must be (pages 160–161 above). Rather, it is this very development, the progress in our understanding of form, that has presumably made it necessary to turn now to the claim of the universal to be ousia: that is, as Aristotle makes clear (1038b1–8), to return to the beginning of the consideration in Zeta of the question "what" ousia is (Z2 1028b31–Z3 1028b36). But to suggest as much is to be confronted with the fact that form is still of interest in connection with ousia even though, as Aristotle also indicates now, the attempt to identify it with the substratum has ended in failure (compare 1038b3–6 with Z3 1029a1–7 and 29–33).

The question "what" ousia is was turned to in Zeta as preliminary to an investigation of the question of primary concern to it: "which" are the authentic ousiai or, in other words, are there any ousiai besides or even separable from the perceptible ones? (Z2 1028b28–32 and Z17 1041a6–9; compare Z16 1040b30–32) As we have seen, the focus of this preliminary consideration, which has already lasted longer than may have been anticipated (Z2 1028b31–32), has hitherto been on form. And, if form has thus far been constrained to vindicate its claim to be ousia by proving to be the substratum (pages 132–133 above), this is ultimately because the substratum is what ousia most seems to be (Z3 1028b35–1029a2). If the claim of form is now to be considered on another basis, then, that basis itself will have to be vindicated or, at any rate, examined. And this means that the ambiguity in our understanding of ousia, which we have supposed all along it was the purpose of the preliminary consideration to remove (pages 126 and 132 above), will finally have to be taken up. That is, more fully stated, the reason why a return to the beginning of this consideration of "what" ousia is has now become necessary. "Since the investigation is about ousia," Z13 begins, "let us go back."

The two words which follow this beginning are the same with which Z3 opened; and here, as there, they serve to introduce a listing of four usages of the term. Moreover, three of the four usages included in the earlier listing are to be found also here, if in each case placed differently. Only "the genus," listed third in Z3, is missing. Its fate may have been settled by what was suggested about it in Z12 (1038a5), a fate which, if this is so, will have foreshadowed the one which will befall "the universal" in this set of chapters (Z16 1040b25–27). And even in the case of "the genus" some continuity with the earlier listing could be said to be maintained by the fact that its replacement, too, is listed in the third place: only to this extent is the order of the listing of Z3 retained here.—But the placement in question is dictated rather by this: in the usage that is here listed third, ousia is called the composite of what it is called in the two usages listed before it. It is said to be what is "from them." That means, moreover, that what those two usages call ousia must be understood now in such a way as permits them to be taken to constitute, in combination, what is said to be "from them." And, as form has in the meantime been identified with "the what it was to be" (Z7 1032b1–2; Z10 1035b32), this would seem to require that "the substratum" be identified here with matter. In Z3, however, it was left open whether the substratum is to be understood as matter, as shape or form, or as what is "from them" (1029a2–7). Those are, at any rate, the alternatives as to the substratum which were given there. And, since they were given in that order, we can make an addition to this catalogue of the differences between the two listings of the usages of "ousia" we are now considering. The listing in Z13, which as we have seen does not follow the order of the listing in Z3, gives its usages rather in an order that corresponds to that in which those alternatives as to the substratum were given in Z3. This holds of course only for the first three of the usages listed here; but just this sets them apart—in their real or alleged link to an understanding of ousia as the substratum—from a fourth usage of another sort. In Z3, on the other hand, three usages which were there distinguished from the one that called ousia the substratum (see pages 133 and 135 above) were thus set apart from it.—But this last difference only partially conceals, and thus in fact calls attention to, a more fundamental similarity. Both listings separate an understanding of ousia as the substratum from another view of ousia that has yet to be precisely delineated. (Compare page 103 above.)

However that may be, Aristotle hastens to correct what he had, in effect, to repeat with regard to the substratum in order to open the chapter as he did. He says that both "the what it was to be" and "the substratum" have already been treated and that the latter (has been said to be) either "some this" (compare pages 133–134 and 140 with pages 103–104 above) or what is as matter to (some) actuality (see pages 145 and 148–150 above). In no case, in other words, is it to be understood as form or as anything with which form can be identified.

He turns then to the consideration of "the universal." To some, this apparently seems to be ousia because it seems to them to be most a cause (compare D8 1017b14–16) and to be a principle. Aristotle leaves it open here whether, or in what sense, a universal might be a cause or, at least, a principle (compare pages 71, 99–100, 126–127, 158, and 162–163 above); but he calls in question the claim of "the universal" to the status of ousia by appealing to other, perhaps related, criteria which those who put the claim forward would presumably have accepted. And, to the extent that they would have done so, the refutation to which they are subjected is a dialectical one (see B1 995b23–24). Accordingly, it cannot be ruled out that Aristotle himself could not have accepted one or more of these criteria or, therefore, the more or less coherent view of ousia which, together, they adumbrate. The question of the tenability of that view may thus be of more importance in his eyes than the question of "the universal."

The first of the criteria to be mentioned requires that the ousia (or, in the reading of mss.EJ, the ousia of each) be proper to each (thing or ousia), that it not be present to another—but it is in the nature of what is universal to be present to more than one. As the same point is put later on, "the ousia is present to nothing but itself and what has it, that of which it is (the) ousia" (Z16 1040b23–24). Is this not already two that the ousia in question is present to (compare 1038b29–30)? The second criterion requires that ousia be what is not predicated of a substratum—but a universal is always predicated of some substratum.

From the first criterion comes as corollary the requirement that those (things or ousiai) whose ousia is one be themselves one. But it is put here as follows: "those whose ousia is one and (whose) 'what it was to be' is one are themselves one." In other words, the ousia which is being distinguished here from "the universal" is, at the same time, being identified with "the what it was to be." And this would entail, in accord with the same first criterion, that "the what it was to be" be proper to a (or each) particular. Now, whether it is possible that a "what it was to be" (a definition) be proper to a particular—as Aristotle occasionally suggests that it is (D18 1022a27; Z6 1032a8)—or not possible—as he has already indicated that it is not (see pages 136–138 and 141–142, as well as page 115, above)—may be left open for the time being. The question will be addressed directly soon enough. It is more immediately important to note that a requirement that "the what it was to be" be proper to that of which it is "the what it was to be" would not stand in the way of the claim of "the universal" to be ousia—to the contrary!

Aristotle brings this out in the following manner. What "the what it was to be" (or definition) proper to a particular (thing or ousia) would consist of is, to say the least, unclear. It can therefore be asked, and he does ask, whether "the universal," which does not admit of being ousia as "the what it was to be" is suggested here to be ousia, may nevertheless be present in "the what it was to be," like "animal" (is present) in "man" and "horse"—that is, in "the what it was to be" (or definitions) of "man" and "horse." But there is clearly a logos of "animal" which, as proper to the species the logos is in, is as much the ousia of "animal" as "man"—"the what it was to be" present in "man"—is the ousia of the "man" in which it is present or, we can add, as "the what it was to be" proper to a particular thing or ousia is the ousia of it. And if something is itself an ousia by virtue of the ousia that is present in it, there is a like claim in all of these cases in this respect as well. This would entail, it is true, that there is more than one ousia in the "this" and the (particular) ousia. Aristotle adds, therefore, that it is impossible and even absurd that the "this" and the (particular) ousia, if it is a composite from something (pl.), not be from ousiai, that it not be from some (other) "this" but rather from a quality. And, since each of these additional ousiai (in the "this") is an ousia of more ousiai than one, he adds further that this is already the case for the ousia held to be present in "Socrates," that is, for "the what it was to be" proper to him (compare Z16 1040b23–24).

Having reached this point, he rather abruptly denies that anything of those (that are) in the logos of an ousia such as "man"—

if "man" and the like are ousia—is an ousia of anything. Nor is it present (anywhere) apart from them or in another: he means, for example, that there is not some "animal" besides those of some sort or other. He grants that in making these denials, which pertain of course to the immediately preceding part of the argument, he is relying on what results from the argument as a whole. But he nevertheless adds that it is manifest from them, to whoever contemplates (them), that none of those (that are) present as universals is an ousia and that none of those (that are) predicated in common signifies "some this" but rather (that a "this" is) of some sort. Why is it necessary to contemplate in particular this part of the argument, together with the denials of its apparent results, before arriving at these conclusions? Or what precisely is it that becomes manifest to those who do so?

As the parenthetical query whether "man" and the like are ousia already suggests, the conclusions apply to "man" as well as to "animal"—indeed, to everything but the "this" (the particular), which remains an ousia. But then they do have some bearing on the "this." If the particulars alone remain (incontestably) ousiai, this cannot be due, as we are now able to see, to their possession of (another) ousia in the form of a "what it was to be" (a logos) proper to each of them. That is, it cannot be due to their possession of something to which universals, too, could lay claim, and with better right than they do.

Referring, as seems likely, to what becomes manifest to those who contemplate his denials, Aristotle says "in addition" that it becomes "clear also in the following way." But, however that may be, what he adds here has, like the conclusions drawn in the light of those denials, a bearing or application beyond the most obvious one. He says that it is impossible that an ousia be from (or a composite of) ousiai that are present in it as actual (ousiai): "what are two in this way, actually, are never one actually."—Whether the application to number that he suggests is in his opinion a valid one depends on whether he shares with "some" the view of number on which it rests (compare D14 1020b1–8 and pages 111–112 above). The remark about number serves to prepare the introduction at the end of the chapter of a perplexity whose explication here admittedly lacks the clarity that is promised from the discussions to follow. It is the question whether there may, after all, be no logos or definition (possible) for any ousia or (if a definition of an ousia is possible) in what manner it may be so and in what manner not.

Z14) In this chapter, as in not inconsiderable portions of the two which follow it (Z15 1040a8–27 and b2–4; Z16 1040b27–1041a3), Aristotle makes a number of observations, mostly critical, regarding those who assert that the "ideas" or "forms" are separate or separable and ousiai. Yet the sentence at the end of Z16 that brings the section as a whole (Z13–16) to a close (Z16 1041a3–5; compare Z17 1041a6–7) confirms that its concern is rather, in the first place, with universals. In seeking the explanation for this anomaly, we may start from the fact that "idea" or "form" and universal have in common that they are alternative answers to the same question: in calling, say, "man" (or a particular man) an animal, what do we mean by "animal"? The discussion of universals in Z13 used as we saw, as example of a universal, "animal," which the discussion of "ideas" or "forms" in Z14 uses as example of an "idea" or "form."

As idea or form, "animal" is taken to be separate or separable and an ousia. Its status as ousia is taken to be independent of any predicating of it (compare Z13 1038b15–16 with Z6 1031b15–18). The animals, on the other hand, "limitless, so to speak," in their multitude, are taken to be dependent on it for being what they are called: animals. On the assumption that the forms are, this is suggested to entail that "animal" be in each of them. (To repeat, in this discussion of form Aristotle seeks in the first place to shed light on the alternative to it: what the one is said to be, the other is not.) Here, then, the question arises whether "animal" is one and the same in "man" and "horse" or different in each. In logos it is clearly one: the "animal" in each of the two will be rendered by the same definition. But if "animal" signifies "some this" that is separate or separable and an ousia, insuperable difficulties confront the attempt to conceive of it, "one and the same . . . just as you are to yourself," as being in "horse" and "man." Can it be conceived then as different in each? Among other difficulties here, there is the question "how it (is) possible for the 'animal' which (is) ousia," that is, which is in each as its ousia, "to be just this," that is, an ousia, "besides 'animal itself'" or the self-subsistent idea. To ask this question is admittedly to confound the two senses of "ousia": to insist that what is ousia in the sense of essence be ousia also in the sense of self-subsistent being. But does Aristotle do more, in giving expression to that insistence, than bring to light a temptation that must from the outset have accompanied, if it did not indeed motivate, the allotment of these two senses to the (same) term?

As there are these difficulties together with others "more absurd" on the level of what are perceptible to the senses—that is, confronting the attempt to conceive, for example, of a relation of "animal" to the particular animals—he concludes that, if it is impossible (that they be understood as what they are) in this way, it is clear that there are not forms of them in the way that some say.

Z15) The chapter opens with an assertion that could be said to draw the full consequences from the conclusion that has just been expressed, as one might well understand that conclusion. The assertion is to the effect that there are these two ousiai, the composite whole and the logos, and that they are different from one another.—What was called in Z3 the shape or the form (1029a2–7; compare D8 1017b23–26) and in Z13 the "what it was to be" (1038b2–3) is now called the logos. It is a question in each of the three passages of what has been "taken together with the matter," as it is put here, when there is a composite whole. That ousia, the composite whole, is understood now as "the logos taken together with the matter"; this different one, as "the logos wholly (or as a whole)." The strange expression can be defended (against Bonitz and Jaeger) by recalling that logos is at bottom a number (Plato Epinomis 977b9–d1). The matter that the logos is taken together with will then be a thing. Prior to being grasped as a member of the group of things to which it belongs, a thing is not fully the thing that it is: the logos taken together with it, in conferring on it a name, identifies it as belonging to the group of the things that bear the name. And the logos itself is at bottom these same things, which are, together, something—say, animals—that they are not apart, when they have not yet been recognized as constituting a group. (Compare pages 99, 160–161, and 162–163 above.)—The assertion in question is introduced as the premise for a further conclusion which is, in its turn, twofold. The first part pertains to as many ousiai as can be spoken of as a logos taken together with some matter: of these, there is a perishing, for (there is) also a coming-to-be. The second part pertains to the logos itself: there is not (a perishing) of the logos such that (it) perishes, for (there is) not a coming-to-be either. This proves however not to mean that the logoi are always; rather, "without a coming-to-be and a perishing, they are and are not." (Compare pages 102–103 above.) As the sequel confirms, the ousiai of the first sort are those perceptible to the senses, the particulars, as to which Aristotle insists, here again, that they are "all" perishable (1039b30–31; compare B4 999b1–5). He leaves it open whether this is the case also for the species of the particulars. But by not insisting on their imperishability, he remains consistent with what he has just said about the logoi. This, then, the impossibility of insisting upon the imperishability of the species, is the authentic source of the problem for science that he reminds us of in the sequel (1039b27–1040a5; compare Z10 1036a2–12).

The proper theme of the sequel, the large part of the chapter which remains to be considered, is definition or rather what can and, especially, what cannot be defined. Three classes of the latter are taken up in turn: the ousiai perceptible to the senses or the particulars; the "ideas"; and such ousiai, like sun or moon, as are "one of a kind" (monacha). Aristotle apparently includes here sun and moon among the (yet to be identified) permanent ousiai (1040a27–29; compare Z16 1040b34–1041a3). But, as particulars perceptible to the senses, are they not among the "all" mentioned previously (1039b30–31)? However that may be, the sensible particulars of the first class are said to be indefinable by virtue of their perishability. They are, then, definable—as members of the group or species to which they belong—but we are necessarily ignorant of the term of validity of those definitions (compare 1040a2–7). The "ideas," on the other hand, are said to be indefinable by virtue of their particularity. Their logoi will consist necessarily of names or words each of which is common to all (1040a11; compare Ross ad loc.: "to all the members of the class denoted by the name"); and, even in combination, those words will apply of necessity to whatever else, besides the particular they are defining, they may happen to describe (1040a11–14, a33–b2). It remains the case, however, that the knowability of an "idea" is dependent, not (like that of one of the sensible particulars) on its being put into the group to which it belongs (Z10 1036a7–8), but rather on its being predicated of the particulars which bear its name (1040a23–27). In this respect, in other words, it differs not at all from a universal. (Compare pages 162–164 above.)

Z16) We said above (page 172) that the ousiai which can be spoken of as a logos that has been taken together with some matter are the ousiai perceptible to the senses. This proves to have been insufficiently precise insofar as it is not yet clear which the latter are. It is true that the bodies—that is, whatever is perceptible to the senses—are thought to be most manifestly ousiai (Z2 1028b8–9), that they are agreed upon by all to be ousiai (H1 1042a6; but compare Z3 1029a33–34 and page 134 above). Twice already Aristotle has provided a listing of them as such (D8 and Z2; compare H1). But now he undertakes, on his own authority, to correct the list. And if it is only now that he does so, that he undertakes to determine more precisely what are to be included among the ousiai and what are not, this is because the determination goes back, as to its basis, to what was implied in that characterization of ousia in Z15, a characterization which was itself the culmination of a long development.

As he explains now, nothing is an ousia, as opposed to the mere potentiality to become an ousia, which is not "one" (1040b8–9). "One" (tò hen) is spoken of just as "being" (tò on) is spoken of (1040b16) and, we can add, vice versa (compare G2 1003b22–25). But to be "one" is to be "some" one (1040b9–10). The question therefore arises of what makes a thing "some" one, that is, the thing or ousia that it is. The cause or element or principle responsible would seem, in accord with the most manifest teaching of the work, to be its ousia. This is, as ousia (essence), proper to the ousia (thing) in question (1040b16–17, 23–24); and for this reason, neither "the one" (tò hen) nor "being" (tò on), "nor anything else (that is) common" admits of being (the) ousia of the things (1040b18–23). Here, however, Aristotle introduces a further consideration (eti): "'the one' would not be at the same time in many places, but what is common is present in many places at the same time" (1040b25–26). Now the relevance of this consideration, as an argument against the responsibility of "the one" for a thing's being "some" one, presupposes that what does bear that responsibility is, after all, something common. Indeed, it is the logos that must be taken together with the matter (or the thing) as we saw in Z15, if the thing is to be fully the thing that it is (which it can be only as a member of the group of things to which it belongs) or as we can now say, if it is to be "some" thing and therewith some "one" (compare D26 1023b27–32). What was already implied, then, in the characterization of Z15, and becomes visible here, is that the authentic ousia, the ousia as understood, is always "one of those." (With Z15 1040a29, compare Z16 1040b34–1041a1: ousiai "one of a kind" were introduced provisionally in Z15 in order to underline the fact that the sensible particulars spoken of earlier in that chapter are not "one of a kind"—which is why their indefinability was not traced there to the particularity proper to them.)

The logos, as common to the ousiai of which it is the logos—in other words, as a universal—is not present apart from or besides those particulars. There is no longer any question here of calling it an ousia (of any sort) in its own right. And the same holds for form, so long as it is correctly understood as a "one over many." But those who separate the forms do so because they have no other imperishable ousiai to propose—besides the sensible particulars, which "we know" and which are, of course, perishable. In response, Aristotle refers, not to the species, but to the stars, although he does not unequivocally affirm the imperishability even of these. Given his silence here, then, on the solution alluded to in Epsilon (pages 124–125 above), this means that the problem for science (Z15 1039b27–1040a7), which the introduction of separate ideas was meant to dispose of, remains unsolved. And this is appropriate in view of the fact that Aristotle is himself still in search of an ousia separated from those perceptible to the senses (Z17 1041a6–9). The repetitions which are necessary to an argument that is meant to teach do not, for that very reason, undermine its fundamentally progressive character.

Z17) To bring Zeta to a close, Aristotle resolves to speak of "the ousia" (compare Z15 1039b20–22): to say "what" and "of what sort" one should say (that it is). He will say this now—it is no longer a question of investigating (compare Z3 1029a32–34, Z4 1029b1–3, Z13 1038b1–2)—having made what is like another beginning. Another beginning, a fresh start, appeared to be necessary because the old one had not led to or even towards the desired result: the discovery of an ousia separated from the ousiai perceptible to the senses. But the departure here is only "like" another beginning. The results of the original beginning are then not set aside but rather presupposed. Moreover, as we see now, the result that we are alerted to anticipate from what Aristotle is about to say is no more than clarity "about" that separate ousia.

What may "perhaps" bring such clarity is a discussion that takes its departure from the fact that ousia is (held to be) a principle and a cause (1041a9–10 and b25–28; compare Z13 1038b1–8). It is a question now of the cause not of the coming-to-be and perishing but of the being (1041a31–32) of the ousiai perceptible to the senses. And so, a question of the cause of their matter, and this is the form, by which (the matter) is "something" (namely, some "this": compare Z7 1032a14–15); and this (that is, either the cause, which is the form, or the "this" that the matter as ousia is) is the ousia (1041b7–9). But the matter is never simple (compare 1041b9–11). And therefore the cause of its being a "this" (an ousia) is at the same time the cause of its parts being put together such that all (of it) is one (1041b11; compare 1041a20–21, 26–28, and b2–7). This then is the aspect of the problem of the oneness of "man" (for example) that was not treated in Z12 (see pages 162–163 above) or in subsequent chapters. Or better: it is the problem of the oneness that belongs to a man or other ousia before it is grasped as "one of those" and therefore before it is knowingly grasped as a "one": that is, before it is fully the ousia that it is.

Aristotle does not provide us here with the solution to the problem, which would be the answer also to the question of ousia as a cause. But he points to it with the help of two examples that are apparently used only to show what cannot be the solution. The examples are the syllable "ba" consisting of the elements (letters) "b" and "a" and flesh (understood as) consisting of fire and earth or "the warm and (the) cold." Neither the syllable nor flesh is its elements, which may continue to be when they themselves, through dissolution, are no more. More precisely, neither the syllable nor flesh is only its elements: they are "also something different" from them. Is this different "something" itself an element or from elements? Aristotle easily shows that it cannot be. But "it would seem to be something and not (an) element and, indeed, (a) cause of this being flesh, that (a) syllable, and similarly also for the others" (1041b25–27).—Since what "would seem" to be the case may, after all, not be the case, the alternative is not excluded that what in addition to the elements makes the syllable, for example, composed of them a syllable, is nothing but the togetherness of those elements. It is not excluded, in other words, that they, too, are something together, or when they are grasped together, which they are not when they are apart.—"And this (is)," Aristotle continues where we left off, "(the) ousia of each, for (this is the) first cause of (its) being (the thing or ousia that it is)" (1041b27–28). And since it is only those things set together in accord with nature that are (strictly speaking) ousiai, this nature "would appear to some" (the reading of mss.EJ at 1041b30; contrast Frede and Patzig ad loc.)—that is, it would appear to some on the basis of the considerations that Aristotle has set forth explicitly—"(to be) ousia, (an ousia) which is not (an) element but (a) principle" (1041b28–31).

A remark made in passing earlier in the chapter (1041a16–17), which might have reminded us of what was intimated about nature in Epsilon, had temporarily returned the discussion to the level achieved there. It was to the effect that there is in all cases "one logos and one cause" that a thing is just the thing that it is (auto . . . hoti auto). Aristotle does not say which logos and cause he has in mind, for it is surely not the alternative that he mentions in the context by way of dismissing it (1041a18–20). And the reason may be that he is referring to the necessity that, as determinative of all particular causes (like the atoms, which are allegedly responsible for everything but their own impenetrability), cannot have been determined by any of them.

H1) The new book, Eta, puts to itself the task of drawing inferences from what has been said, presumably in Zeta, and adding a conclusion to the discussion on the basis of a drawing together of its chief point. Since the declared intention of what proved to be by far the largest part of Zeta (Z3–17) was to clear the way for an answer to the question of which the authentic ousiai are (Z2 end; compare the reminder at Z17 beginning), we might reasonably expect now a definitive answer to it. But in this regard Eta appears to be anything but definitive (H1 1042a22–24; H3 1043b18–19). We must allow then the book itself to instruct us as to what it regards as the chief point of the discussion we have just worked our way through and as to what sort of conclusion it wishes to add now to that discussion.

The summary of the contents of Zeta offered in this first chapter does indeed include many of the topics taken up in that book. But in mingling indiscriminately what had been mentioned (in Z2) as answers to the question "which" the ousiai are with what had been mentioned (in Z3) as answers to the question "what" ousia is, the summary appears to disregard a distinction upon which the structure of Zeta as a whole was based. And a relaxation of the rigor of Zeta may be seen also in the fact that, in listing those ousiai which as it claims are agreed upon by all, those which had been listed in the first place in both Z2 and D8, it takes no notice of the tightening of the list that Z16 has shown to be necessary. Other examples, as well, of what we are tempted to call Eta's more rhetorical character (Art of Rhetoric A1 1355a24–29) could be given (H1 1042a30–31 and b1–6; H4 1044b6–8; H3 1043b14–16 and 18–19). However, a relaxation of rigor in some respects may be compatible with a tightening of it, or at least a greater explicitness, in others.

That "the what it was to be" and the substratum are (held to be) ousiai, for example, is said here to result "from the logoi." In other words, these two do not belong among the most manifest ousiai or those generally agreed to be ousiai but come to sight as ousiai, if they do, rather from the examination or analysis of those others (compare page 165 above). Having remarked that the ideas and the "mathematicals" are said by some (to be ousiai) besides the ousiai perceptible to the senses, Aristotle adds that the ousiai perceptible to the senses all have matter.—The words omitted by mss.EJ at 1042a24–25 may have been added by an editor attempting to supply the transition which, as the text stands without them, is less than transparent. But they do more to obscure than to reveal a transition that becomes visible (against the background of Z16 1040b27–1041a3) in the light cast by subsequent references in Eta to a matter that is exempt from coming to be and perishing (H1 1042b1–6 and H4 1044b6–8; but compare D8 1017b10–13 as well as Z2 1028b10–13).—Next, he speaks of three ways in which the substratum is ousia, and matter is mentioned first in this connection. In other words, matter is ousia insofar as the substratum is ousia. But he goes on to make this clear: that matter is ousia—something which he fails to do either for "the logos and the shape" or for what is from it and the matter. That the latter is ousia, the composite, is perhaps not in need of being shown; and, as for the former, it is admittedly separable (from the matter or the thing) only in speech (but compare 1042a30–31). The matter which was said to be ousia as substratum was distinguished from "the logos and the shape"—not to mention the composite—by being said to be "some this" only potentially. But the matter which, as substratum of changes, is shown to be clearly ousia is in each case but one already some (thing) or "some this." The exception concerns change in respect of ousia itself. The matter which is said, at least, to be the substratum for the coming-to-be of an ousia or thing is the thing which is coming to be and which is present therefore (during its coming-to-be) only "by privation." Whether the exception is a genuine one will depend on how coming-to-be simply is to be distinguished from the other cases of coming-to-be or change considered here. Aristotle refers us therefore to the scientific writings in which he has already treated this question (On Generation and Corruption A3, for example).

H2) According to what is suggested at the end of this chapter, in which the focus continues to be on "the sensibles" or the ousia perceptible to the senses, it is manifest "from what has been said" which this ousia is and how it is: the one (is ousia) as matter, the other as shape, and the third is the one from these. The first chapter of Eta had spoken of the substratum as an ousia which is in one way the matter, in another the shape, and the third what is from these. The division applied there to ousia understood as substratum is applied here to ousia understood more simply, and perhaps more adequately, as something perceptible to the senses. But the division itself carries with it, if not the name, then the notion of a substratum. And the chapter's beginning acknowledges as much by identifying ousia as substratum with ousia as matter. The purpose of this identification is to introduce the chapter's task or theme. A matter or substratum which is (only) potentially (1042b9–10; compare H1 1042a27–28) would require as complement some "energeia": the actuality of being in a certain state or activity (compare Z13 1038b6). And what remains to be said, at the chapter's beginning at least, is this: which is the ousia (that is ousia) as energeia of the sensibles?

To explain what he means by energeia, Aristotle turns to the differentiae, and in the first place to those that seem to have been recognized as such by Democritus. According to Democritus, the body which serves as substratum, the matter, is (everywhere) one and the same; but (these bodies) differ in shape, setting, and position (compare A4 985b16–19 and context). Now the body—each body—which is, as matter, available to be determined by the three differentiae is of course already determined by all of them: it is of some shape, is set in some way, and is in some position relative to the others. (We can disregard here the question of whether it can change in all of these respects.) The body or matter which, as free from all such determination, is nothing but the potentiality to receive it, is known (to the extent that it is known) "from the logoi" (H1 1042a12–13): it "is" in the logoi.

The only objection that Aristotle makes to Democritus here is that there are manifestly many differentiae. The examples that he offers first (1042b15–21) are admittedly not decisive with a view to what he ultimately wishes to make clear (1043a4–7; compare H3 1043b21–23 as well as Z17 1041b28–31).—They share this difference from the differentiae of Democritus: the matter which they determine is in each case already determined (independently of them) and is therefore identifiable. They are but a further determination of it. And although Aristotle does not identify that matter—he identifies only one or more of the bearers of each of the (further) determinations that he mentions—its identity is in all of these cases easily inferred and in some of them also mentioned further on (1043a7–8 and 22–23; compare also 1043a9–10 with 1042b27–28).—But at the end of the list an example is added that is different from these and treated somewhat differently, one that seems to be of a significance greater than theirs. The differentiae in question are qualities (affections) of the sensibles: for example, hardness and softness, density and rarity, dryness and wetness. In this case, Aristotle does not mention any particular bearers of the determinations. Could he not have in mind the sensibles as such, that is, the bodies, and especially the natural bodies? Fresh light would thus be thrown on the meaning of the criticism that he has made here of his predecessor: in treating of the differentiae of bodies, which are as such sensible, Democritus had acknowledged only three of their "many" differentiae. But we would be compelled also to admit that we are as little able, as we were in the case of the differentiae of Democritus, to identify any matter determined by these qualities (compare On the Soul B11 422b25–33)—unless we are to say that they are themselves the parts of matter that were alluded to in Z17 (page 175 above). What they determine are just the bodies which bear them; and they are together, in their various combinations, those bodies or, at any rate, all that we truly know of bodies. (Compare pages 119–120 above.)

In the latter part of the chapter, Aristotle takes a step back from the point to which his examples of differentiae have led us; and it is here that he first identifies, for one or more of them, a matter that they determine (1043a7–10; but compare 1043a10–11). In the meantime, he has suggested that the differentiae, if not singly, then in their various combinations (1042b24; compare 1043a4), are nothing less than the "to be" of what bears them: the "(it) is" is said in just so many ways (as the differentiae or their combinations) (1042b25–26; compare 1042b16 and context). And for those (things) whose "to be" will be "to have been mixed," the "not to be" (is) set over against (this) (1042b36–1043a1). It follows that one is to look among the differentiae or their genera for the cause of the "to be" for each of those that bear them, only if the ousia is the cause, for each, of its "to be" (1043a2–4; compare Z17 1041b25–28 as well as pages 175–176 above).

It is only after he has clarified in this way or to this extent what the differentiae are, that Aristotle returns to energeia, which thus comes to sight above all as that combination of differentiae which determines a given matter (1043a12–14 and 19–20; contrast 1043a23–26). He gives a further indication of what he intends, by associating with energeia each of the following, in turn: logos (1043a12–13), form (1043a20), ousia (1043a23–24), and shape (1043a25–26). He is concerned above all with that energeia which is predicated of the matter in the case of the ousiai (1043a4–7). Therefore he concludes the chapter, as we have seen, by speaking of the ousia perceptible to the senses, which (among other ways that it is) is as shape "because" (it is as) energeia (reading "hoti" at 1043a28 with the manuscripts).

H3) This chapter, "a collection of ill-connected remarks on various topics relating to essence and definition" according to Ross

(Vol. II, p.231), is the most important in Eta and among the most important in the work as a whole. The remarks to which Ross refers are for the most part rather terse; and they are ill-connected in the sense that the transitions between them are not made explicit—the thought, if any, linking one remark and grouping of remarks to another and determining the overall sequence of their presentation. This need not mean, however, that no thought has gone into their arrangement or that, in addition to being "ill-connected," they are also ill-placed. But if they are in fact carefully arranged, the unspoken thought that is made visible in the order of their presentation becomes part of their presentation. It supplies something of what they, in their terseness, withhold; and it does so in a manner consistent with the reserve underlying that terseness.

The first part of the chapter (1043a29–b4) warns us not to be ignorant of the fact that it sometimes escapes notice whether a name signifies "the composite ousia" or the energeia and the shape. (Here, as in H2, shape, form, and ousia, in one of its usages, are taken to be the same as energeia.) For example, (it may escape notice) whether what is being referred to as an animal is a soul in a body or a soul, (the) ousia and energeia of some body. "Animal" might be applied to both, although not as rendered by one definition. But whatever importance these (questions) have in some other respect, they have none for the investigation into the ousia perceptible to the senses.

That investigation continues to be of concern to us then. Although the end of H2 declared it to be manifest (from what had already been said) which this ousia is and how it is, we are evidently still in pursuit of an adequate understanding of it. The end of H2 had declared manifest, in particular, that there is an ousia which is from (or of) matter and shape or energeia; and the first part of this chapter appears to speak with as little hesitation of "the composite ousia."

That the questions dismissed here have an importance in some other respect (than as bearing on the investigation of sensible ousia tout court) is indicated by the last remark in this part. Whereas soul is the same as (the) being for soul—since the form and the energeia is that which "the what it was to be" is present to (or the same as)—man is not the same as (the being) for man, unless the soul, too, will be said to be man. (Compare 1043b18–19 as well as Z10 1036a13–25 and pages 158–159 above.) But it cannot be excluded that this remark also belongs, along with the earlier reference to "the composite ousia," to the indications Aristotle gives of the ground or grounds for his suggestion that the investigation into the ousia perceptible to the senses needs to be pressed further.

From speaking of man and his soul, Aristotle turns abruptly in the second part of the chapter (1043b4–10) to speaking of the syllable once again (compare Z17), among other things of lesser moment. But the assertion that he ventures in their regard is no less remarkable for being applied here expressly only to them. Making explicit what he had at most silently suggested in Z17 (pages 175–176 above), he says now that it is manifest (not "from what has been said" but) to those who are investigating that the syllable is not from (or of) its elements and a "synthesis" (a putting together). If it were, or if more generally things, each of which is a synthesis or mixture of elements or parts of matter, were from (or of) those elements or parts <u>and</u> a synthesis or mixture, then the latter would be from (or among) the very elements or parts of which it is, rather, the synthesis or mixture (following the suggestion of Bonitz conveyed though not accepted by Ross <u>ad</u> <u>loc</u>.; compare D24 1023a31–33). To begin to appreciate the weight of this remark one must recall that "synthesis" and "mixture" were presented in H2 as preeminent examples of energeiai (H2 1043a12–14; compare 1042b36–1043a1).

In the third part of the chapter (1043b10–23), Aristotle turns back to man. He thus makes his silence on man in the second part all the more conspicuous. It would be wrong to say that his remarks here are entirely unaffected by that second part, since the question "what is man?" is approached now by starting from parts that are acknowledged to be or are regarded as matter (1043b10–11; compare 1043a34–35 and b2–4). But he goes on to insist—in language reminiscent of that which he had used in Z17 (1041b4–28), though not entirely in his own name—that there needs to be something (ti) besides those material parts, which is neither an element nor from one but the ousia, something which "they" speak of without reference to (more literally: taking away or removing; compare Z11 1036b22–24 and context) the matter. If then this (additional something) is cause of the "to be" (of man) and is (also) ousia, "they" would be speaking of the ousia itself.

These remarks retreat, then, from the point that had been reached in the second part. But they shed light on it by the very contrast they afford, by reminding us, that is, of the alternative view that it threatens to replace. And we must keep this in mind also in considering the remarks added now, which are (in part) to the following effect. This (the ousia of which "they" speak or would speak) is necessarily either permanent or perishable without perishing, having come to be without a coming-to-be. Whether the ousiai of the perishable things are separable (from them) is not yet at all clear. There are admittedly exceptions, cases that clearly do not admit (of such separation): for example, house or implement, which cannot be besides the particulars. But perhaps the latter and their like, which have not been set together by nature, are not ousiai even. For someone might make (suppose) nature alone (to be) ousia of those (reading "tōn" at 1043b23 with the manuscripts) among the perishable things (that have an ousia). (Compare Z17 1041b28–33.)

The fourth part (1043b23–32) presents itself as a mere continuation of the third ("hōste" at 1043b23); and this would not be misleading if the third part had truly been, as it presented itself as being ("oude" at 1043b10), a mere continuation of the second. Here Aristotle turns abruptly to definition. Given the affinity and more than affinity of definition and "the what it was to be" (1044a1–2; compare D8 1017b21–22 with Z4 1029b13–14), we can say that definition has been referred to once before in the chapter. "The what it was to be" was said in the first part to be present to the form and the energeia (1043b1–2). And this was consistent with what we have heard more than once in the work: that "the what it was to be" and definition belong preeminently, if not even exclusively, to form (Z10 1035b31–34, for example, and Z11

1037a26–30). It is, however, the sole function of this part of the chapter to retract that long held or long asserted position (compare Z13 1039a14–20): to deny that shape (that is, form) is definable. For the reason alleged for the retraction must be disregarded, as appealing, in its account of what is and is not definable, to a view of ousia (ousia as composite of matter and shape) that has been shown in the second part to be untenable.

According to the fifth part (1043b32–34), it is manifest why (or that), if the ousiai are somehow numbers, they are in this way and (are) not, as some say, of monads. The ousiai which are suggested here, however tentatively (compare Z12 1038a5 and pages 162–163 above), to be numbers, somehow, are the forms (1044a9–11). It is a question then, in both the fourth and the fifth parts, of the forms: in the fourth of their being indefinable; in the fifth of their being numbers. Could it be due to their being numbers, or to the way in which they are numbers, that they are indefinable? Aristotle suggests as much, perhaps expressly (the term "houtōs" that we have translated here as "in this way" can refer back, to what has just been said, as well as forward) but certainly by his juxtaposition of these two parts.

The sixth part (1043b34–1044a11) turns therefore to a discussion of number, or of number and definition, coming back to ousia or form only at its end. The number in question now is not that which belongs to form as class or universal or logos (H1 1042a28–29, H2 1043a12–13, Z15 1039b20–22), for that number is of an indefinite multitude of things (compare pages 162–163, 171–172, and 173 above). Nor can one leave it at saying that it is the number which is shown here to belong to definition, one that is always "some" number: of a definite multitude of parts, such that the subtraction or addition of even one part suffices to make it a different number. It is true that form is a number also of this sort (1044a9–11), form as we were confronted with it in Z17 and H2 (pages 175–176 and 181 above) and reminded of it in the second part of this chapter. And in compelling us to recall the two ways in which form is number, Eta does indeed draw together the points in Zeta that could be regarded as the chief one or ones (H1 1042a3–4). But what concerns Aristotle now is what also makes form indefinable (compare Z13 1039a17–19); and that is not so much even its limited manyness as the respect in which it is, precisely as limited or as "some" number, also one. He first raises, without expressly answering it, the question "by what" a (definite) number, or a definition, is one. And then he says that the ousia too (that is, the form) is one "in that way" (houtōs). The ousia is one as some definite number or definition is one—it is not the cause of anything's being one. Each ousia is one therefore, not as something simple, as a monad or a point, but as some nature or an actuality or completion ("entelecheia," a term used more or less interchangeably with "energeia": compare H6 1045b16–17 with b19, 21, and 22). And this means, in accord with what we were reminded of in the second part, that it is one as the synthesis of the parts of the ousia (thing) of which it is the ousia (form). Now, precisely as their synthesis, it is not (1043b33–34) or not simply (Z13 1039a11–14) those parts. As in the case of the six (monads) of which Aristotle had spoken much earlier in the work (D14 1020b6–8), the ousia (as form) is the parts of the ousia (as thing) taken "once," that is, in their togetherness.

Finally, in concluding the chapter, he indicates that what has been determined here would, if fully developed, dispose of the question of the coming to be and perishing of what are said to be ousiai (compare 1043b14–23), as well as of the closely related question of the leading (of things) up or back to number (compare Z11 1036b3–13 and context).

H4) In this chapter Aristotle says something about scientific investigation: how the cause or rather the causes are to be pursued (1044a32–b5). At the same time he shows again by deed that there are limits to this pursuit (or to the way in which its results are presented) which the scientist would do well to respect (1044b6–8; compare H1 1042b3–6, as well as Z11 1037a10–14 and Z16 1040b34–1041a3). And he gives an example of the freedom that the scientist who shows such respect can permit himself on occasion (1044b12 and context; compare Thucydides VII 50.4). Since what is under consideration is scientific investigation, it is of course a question here of the material ousia. According to the beginning of H2, agreement has already been reached as to the ousia (which is ousia) as substratum and as matter. But there may be agreement of a sort about something, without sufficient clarity in its regard and even because such clarity is lacking (Xenophon Memorabilia IV 6.13–15). Among the questions which remain with regard to the material ousia is that concerning a first matter (one or more) for all things. While this question must, it seems, be left unsettled, and in part perhaps because it must, the attention of the scientist is directed to the matter or other cause nearest to what is to be explained (1044a15–20 and b1–3). (There is not, in every case, a material cause strictly speaking: 1044b8 and following.) A most vivid illustration of the correct approach is provided by what Aristotle says at the end of the chapter as to how sleep is to be investigated.

H5) According to the statement with which the chapter begins, the forms are and are not, without a coming-to-be and a perishing (1044b21–22 and 28–29). When ousia of this sort was mentioned in this connection in H3, an alternative was considered which is no longer in question here (H3 1043b14–16: see also b18–19)—the earlier chapter itself may be in part responsible for its omission (page 186 above). After this beginning, the chapter appropriately turns in its second half to what one may call a meditation on death. As an old Jewish saying has it, there is no death without sin. Aristotle does not go so far. But he does wonder out loud whether perishing generally, and that of a living being in particular, is not in accord with accident (1044b36–1045a1) or against nature (1045a1–2 and 1044b32–34). It is a question of how the potentiality that is or belongs to the matter of an animal is to be understood. Having disposed in its first part of the forms, which are said there to lack matter (1044b28–29), the chapter thus takes up again, in its second part, the concern of its predecessor with the material ousia.

H6) This chapter adds a footnote to H3 by providing the answer to a question to which we are led by that chapter. It is not the question from which the discussion begins here and which had been raised explicitly, in almost the same terms, in H3: what is the cause that definitions and (definite) numbers are each one? That question, which is recognized in both chapters as equivalent to the question of the oneness of ousia as form, can be raised again because it was not answered explicitly in H3. Is the new chapter unaware of the answer that, suitably prepared in H2, was in fact given in H3? It speaks of "the whole" as being something besides the parts (1045a10). Where it refers on its own to matter and shape (1045a23 and 29, b18), it is silent as to any composite of the two of them. It suggests that life (tò zēn) cannot be understood as a binding together of soul with (a) body (1045b11–12). Above all, it understands matter as what has the potentiality to be that which, as shape, it will be in actuality; and shape as what is in actuality that which the matter has the potentiality to be (1045a23–24 and 29–30).

The new chapter thus gives every evidence not only of being aware of but also of accepting the answer given in H3 to the question, especially regarding the oneness of form, that it professes to regard here as still unanswered. Moreover, it makes the surprising suggestion that that question can be answered by answering the question of the cause that matter and shape (that is, form), understood as we have indicated that they are here, are one (1045a20–29). It appears to go so far even as to claim that these two questions or perplexities are the same (1045a25). Yet the answer that it gives to the second of them (1045a30–31 and b21–22) makes no immediately discernible contribution to answering the question of the oneness of ousia as form.

But perhaps it is less the answer to it than the question itself which constitutes a step towards removing (1045a24 and 29) a perplexity that the authentic answer to the original question has left us with. For if form is nothing but the synthesis of the parts of the thing—that is, of the matter—if it is nothing other than those parts in their togetherness (page 183 above), the question that must be put, it would seem, is what remains to distinguish form from matter. And the answer that Aristotle gives here is that the ultimate matter (compare H4 1044a15–18 and b1–3) and the shape (that is, the form) are the same (1045b17–18). They are the same even in potentiality (the reading of mss.EJ at 1045b18–19): matter is potentially the shape that it will assume as the ultimate matter, and shape is potentially the shape of that ultimate matter. And again (they are the same) in actuality (1045b19): the shape is the parts of the matter in the togetherness which they have as the ultimate matter; and that is to say that those same parts are in their togetherness the shape. There is thus no need to search either for what differentiates potentiality (as matter) from actuality (as shape or form) or for what makes them one (1045b16–17). And as for matter in the sense of what has potentiality and form as the actuality corresponding to it, even they are "somehow" one (1045b20–22; compare 1045a30–33).

Th1) Theta is divided into two parts. The greater of them by far in length (Th1–9) is devoted to the single task of the precise determination of potentiality (power/capacity) and actuality (completion). The task is undertaken with a view to the fact that being (tò on) is expressed not only by the predications—of "what" or "what sort" or "how much" and so on—but also with a view to potentiality and actuality and to the work (deed/fact). This was one of the four ways, taken up in D7, in which "tò on" is used; and the suggestion made there (1017b8–9) of something in its regard that requires determination elsewhere may suffice to explain the return to it here. It was mentioned also in a similar listing of the usages of "tò on" in E2, but not when they were taken up again in E4. Being as truth, another of those usages (mentioned in all three places), was suggested in E4 to require subsequent investigation (1027b28–29). And the other part of Theta (Th10) is devoted to the determination or investigation (1051b5–6) of this sort of being. The book as a whole thus comes to sight as a continuation of the discussion of being, after what was to have been said about ousia has been said (that is, in Zeta and Eta)—as the sentence with which Theta opens declares that it has. Ousia is called here "the primary being" (1045b27); and in E4 being as truth was said to be a different being from those which are beings authoritatively (1027b31). One may be tempted, therefore, to go so far as to speak of a continuation of the discussion on a lower level, at least thematically. Yet the very being that was said in E4 to be different from those which are beings authoritatively is said in Th10 to be that which is most authoritatively being (1051b1–2). We have to do here, then, not with mere continuity but with a turning point in the argument, one that is perhaps prepared by the consideration of being as potentiality and actuality (about which, to repeat, E4 had been silent: see pages 125–126 above) that precedes it. And Aristotle may have wished to alert us to the possibility of some such development by referring in this context to an earlier remark as one made "in the first speeches" (1045b31–32). The remark in question is to be found in Z1 (1028a35–36); and he could therefore have referred to it, indeed more precisely, as occurring "in the speeches about ousia" (compare Th8 1049b27–28). But to have done so would not have served, so well as a reference to "the first speeches" does, to mark off the discussion to which we are about to turn from what has gone before as a whole.

Early in this first chapter, Aristotle refers to "what we wish now": first to be determined is a potentiality (power/capacity) that is most said (to be) authoritatively (such) (see 1046a9–11), "though it is not (the one) most useful for what we wish now." By way of explanation, he says that potentiality and actuality (here "energeia," earlier in the chapter "entelecheia") extend beyond those said only with a view to motion (to be such). But having first discussed this (one), he will in the determinations regarding actuality (energeia) bring clarity also regarding the others (compare Th6 1048a25–30). The focus of attention in this discussion of actuality will then continue to be on potentiality, although potentiality itself, and all the more that to which he turns first, is to be considered for the sake of some further end, which he leaves for the time being unidentified.

The potentiality (power/capacity) in question has been considered before (in D12). Aristotle presents again, with apparently minor variations, the chief points of the earlier treatment of it. But by reminding us here of that treatment, he directs us to take such variations as there may be into account in attempting to grasp the character of the present discussion.—The reminder consists in his saying that "it has been determined . . . elsewhere that potentiality (hē dunamis) and being capable (tò dunasthai) are spoken of in many ways." Since he intends to add in Theta to the ways enumerated in Delta, he does not say, as he will in a later reference (Th8 1049b4) to another chapter in that book, that it has been determined "in how many ways" they are spoken of.—In dismissing from consideration now what he calls here "homonymous" uses of the term, he includes among them uses of "possible" (dunaton) and "impossible" (adunaton) in geometry. He thus seems to conflate two classes that were distinguished earlier (compare D12 1019b33–34 and the note of Ross ad loc. with 1019b22–33). However that may be, he says nothing in particular here about the former of these classes, about which he had said not a little in Delta. On the other hand, he says now explicitly, what could only have been inferred from the earlier treatment (compare, for example, D12 1019a19–22 with a33–b1), that (the potentiality or power) to do and to suffer is in a sense one potentiality (1046a19–20). In the elaboration of this remark, he appears to treat the potentiality to suffer as the root potentiality (1046a20–21; compare 1046a9–11 as well as D12 1019b35–1020a2). And the discussion of the complementary remark, too, appears to devote more attention to suffering than to doing (1046a22–29). It is in this context that matter is referred to: as some principle on account of which what suffers (something) suffers, or rather on account of which what suffers in a particular way suffers in the way that it does. There had been no mention of matter in the chapter in Delta.

Th2) This chapter draws a distinction within the form or class of potentialities (powers/capacities) said in both Th1 and D12 to be the one by reference to which the others are to be understood (compare 1046b3–4 with Th1 1046a9–11 and D12 1019b35–1020a2). Some of the principles (compare D1 1013a7–8) of this sort are present in inanimate (things), while the others (are present) in the soul and in that (part) of the soul that has logos (speech/reason); so it is clear that of the potentialities (powers/capacities), too, some will be without logos, while the others will be with logos. Now, all of those that are with logos are, the same ones, (capacities for the production) of contraries—as medicine is for sickness and health. And this much is easily explained by recourse to the facts that a science capable of this is a logos and that the same logos makes clear the thing (that the science aims to produce) and its privation (1046b7–9) along with the means to each of them (compare 1046b21–22). More difficult to explain is why—given that the contrary ends are of different rank (1046b9–10, 11–15, and 20) and that the moving principle in the soul that has the science or art is in each case the same (1046b17 and 20–22)—the knower does produce (poiein) both of them (1046b18–20).

The reason may have to be sought in the fact that the single principle from which the soul acts in doing so is encompassed by the logos (the reading of mss.J and Ab at 1046b24). In other words, the science which determines the means to the contrary ends, and in the first place to the better of them, is a logos (1046b7–8), but not "the" logos (1046b24) or logos simply. Adding a remark at the end of the chapter which has no (other) discernible connection with the rest of it, Aristotle finds occasion to say that it is not necessary that the one who does or acts (poiein) do or act well (eu poiein; compare Republic 335a7 and 9). His assertion, as we have suggested that it might be understood, is perfectly compatible with the thought that it is necessary for the one who does or acts to act in accord with the moving principle in him, as that principle is affected, or even if it should be unaffected, by reason.

Th3) Aristotle discusses here the assertion made by some to the effect that someone or something is capable (dunasthai)—capable of being at work (energein)—only when it is in fact at work, and otherwise not capable. He tells us neither the ground to which they appeal in making the assertion nor the reasoning that leads them to it from that ground; and little is now known of the views of the only ones among its proponents that he identifies by name: the

Megarics. But he points out the "absurd consequences" which follow for such proponents from what they say. It follows, for example, that they say (also) "the logos of Protagoras" (1047a6–7).—The context suggests that Aristotle is thinking here more of the exposition of that logos which was given in the Theaetetus than of his own treatment of it in the fourth and fifth chapters of Gamma. (Compare 1047a4–8 with Theaetetus 152c8–e1, 153d8–154a2, and 156a3–157a7.) Plato had in a way ascribed authorship of that dialogue, which fails to answer the question (what is knowledge or science) that it raises, to a Megarian by the name of Eucleides (142a1–143c7), the same who is credited with being the founder of the Megaric school (Diogenes Laertius B10.106).—Above all, the logoi of its proponents, in making potentiality (dunamis) and actuality (energeia) the same, seek to make away with "no small thing" (1047a19–20). As a remark later on in Theta (Th8 1049b8–10) confirms, the no small thing in question is likely to be nature, which can be understood as a principle or capacity for motion that is intrinsic to the natural beings as such. (Compare D4 1014b18–20 as well as Physics B1 192b8–23.)

Since he does not mention, let alone criticize, the ground to which its proponents appeal in making the assertion he is combating, we are free to suspect that Aristotle may have accepted that ground himself. And if the ground should prove to be one that science as such requires, our suspicion would approach certainty. But we would then be confronted with the paradox that a ground which must be presupposed, if science is to be possible, can be appealed to in support of an assertion that entails the denial of the possibility of science. Or have we already met with just such a ground without, however, having grasped its Janus-faced character?

In our consideration of the second and third chapters of Epsilon, which treat of accidental being, we were struck by the remark that, if the accidental will not be, "everything will be of (or by) necessity" (E2 1027a12–13). Now, as became clear upon reflection, accidental being is only in a manner, not fundamentally, an exception to the rule of necessity (page 124 above). The necessity for there to be then, for everything which is coming to be and perishing, some (sufficient) cause (E3 1027a30–32) is presupposed on either alternative: whether the accidental is or it is not. What the accidental proved to depend upon is the existence of beings which are in the same way (only) for the most part (page 124 above). And this was suggested to be at the same time the minimum that the possibility of science itself requires (E2 1027a20–21 and page 125 above): what is in the same way for the most part can also be said to be "by its nature" in that way (Prior Analytics A13 32b4–10; compare 32b18–21). But in the same context in which all of this was spelled out, Aristotle put the question "whether there is nothing that is either always or for the most part" (E2 1027a15–16 as well as pages 125 and 124 above). One might respond that the existence of what is for the most part is manifest. But his putting that question shows, as we pointed out in discussing it, that Aristotle could conceive of a state of affairs in which there is nothing which is for the most part or "by its nature" in some way. Indeed, he could wonder whether such a state is not the natural one, with ours an exception of comparatively short duration (On the Heaven G2 301a4–11; compare On Generation and Corruption B11 337b12–13). And there is only an apparently short step from this point to a denial of the possibility of science altogether.

But Aristotle seems not to have taken that step—whereas, according to his indications (Th3 1047a19–20 and Th8 1049b8–10), those who made potentiality the same as actuality did take it. The reasoning they may have followed from the ground which they shared with him to the assertion that he rejected is again indicated in Epsilon (E3 1027a30–b9). For if every coming-to-be is either necessary or impossible, there would seem to be no room for any potentiality other than the possibility that is implied by necessity itself (pages 109–110 above). As for his own resistance to that reasoning, it cannot be due simply to his recognition of the positive role that our very limitations play—our ignorance, for example, of how even that will occur of which we know that it will occur—in our grasp of the world (E3 1027b9–14 and the conditional formulations in Th3 1047a24–29): opposite conclusions could be drawn, and no doubt were drawn, from such recognition. It may have to be traced then to a manly insistence on the significance, in its own way timeless or universal, of what is manifest to us—to an unwillingness, to begin with, in the face of the thought of an absence of order of perhaps limitless duration, to be so overwhelmed as to refuse to the here and now, to what is around us, to the order in which we live and move, its undeniable evidence. (Compare G5 1010a25–32.)

Th4 & Th5) Toward the end of the chapter we have just been considering, Aristotle gives an account of potentiality (power/capacity) that renders what one might call the flooring that belongs to any potentiality, as such (compare Th4 1047b3): if the actuality or being at work (energeia), of which it is the potentiality (dunamis), should be present, there will be (in or resulting from it) nothing impossible (Th3 1047a24–29). One can speak accordingly of something capable (dunaton) of coming about, if its doing so would entail nothing that is impossible (adunaton). But among what are capable, in this sense, of coming about, are those which will not come about, since a cause sufficient for their doing so is lacking (compare On Generation and Corruption A3 317b14–18 together with A5 322a4–6). For the sense in which "A" is capable of coming about, if "B" (whose existence its existence entails) is capable of doing so, is different from the sense in which "B" (whose existence the existence of "A" would entail) is capable of coming about, if "A" is bound to do so.

Having indicated this much in the latter part of Th3 and in Th4, Aristotle returns in Th5 to the distinction which he drew in Th2 between potentialities with logos and those without logos. Of the latter, he says now that whenever, in a manner that accords with the potentiality in question, the (potential) doer and the (potential) sufferer are in proximity to one another, it is necessary that the one do (poiein) and the other suffer (paschein). The potentialities with logos, on the other hand, are not subject to this necessity. But why not? The reason given is that they are (capacities for the production) of contraries, so that (were they subject to it) one would at the same time be doing/making (poiein) those contraries—which is impossible. It is necessary, then, that something different (from the potentiality in question) be what is authoritative (compare 1048a2–5): "I mean, by this, appetite (orexis) or choice (prohairesis); since, for whichever (of the two contraries) the appetite is authoritative, this one will do (poiein) whenever one is, in a manner that accords with the potentiality, in the presence and proximity of the (potential) sufferer." This necessity extends, according to Aristotle, to "everything" that is capable (dunaton) in respect of logos. When appetite and capacity (dunamis) coincide, under the conditions required by the latter, what is capable will do that of which it has the appetite; and when those conditions are absent, it will be incapable of this. Indeed, as he insists here (compare Th7 1049a5–7 and 13–14), those conditions are presupposed whenever one speaks properly of potentiality (power/capacity).

Th6) In turning to Theta, whose first part on potentiality (dunamis) and actuality (energeia) we are now considering, we failed to raise the question of the thematic link between this part and Eta, where Aristotle had been at pains to identify form with energeia or to reinterpret it as energeia (see, in particular, H2 end and page 181 above). This was due only in part to the fact that, in introducing Theta, he directed our attention rather to its relation to the consideration of ousia (in Zeta and Eta) as a whole. The deeper reason was that we had not grasped the significance of the identification insisted upon by Eta.—The four chapters which begin with Th6 may cast some retrospective light on its significance. In doing so, they would at the same time establish the thematic link between the two books that we failed to anticipate.

The beginning of Th6 indicates that the treatment of the potentiality said with a view to motion (to be such) has been completed. The discussion is now to turn to the determination of actuality—both what it is and of what sort—that is, to the determinations that were to bring clarity also regarding the other sorts of potentiality, including presumably the one "most useful for what we wish now" (compare Th1 1045b34–1046a4). In repeating that promise or prediction here, Aristotle describes what is, in the manner already treated, capable (dunaton) as what is "by its nature" such as to move another or to be moved by another (1048a28–29; compare Prior Analytics A13 32b4–8 and 10–13); and he suggests that the consideration of it has been for the sake of what are capable in the different manners now to be made clear (1048a30). That its consideration may prove to have been useful for this end should not be altogether surprising, since (a consideration of) it was not said to be useless even with regard to the further end to which this end too is but a means (Th1 1045b36–1046a1 and pages 190–191 above). But Aristotle does surprise us at the conclusion of Th6 by claiming to have brought clarity as to actuality—both what it is and of what sort—without adding a word about the clarity as to potentiality and what are capable that was supposed to come "at the same time" (1048a27). On a closer look, we see however that even as to actuality he says only that clarity "will" come (the reading of mss.EJ at 1048b36) or that one should allow that it comes (as one might take the reading there of ms.Ab and Alexander) from "these things" (that have been said) and "things of this sort" (that have not). Moreover, looking again at the beginning of the chapter, we see that the clarity as to potentiality that was to come from the determination of actuality was promised there only to those who make (some presumably further, though unspecified) distinctions (1048a27–28; compare H3 1043b4–5 and page 183 above). This much then on the frame, as well as the setting, of the chapter's substantive discussion.

The discussion has three parts. In the first of these (1048a30–b9), Aristotle tells us that actuality (energeia) is the being present of the thing (tò pragma) in a way that is not the way we speak of (it) as (being present) in potentiality. Actuality, then, or the actuality spoken of here is the correlate of some potentiality, which it presupposes, even if the potentiality in question should be known or knowable, to the extent that it is, only from the given actuality (Th8 1049b12–17). "What we wish to say" (will be) clear in the particulars, by induction (from them). And in place of a definition—which he warns us is not to be sought (1048a36–37), apparently because of the diversity of what is said (to be) in actuality (1048b6–8)—he offers many examples, without however claiming that those offered are sufficient with a view to what he wishes to indicate. In the typical case (compare 1048b1–2), an actuality is paired with the potentiality that it presupposes. And, although the examples are apparently introduced to illustrate the indefinable diversity in question, they prove to fall into two classes (compare Th1 1046a3–4): some are related to the potentiality they presuppose as "motion to potentiality" (that is, to the potentiality treated in Th1–5), others as "ousia to some matter."

In the second part of the discussion (1048b9–17), Aristotle broaches the question of the way in which the limitless (tò apeiron) and the void (tò kenon) and everything of this sort (hosa toiauta) are said (to be) in potentiality and actuality. Only the limitless is discussed. It thus emerges that—while it admits of being simply true "at some time" (pote) to say, of what is then being seen for example, that it is being seen—the limitless is not such as ever to be a separate (distinct) actuality (compare Physics Th2 252b27–28). But since there can be a dividing (within things) and, so far as we know at least, the dividing (of them) need not leave off, one can speak of "this actuality" (the limitless) as being potentially (in each of them).

In the third part (1048b18–35), Aristotle draws a distinction within actions (of human beings) between those which have a limit, that is, a "for the sake of which" that lies outside of the action, and those which are themselves an end (telos). The latter are already complete (teleia) as actions—at any moment, so to speak. Otherwise, they would have to cease sometime (pote): on reaching the end extrinsic to the action itself. They may, of course, have to cease for other reasons. Only complete action is (truly) action; and such action is called by Aristotle "actuality." The other sort he calls "motion" (kinēsis). "Every motion is (as motion) incomplete" (1048b29): does this refer only to motions that fall within the (broadly understood) class of actions (praxeis)? However that may be, what holds for motion holds also for coming-to-be (1048b30–33).

At the end of Th3 (1047a30–b1), Aristotle had suggested that the name "actuality" (energeia)—he is thinking of the actuality which is conflated with completion (entelecheia)—has come especially from (its use for) the motions to its other usages. The reason given is that motion is what especially seems to be actuality: therefore motion is not attributed to non-beings, on the ground that to attribute motion to what are not, in actuality, beings is to attribute being, in actuality, to them. Th6 thus comes to sight as an attempt, or the beginning of an attempt, to see whether any of the things to which actuality is attributed in the other usages of the term is free from motion (or change) in the most fundamental respect. To mention just one point: insofar as the actuality that is ousia comes from some matter (1048a32–33, b3, b8–9), it is also, of course, of (some) matter. In other words, it is capable (dunaton), as are all things which come into being, whether by nature or by art, both of being and not being (Z7 1032a20–22).

Th7) In this chapter, Aristotle returns to the question regarding potentiality that he had called to our attention when he first listed it as one of the ways in which "tò on" is used (D7 1017b8–9).—More precisely, potentiality and actuality (entelecheia) were listed there not as signifying beings alongside of others, such as those signified by simple predication or by saying of something that it is true, but rather as signifying ways in which those others are present, as one might put it (D7 1017a35–b2; compare Th6 1048a30–32). In other words, the division potential/actual is comprehensive or exhaustive with respect to beings (compare Th3 1047b1–2).—It is the question of when something can be said to be potentially (present) and when "not yet." In repeating the question here, Aristotle replaces "not yet" with "not."

It follows from potentiality, as understood and defended in Th3, that uncertainty attends even what is in the most demanding sense potentially (present) as some thing or what is (the proximate) matter of the thing (1049a23)—uncertainty as to whether it will ever actually be present as or become that thing. This is the immediate bearing of Aristotle's retreat here from an extreme position with regard to potentiality that he had experimented with, in another context, at the end of Th5 (see page 196 above). But the uncertainty attending potentiality as such (compare Th8 1050b8–16) increases, of course, as one moves away from the ultimate matter, which is identical to the thing or to its form (page 188 above), and towards (its) matter in a more remote sense. This is the indeterminacy of matter (1049a36–b2), which increases as one approaches a first matter, whether there is some first matter or there is not (1049a24–27).

Th8) The chapter, which argues for the priority of actuality to potentiality, opens by indicating its reliance on an earlier determination (presumably that of D11 rather than of Categories 12) of how many ways "prior" is said. It thus prepares us to observe that it makes no explicit use of one of those ways, in particular, a way that figured prominently in each of its possible sources (D11 1019a1–14 and Categories 12 14a29–35; compare D11 1019a2–4 with Th8 1050a4–5 and following; whether 1050b16–17 and 18–19 constitute a tacit use of that way remains to be seen). The second observation that we need to make has been prepared by all of Theta hitherto but especially by what was said in Th1 and Th6 about the sort of potentiality "most useful for what we wish now." For actuality is asserted to be prior not to that potentiality, whatever it may be, but rather to the old Adam which has to do with motion: the enlargement of the old notion here, which serves to bring nature within the circle of what actuality is said to be prior to (compare Physics B1 192b34 as well as G1 200b32–33), leaves entirely intact the distinction that was drawn in those chapters between it and the potentiality "most useful . . ." (compare 1049b5–10 with Th1 1045b35–1046a4 and Th6 1048a25–30). It is, then, to "all such" (to every principle, whether external or internal, of motion or rest) that actuality is asserted to be prior (1049b10–12 and 1051a2–3)—in both logos and ousia. As for time, there is a way in which actuality is prior in time and a way in which it is not.

The priority of actuality in logos or knowledge (1049b17) is taken up first. It is the only case in which Aristotle says that a priority of actuality is clear (1049b13); and the priority may be said to consist in this: that we know of a capacity to do or to suffer—to see or to be seen, for example—by looking back to it from an actual doing or suffering in which it has issued (compare 1050a15–16, 17–19). One might object only that actuality is prior, in this respect, to every sort of potentiality, as Aristotle perhaps acknowledges by an unspecified reference to "the others" at 1049b16 (compare 1049b13–14, as well as the transition at 1050a16–17).

Next should come priority in ousia (compare 1049b11–12). But before turning to it, he takes up the admittedly ambiguous case of priority in time. The actualities offered as examples here all presuppose some potentiality that precedes them (1049b19–23).—And here, too, we should note, the potentialities considered are not merely those for motion or rest.—It is therefore only in form (eidos) that the actuality which is prior to each of the potentialities in question (1049b23–24) can be the same as the actuality which presupposes the potentiality (1049b17–19). Is it in every instance the same even in that way? In support of the suggestion that it is, Aristotle appeals to what he had said to this effect "in the speeches about ousia" (1049b24–29: compare Z7 1032a22–26 on natural coming-to-be): he thus reminds us, at the same time, of the exceptions that were alluded to there (Z7 1032a28–32). But even if we should disregard such exceptions, we would still have to face the question that they raise, unless we can assume that the order of coming-to-be, as we know it, is a permanent one (that is, that it extends without limit in both directions). And this may account for the addition which Aristotle makes to his discussion of the priority of actuality in time when, later on in the chapter, he repeats in condensed form its chief result (1050b4–6; compare 1049b24–27 and see the note of Ross to 1050b4).

The repetition interrupts the treatment of the priority which is considered at greatest length, priority in ousia, dividing it more or less neatly into two parts. In the first of these (1050a4–b4), which seems to constitute a single argument (1050b3), actuality is suggested to be prior in form and ousia (1050a5) ultimately because it is what ousia and form are (1050b2–3; see page 196 above).—

Here again the potentiality to which actuality is argued to be prior is not merely that for motion or rest: we have already referred to the transition at 1050a16–17.—Its priority in this respect is therefore compatible with and even presupposes its posteriority in coming-to-be: that is, in time (1050a4–5, 7–9, 15–16). And this is the more immediate context of the addition Aristotle makes in referring to "the actuality of what is always moving (causing motion) first," when he repeats here the chief result of the discussion of priority in time. With or by virtue of the addition, the repetition serves to introduce or to open the second part of the treatment of priority in ousia.

In this part (1050b6–34), he treats of the actuality or actualities which are in a more authoritative manner prior in ousia, for they are prior as the permanent (beings) are prior to the perishable (ones). The latter too, then, are actualities—indeed, the very actualities whose priority in ousia was argued for in the first part—but not permanently so. Their perishability is due to their being also potentialities (1050b7–8). They are potentially that which will come to be on and through their dissolution (D11 1019a6–11 in the latter part of the chapter to which Aristotle had referred at the beginning of this one). Every potentiality is, of course, also an actuality of some sort (compare On Generation and Corruption A5 322a4–6); but it is at the same time the potentiality for the negation of the actuality that it is (1050b8–9; compare Z15 1039b27–31 with Z11 1037a10–13). The only question is whether there is, as Aristotle contends, an actuality that is permanent in the only way in which this would seem to be possible: as free from potentiality or matter, at least in the most fundamental respect (1050b16–22). And since such actualities could seem to be the only warranty for the permanence of this whole order of things (compare On Generation and Corruption B11 337b12–13 and 338a14–b5), this is at the same time the question of the knowability of the limits to the potentiality that it also is.

The brief remarks on the subject that are offered by Aristotle here present a number of puzzling features, which we can do no more than to note. The necessary beings are distinguished in them from the imperishables, although they are said, like the imperishables, to be free from potentiality in the most fundamental respect (1050b16–17 and 18–19). It appears to be only the necessary beings on which the existence of all others is said to depend. The questions of whether there is some permanent motion and of whether there is some thing permanently moving (in motion) are pointed to, as questions (1050b20–22). They may be said to be answered by the immediately following affirmation of the permanence of the motion of sun, stars, and the whole heaven (1050b22–24). But no ground is offered for supposing that the condition for such permanence (stated at 1050b20–22 and reiterated at 1050b24–28) is fulfilled in their case (compare Z2 1028b10–13). The elements, such as earth and fire, which are distinguished from the imperishables as undergoing change (transformation), are nevertheless said to imitate the latter in the permanence of the motion that is in them (and belongs to them by nature or) of themselves (1050b28–30). Aristotle does not go so far as to claim that, in the absence of the heavenly motion, their motion would or even could retain the regularity that we observe it to have (On Generation and Corruption B11 338a14–b8). Are these potentialities (Z16 1040b5–10) truly to be distinguished then from the others, all of which are potentialities for contradictories (1050b30–32)? Do they constitute an exception to the rule (1050b8–9)?

At the end of the chapter, Aristotle indicates that what he attempts with the actuality or actualities without potentiality is meant to be a superior version of what Plato attempted with the ideas. (Compare page 140 above.)

Th9) This short chapter opens with an argument purporting to show that an actuality, if good, is better and more honorable than the worthy (spoudaia) potentiality that it presupposes. Such an argument could be regarded as a continuation of the treatment of the priority of actuality to potentiality of Th8 (see Categories 12 14b3–8); but Aristotle gives no indication of wishing this argument's function to be understood in that way. In judging of its function, we should note the facts: (1) that he makes no use in it of considerations mentioned in Th8 (1050a4–14 and 23–29) that would have settled the question definitively; (2) that he blurs in it a distinction (between contraries and contradictories) which he had been careful to observe in Theta hitherto (see the note of Ross at 1051a5); and, above all, (3) that he has himself supplied in advance an appropriate response to it (H5 1044b29–34). The chapter in which he did so asserted that the forms (ta eidē), which were also said there to lack matter, are and are not, without a coming-to-be and a perishing. What follows, that is, from their alleged lack of matter (potentiality), or what such a lack means, is that they are not subject to coming-to-be and change (transformation) into one another, but are and are not, without (such) change. (H5 1044b21–29; compare G5 1010b19–26) The chapter now before us is the last of those in Theta which are devoted to the precise determination of potentiality and actuality.

The two parts of which it is composed appear to have little to do with one another. In the first of them (the argument that we have just been speaking of), Aristotle draws a noteworthy conclusion from the fact that, with evils, the actuality is worse than the potentiality: it is clear, then, that evil is not, besides or beyond the things, for evil is posterior in nature to potentiality (1051a15–19). This suggests that potentiality, or some potentiality, is besides or beyond the things (ta pragmata). It is not immediately clear what this could mean.

In the second part, he speaks of the way in which certain propositions—that the sum of the angles of a triangle is two right angles, that the angle in a semi-circle is a right angle universally—are discovered (to be true). The lines which must for this purpose be drawn for each of them, to make manifest why it is so, are said to be present, potentially, in the figure that presents or illustrates the proposition (1051a21–24). Here, then, is a potentiality that is not beyond what, with some license, may be called "the thing." The reason supplied in the context (1051a30–31) is that the actuality from which the potentiality in question is derived is (an act of) thought (noēsis). Now the things, too, of which our world is composed are (acts of) thought—namely, as Aristotle has with great care spelled out, insofar as they are things. But they are only in part (such acts of) thought. And therefore the potentiality that belongs to them as things—which is to say, insofar as they are thought—and that, when it is internal to them, we call their nature, is not the whole of the potentiality that they presuppose and, in a way, also are. To this extent, then, there is a potentiality "beyond the things" (though not, of course, beyond actuality tout court: see page 202 above).

Th10) The treatment of being as truth in E4 had promised a further consideration of it (1027b28–29), which it is the evident purpose of this chapter to supply. The new treatment differs from the earlier one, according to which being as truth is a different being from those which are beings authoritatively, in the manner that we have already mentioned (compare 1051b1–2 with 1027b31 and see pages 190, 125–126 and 31 above). And this has tempted editors to tamper with the text of this chapter in such a way as to remove the inconsistency. It would have been more cautious and more respectful of the character of the Metaphysics, as a work from which one can be expected to learn something of importance on virtually every page, to have considered whether what has become clear in the intervening passages, in Zeta and Eta and in the first nine chapters of Theta, has not necessitated the change of perspective.

The difficulty with which the chapter confronts us is brought to our attention in the very first sentence. It is there that being as truth or (the) true is called that which is being most authoritatively (1051b1–2), while at the same time the subordination of truth to the things—which, insofar as it is about them, supply its measure—is once again, as in E4, acknowledged (1051b2–5; see also b6–9). That is, Aristotle apparently reaffirms the consideration that led to the assertion that being as truth is a different being from those which are beings authoritatively, even as he takes back the assertion itself. And he thus poses the question in which the sentence culminates: "when is (it) or is (it) not, (the being) spoken of as 'the true'. . . ? For," as he adds, "(it is) this (that) one must investigate: what we mean (by it)." (1051b5–6)

On a somewhat closer look, we see that the reaffirmation is lacking in the emphasis which the original had placed on the distinction between what is present in (the) thinking that joins and separates predications (dianoia) and what in the things (1027b29–33 and b25–27). The distinction may be said to be implied by what is said in the first part of the chapter (see again 1051b2–5 and 6–9 as well as b9–17) and to be accepted here. But it is no longer presented in just those terms. Their use for that purpose, insofar as it might have given the impression that a clear line can be drawn between thought (noēsis or noein) and thing, would have been ruled out by what has been brought to light in Zeta and Eta about ousia.

The second part of the chapter turns to "the non-composites" (1051b17) or what are called in E4 "the simples" (1027b27). What these "simples" or "non-composites" or "not composite ousiai" (1051b27) are is not explained, nor is any example of them given. But they are associated in both places with the "what it is" (1027b27–28; 1051b25–27), that is, with the characters of things or of classes of things (compare 1051b30–31). What holds for the characters of things, with regard to the questions at issue, is said to hold also for the simples or non-composites. So we will disregard the latter, except in name, as our ignorance of them compels us to do, and direct our attention to the former—which is all the more appropriate, since (as we have seen) there is a respect in which the characters are, each of them, simple or one (pages 176 and 185–186 above).

The questions at issue are those of the being or non-being and the true and the false: what these are for "the non-composites" (1051b17–18). These are still distinct questions then; and that of truth and falsehood is therefore subordinated to that of being or non-being (1051b18–22). A reformulation, however, subordinates (the question of) being, in their case, to (that of) truth (1051b22–23). As to the true and the false, then, for "the simples" and the characters (ta ti esti), the earlier chapter had said (1027b27–28) that they are not to be found even in (the) thinking (that combines and separates predications). And Aristotle says now, with regard to the true or false in their case, that to touch them and to say (name) them is true or truth (1051b23–25). There is also ignorance here, which is not to touch them, but no being deceived (that is, falsehood: 1052a1–2); for this is possible about character (tò ti esti) only incidentally (1051b25–28): for example, one might be deceived as to whether there are things of the character in question or there are not (1051b32–33; compare 1052a8–9, in the discussion of "the motionless"). By the "touching" of the characters, Aristotle means the grasping of them in thought (noein: 1051b32 and 1052a1; compare 1027b23–25). And all of them—"the not composite ousiai" and the characters—are in actuality, without potentiality (1051b26–28 and 30–31). This means that they neither come into being nor perish (1051b28–30). It does not mean that they always are (page 204 above). When are they, then, and when not? Is it not as follows: that when they are thought—that is, when they are true or truth (compare 1051b5–6)—they are; and when they are not thought, they are not? But they are always thought, for ignorance here is not like blindness, as if someone lacked that which thinks (tò noētikon) altogether (1052a2–4). The world that we live in and reflect upon is the already articulated world. But precisely if the things as things are already thought (page 204 above), it is in the thinking of them as that thought (compare pages 31 and 103 above) that they will become most fully what they in some sense already are. And thus being as truth will be, not different from what are authoritatively beings (the things with their predicates), but what those beings themselves are, in their most authoritative form.

But the last chapter of Theta has been prepared not only by the discussion of ousia (in Zeta and Eta) but by the first nine chapters of Theta itself (pages 189–190 above). In arguing as he has for the authority of truth as being, Aristotle corrected but also presupposed the common view that he had given expression to in E4, according to which this place belongs to the things with their predicates: it is, to repeat, as those things, rather than as distinct from them, that truth is most authoritatively being. Before making the argument, he reminded us therefore of <u>their</u> subjection in particular to the division potential/actual (compare1051a34–b1 with

D7 1017a35–b2 and context, and see page 199 above). For, as we have seen (page 204 above), there is a potentiality "beyond the things"—and therewith beyond the truth that they are. Their truth may well remain, then, the measure even for that potentiality (page 195 above). But Aristotle would not have been the man that he was, if he had not also wondered about the adequacy of the measure.

I1) In the course of my discussion hitherto I remarked, too glibly as it turns out, "that logos is at bottom a number" (page 171); and I paid insufficient attention to Aristotle's indication that forms are only "somehow" numbers (page 185). The latter failure had as immediate consequence that I assimilated, to the way in which a synthesis of differentiae (pages 181 and 183) is distinct from its parts, the way in which a definite number of monads is related to its (page 186; compare page 112, but see also page 169). It may indeed be the case for both a number and a synthesis that, though there is no ingredient of either besides its parts (pages 175–176), both are as wholes something besides or distinct from them (H6 1045a8–10). Yet they may be distinct in different ways or to differing extents.

These, then, are difficulties of my discussion that cannot be traced to an attempt to reproduce in its complexity the progress of the argument of the work before us. This is not to deny of course that the argument, as it continues, may help to remove the confusion which underlies them. For example, Aristotle returns now, in Iota, to the account that he had given in D6 of "one" and therewith of number (I1 1052a15–19; compare D6 1015b16–17). Perhaps he was induced to do so, in part, by an awareness of the greater and lesser obscurities of the earlier passage (page 97). However that may be, his taking up its questions (again) in Iota serves to provide something of an interlude between the treatment of the grave theme addressed in Theta—indeed in the whole portion of the text, beginning with Epsilon, which is brought to a conclusion by Theta—and what is, according to Thomas (pages 84–85), the beginning of the ascent to the high theme of Lambda. (Compare

I1 1052b9–11 and 1053a35–b3 with 1052a27–28 and 1053a10–12.)

Aristotle says in the course of the sixth chapter of Iota that each number is many (in part) because it is one (the reading of mss. EJ at 1056b23). Every "many" is then, as we can add, also one: without being one, it could not be many. And he says also that not everything which is one is a number (1057a6–7). This is consistent with the fact that multitude is only the genus, or something like the genus, of number (1057a2–3). Number, each number, is a multitude which is measurable "by one" (1057a3–4; compare 1056b23–24)—clearly by a different "one" than the one that it is.

The question what it is to be one and which is its logos is raised in the first chapter of the book (1052b3). And it is also answered here, in a way that appears to be similar to the way in which the earlier chapter (D6) had answered it (without explicitly raising the question). There it was said that to be one is to be (the) principle for some number (1016b17–18); as I1 has it, "the one" is (the) principle of number as number (1052b23–24). The primary question of both chapters, however, is in how many manners "one" or "the one" is said or, as it is also put in I1, which repeats the portion of D6 that is devoted to non-accidental ones, what sorts (of objects) are said (to be) one. And I1 insists on distinguishing this question from that of what it is to be one (1052b1–3). We are all the more surprised, therefore, to find that the distinction is blurred in the immediate sequel (1052b3–7 and 15–24): the various manners in which the term is said here to be used are said also to represent another understanding or other understandings of what it is to be one. But this ambiguity (of which we have a glimpse also in I6) prepares us perhaps to return briefly to the earlier chapter. The articulations of D6, which are not less visible than those of its repetition, may help us in our attempt to come to grips with I1.

First to be mentioned in D6, among what are said of themselves or with respect to themselves to be one, are continuous magnitudes (1015b36–1016a1; compare 1016a7–9). What is said to be continuous, in turn, is that whose motion is of itself one and cannot be other than one (1016a5–6). There is no circularity, since "one" as applied to motion can be explained or replaced by "indivisible" with respect to time (1016a6). We thus have a clearly defined class, which can be further refined or divided as Aristotle indicates, and to whose members the term "one" or indeed, insofar as the term is explained by the class rather than vice versa (compare page 173 above), any other name can be applied.

There is, in addition, another manner of using the term, in accord with which that (1016a20, 21) or those (1016a18–22) are said to be one whose substratum is indistinguishable in form. And this is the case if the form is indivisible so far as sense perception can determine—if, in other words, sense perception is unable to divide the substratum, or to divide substratum from substratum, by discerning that they are qualitatively different. It may, of course, be able to divide them by discerning that they are (discrete) continuous magnitudes. But Aristotle does his best to divert our attention from this possibility by using as examples only fluids (1016a20–24): a fluid, as he will suggest in I6, may be "much" without being also "many" (1056b11–13 and 16). And this helps us to see that not only the second but also the first (non-accidental) usage of the term that he treats in D6 points back to an awareness that may have been, somehow, of a one that is neither itself also many nor even a one of many. There would not have been then for such an awareness, taken by itself, a class of such ones—nor, lacking that, the application of a significant name to any member of the class.

But they, too, are said to be one whose genus is one, though it differs (that is, the individuals or species belonging to the genus differ) by virtue of opposing differentiae (1016a24–25). They, too, are all said to be one, because the genus, the substratum to the differentiae, is one (1016a25–26)—in a manner approaching that in which the matter, the substratum spoken of in the section preceding this section, is one (1016a27–28). The manner in which the genus is one only approaches that in which the matter was said to be one: there is no question here of an inability of sense perception to discern differences. What are said to be "some" one are, for example, horse, man, dog, because they are all animals (1016a27). They owe their being animals, therefore, to a putting together, a combining, or alternatively—as in the case of isosceles and equilateral triangles, which are one figure (different from others) because they are both triangles (1016a28–32)—to the separating or dividing that accompanies any combining. Now, in this dividing and combining, there is necessarily awareness of multiplicity—if not yet, not necessarily, of multiplicity as multiplicity. And this would seem to be a sufficient basis for speech—first in the most elementary form of naming the members of a class as members of the class—though not for number. Horse, man, and dog are one because they are animals; the isosceles and the equilateral, because they are triangles.

The series of sections, each treating a distinct usage of the term, or what is presented as a usage of it, can thus be brought to a conclusion by what Aristotle says next: that, in addition, those are said to be one whose logos, which states "the what it was to be," cannot be divided from another that makes clear what it was to be the thing in question (1016a32–34). In this way, even what has grown and is (now) declining is (the) one (that it was), because the logos is one, just as in the case of plane figures (triangles, for example) the logos of the form (is one) (1016a35–b1). Another passage, which could claim inclusion in the series—its counterpart is in fact included in I1, when the series is repeated—is to be found in D6 only somewhat later on, as if added as an afterthought (1016b11–17; contrast 1016b8–11 as well as 1017a3–6). Its inclusion, in what would appear to be its proper place (I1 1052a22–28 and context; but compare 1052b15–18), could have made it more difficult than it already is to discern the progress in awareness that is traced by the series as presented in D6.

This can be seen from what happens here in I1, where the passage that is its counterpart forms the second section of the series, after that which treats of what is one as continuous magnitude. The placement makes sense, given the kinship—stressed here (1052a22–25, 29, 34–35) and pointed to already in D6 (1016b11–16)—between the usages treated in the two sections: between what is one as a continuous magnitude and what is still more one as such a magnitude that is also, by virtue of having some shape and form, a whole. But it becomes difficult then to see how this second usage differs from that treated here either as fourth (1052a31) or third (1052a31–33, 35–36 and b1).—In order to bring out the problem that he is pointing to, Aristotle had to treat the third and fourth as two usages: he had treated them in D6 as one (compare 1052a29–33 with 1016a32–b1, but see also 1016a24–32).—For will not that whose logos is one and which is perceived as indivisible not only in form but also in number be, by virtue of its possessing that form, a whole?

Aristotle insists, however, that there are four usages treated in I1 (1052a15–19: there is no comparable assertion in D6), which are the four already referred to. And this means that he insists that the second usage does differ from what we will call the third. What then does he take the difference to be? He calls the object of the third usage—and not that of the second—"the particular" (1052a34–36). There is, indeed, in the case of both of them awareness of a one as possessor of some form; and perception of form is necessarily, in the first place, perception of a particular that has the form (M10 1087a15–21; Posterior Analytics B19 100a16–b1). But this first perception is not yet perception of the particular as particular. For that, for the completed perception (pages 159–160 above), logos is required: the recognition of what is one only in form or of the class. That is to say, the particular is seen, as particular, by reference to the class to which it belongs. And it may be for this reason that, when he first mentions what is indivisible in number—that is, as particular—Aristotle puts the usage pertaining to it fourth rather than third, after and not before what is indivisible only in form. It may also be why he all but explicitly identifies, in this context, the universal as what is responsible for (each of) the ousiai being one (1052a34–36 together with a 32–34; compare D26 1023b29–32).

I1 is not then, after all, indifferent to the progress in awareness of what is "one" to which our attention was drawn in D6. And in stressing, as the earlier chapter had done, the complexity of the later stages of that awareness, it too helps to make us mindful of the significance of the earlier stages that those later stages presuppose. Now, it is at this point that Aristotle turns to the question which it is the chief task of I1 to address: what is it to be one and which is its logos? But by turning to it after his survey of the progress in our awareness has been concluded (it is answered in a similar context in D6), he indicates that the question has not yet been answered by that survey. In other words, the survey has not been carried forward to the point where there is awareness of the one or therefore of number, as number. What, then, is responsible for that awareness or in what does it consist?

According to the sketch of an answer given in D6 (1016b17–24), to be one is to be (the) principle for some number (of things). It is a principle, because it is the first measure of a genus; and it is the first measure, because it is the first by which we know or become familiar with the genus. This principle is "the one"—for that genus: "the one" is not the same in all the genera. There is no explicit restriction here to genera of quantities (1016b23–24) or to genera of things considered as quantities (see the words added at 1016b24 by mss.EJ). And for this reason, if not also others, it remains somewhat unclear what is meant in this context by calling the principle of each genus a one and the genus itself a number (page 98 above). In other words, in what sense or to what extent is the genus in fact a number?

The passage in I1 corresponding to that of D6 is prefaced by the statement already referred to, which distinguishes the question addressed in the two passages from the question that is raised and addressed first in each of the chapters. As the preface itself indicates however, by blurring the very distinction that it has insisted upon, the questions are not simply distinct from one another or, if distinct, they are not entirely separable. The reason is twofold. On the one hand, what is one in the most precise sense—so far as it is not merely the product of an abstracting or positing (1052b33–1053a2)—is so because something accrues to what is already one in some looser or more elementary but nonetheless real sense.—In this same way fire (or perhaps the limitless or something else of this sort) is an element, not or rather not simply by virtue of being fire, but also by virtue of what accrues to it: that something is from it, something of which it remains the first constituent (1052b7–15).—On the other hand, what is one in that looser but still indispensable sense (1052b1–7) will not be grasped fully, as the one that it in some way already is, before it is seen as or in the light of what is one in the most precise sense or, as one can perhaps also say, before the one, as one, is named (1052b5–7 and 1053b4–6 together with 1052b15–20 and 23–27). And the passage which has been thus prefaced and to which we now turn takes as its task to explicate the sense of "one" that comes closest to what is implied by the name.

The naming of a one requires, what is required in the case of any other recipient of a significant name, that it be put into the class to which it belongs—not to say that the naming consists in that placement. To which class or group, then, does a one, as one, belong? In attempting to answer this question, our passage refers to the role of the one as the first measure of each genus, as its predecessor in D6 had done (1052b18; 1016b19–20). Unlike its predecessor, however, it speaks of the role of the one as the measure of quantity as being decisive ("most authoritative") in this respect: "from thence (the name) has come to the others" (1052b19–20). But further, "quantity, as quantity, is known (that is, measured [1053a7–8]) by (a) one or (a) number," but every number by a one (1050b20–22): so that that by which quantities are first known is "one itself" and "the one" is the principle of a number, as a number (1052b22–24). "And from thence" the measure of each is said to be one, also in the case of the other quantities (1052b24–27).

A one, as one, is then always the measure of some number. In the words of I6, it is only as number that multitude is opposed to ("lies over against") the one (1056b19–20; compare 1057a14–17). And, as we have already heard by looking ahead to that chapter, a number is a multitude that can be measured by a one (1056b23–24, 1057a2–4)—or, still better, a multitude that has been so measured (1056b21–22; N1 1088a4–6). Now, as this implies, a number is always some (definite) number, consisting of just the ones of which it is composed. Is then the group or class to which a one belongs, as named or nameable, (a) number?

I1 makes clear that it is not. Unlike magnitudes of every sort, a number is not measured by what is akin to it (1053a24–30); but to be named is to be placed among kindred things or objects, in a class that bears the name that is applied also to each of them. A number, then, is a group in a different manner than a class is a group.—It has more in common with the synthesis of parts that may constitute each of the members of a class (H3 1043b34–1044a2); but, as we have to some extent already seen, Aristotle balks at understanding number as a synthesis of parts (Z13 1039a11–14; compare D14 1020b6–8 as well as N5 1092a23–24 and 26–28).—And if a number is not a class, it cannot be the class of the ones which constitute it. But this is not to deny that it is by virtue of a relation to number that a one is a member of the class to which, as a one, it does belong. For, as we have also heard from I6, number and the one are complementary terms. They are opposed to each other as what are "towards something" (pros ti) in such a way as to be, each of them in this case, what it is, by virtue of the fact that something else, the other, is spoken of only in relation to ("towards") it (1056b32–1057a1, a3–6 and 12–17).

I2) Just as I1 began by referring to a chapter in Delta, whose problem it took up again, I2 begins by posing a question that "we went over in the perplexities," that is, in Beta. But does the question of Beta retain, in the light cast by the discussion in D6 which has now been brought to its completion in I1, the evidence that it seemed there to possess (B1 996a4–9, B4 1001a4–8)? We arrive at the same difficulty if we say by way of transition to I2 what Aristotle does say, that with respect to the ousia and the nature (from which the other beings are presumed to come to be—1053b29–30, retaining "ei" with mss.AbE at b29) one must seek the answer to the question of Beta. For, as that question is put here, it asks whether the one is by itself some ousia (namely, <u>that</u> ousia—see M6 1080b6–7), as the Pythagoreans and Plato say, or rather some nature underlies it, as is more intelligibly asserted by those (concerned) about nature, one of whom says that the one is love (compare B4 1001a12–15), another that it is air (compare B4 1001a15–17), another that it is the limitless (consider B4 1001a15 together with I1 1052b9–11). But is there in this matter only the alternative which has been mentioned? Is it necessary to accept the assumption shared by the two rival doctrines (or species of doctrines) that ultimate responsibility for things lies with a one? (Compare L7 1072b13–14.) Has not the just completed account of the meaning of "one" taken away at least some of the allure of that assumption?—In response, one must say that Aristotle no longer insists here on a precise understanding of (what is) one (compare L7 1072a32–34), any more than he insists in this context on a precise understanding of being, and that he lets the alternative stand, without further justification than what may be provided by that very allure.

As for being (on), in the precise understanding of it the beings (onta) are taken to be the attributes of things—as predicated of them in the various categories or forms of predication—and it is tacitly granted that the things (ousiai) themselves are not meaningfully called beings (pages 64–65, 100–101, and 108–109 above). Here, on the other hand, it is the ousiai that are regarded as the beings (compare 1053b32 and 35, as well as 1054a1–2 and 3, with 1054a5–9), a step that is perhaps prepared by a prior assimilation of "ousia" and "on" (1053b17–18 and 23–24; consider also b18–21, taking "ousian" or "ousia" in b18 as subject, as does Bonitz according to Ross _ad_ _loc_.). Of course, it is unreasonable to insist everywhere and always upon precision; and the demands of precise speech with respect to being have been relaxed before in the work: for example, in order to bring out more simply or effectively the place of thought in the composition of things or, what amounts to the same point, the authoritative character of being as truth (pages 205–207 above). But, as the example indicates, one must consider in each case whether there is a particular reason for the relaxation of those demands, especially if Aristotle supplies at the same time a reminder of the stricter usage that he is departing from (1054a16–18, which recalls G2, both 1003b26–30 and generally).

The positive meaning of his option for the anti-Pythagorean, anti-Platonic answer to the question that he has posed anew here must therefore be understood against this background. He objects neither to the role ascribed to a one (1053b29–34) nor, in the decisive case, that of the ousiai, to understanding that one as a being. (Compare pages 126–128 above.) He insists only that the one ousia is some ousia, an ousia of some definite character, and only as such a one and a being (1053b24–28, b34–1054a1, 1054a4–11). And from this follows, understandably, his injunction to seek that ousia (1054a11–13; compare Thomas, Commentary on Aristotle's Metaphysics, para. 1973).

I3–I10) "The one itself" (I2 1054a12–13) is then some ousia, and a one and a being only as such. And that one ousia, an ousia of some definite character, is what we must seek. Yet, in the remainder of Iota at least, Aristotle refrains from seeking it. He treats instead of the opposition of what he calls here "the one" (without further determination of it) and "the many" (I3 1054a20–21). Nevertheless, some continuity is maintained in this way with the thesis or conclusion of I2.

The one and the many are said to be contraries, even the first of the contraries or their genera, those to which the other contraries are led up or back (I4 1055b26–29; compare G2 1004b27–1005a5). And coming-to-be is said to be from the contraries (I4 1055a8, b11–12 and 16–17; I7 1057a18–19, b2–4 and 29–34). Moreover, it is suggested of the first contraries, in particular, that one of them is (merely) the privation of the other (I4 1055b26–29; compare b11–15, as well as I2 1053b28–34). And thus paramount responsibility for coming-to-be is in effect ascribed to the (undefined) one in question here. This, then, is the first step.

The fuller argument of this last portion of Iota, which we will attempt to reproduce in outline, presents itself—with a partial exception that will be noted below—in four pairs of chapters. (See page 15 above.)

* * * *

The assertion that the one and the many are contraries occurs near the beginning of I3. (The ground of the assertion is not entirely clear, regardless of whether one accepts the reading of mss.EJ at 1054a24 or not.) It is then said that to the one belong, "as we delineated in the division of contraries" (compare G2 1003b33–1004a2, where the species of being are assimilated to those of the one), the same and like and equal, while to the many belong the other (heteron) and unlike and unequal. And the enumeration that follows of the usages of some of these terms leads, at the end of the chapter, to a discussion of difference (diaphora). Difference is other (allo) than otherness (heterotēs): everything—everything that is—is the same as or other than everything; but what are different are also the same in some respect; and the respect in which they are the same is also that in which they differ (1054b23–27; compare I8 1057b35–1058a8). This proves to mean that they belong to the same genus at least (1054b30–31; compare I4 1055a26–27): if they did not, they would lack a common matter and there would be no coming-to-be of one of them from the other or vice versa (1054b27–29; compare I4 1055a6–7). And it thus prepares the conclusion that contraries are (among the) different and that contrariety is "some" difference, a difference of some sort (1054b31–32; compare b32–35, retaining "and the same" in b34 and putting a full stop after "onta" in b35).

I4 therefore undertakes (in its first half) to establish which difference that difference is. It is the greatest difference that Aristotle calls contrariety (1055a3–6).—Difference in genus is ruled out of consideration on the ground already mentioned: that (things) differing in genus have no path from one to the other or vice versa; whereas for (things) differing in species the comings-to-be are from the contraries as extremes (1055a6–10; compare a25–27 and 30, as well as I3 1054b27–31).—But the greatest difference is also the perfect difference (1055a10–17). And, if these things are so, it is manifest that there does not admit of more than one contrary to a contrary (1055a19–23).

The second half of I4 turns then rather abruptly to privation. (The judgment of how abruptly will depend on the reading to be adopted in I3 1054a24.) It identifies contrariety, or the "first" contrariety, with perfect privation (1055a33–35 and b13–16, as well as b18 and 26–27). There is no mention of difference (diaphora) in this part of the chapter. If there are, including contrariety itself, four sorts of opposition (1055a38–b1; compare D10 1018a20–25), there are three with which contrariety could conceivably be linked. Of these, contradiction is explicitly ruled out, on the ground that there is no "in-between" between contradictories, whereas there admits of being an "in-between" between contraries (1055b1–3; compare I5 1056a12–15). The same ground speaks for the link of contrariety with privation: although privation is some (sort of) contradiction, there is an "in-between" in the case of some (sort of) privation (1055b3–11). And a perhaps related ground (see I7 1057a18–b4) would speak (more) clearly for the identification of contrariety with some privation: if the comings-to-be for matter are from the contraries, but what come to be do so from the form and the possession of the form or from some privation of the form and the shape (1055b11–17; compare 1055a33). And so the conclusion is drawn that it is manifest that one of the contraries is always called by way of privation what it is called (1055b26–27; compare b18). "But it suffices even if (this should be manifest only with regard to) the first and the genera of the contraries, for example, the one and the many; for the others are led up (or back) to these" (1055b27–29). The text had been silent for some time on the one and the many. This addition reminds of them and of what has already been claimed in their regard. And in thus taking us back to the beginning of I3, it brings the first section of the argument to a close.

* * * *

I5 makes use of the conclusion of the first half of I4 to introduce a perplexity. Since there is only one contrary to a contrary, someone might be perplexed as to how the one and the many are opposed. The perplexity clearly bears directly on what had appeared to be the argument of this last portion of Iota (page 217 above). But Aristotle takes it up only in I6—not in I5, where he turns instead to the question, prompted by the same conclusion, of how the equal is opposed to the great and the small. Yet, as he has assigned the equal to the one, in accord with "the division of the contraries" (I3 1054a29–31), his treatment of this latter question is unlikely to be without interest for someone perplexed about the one and the many (compare I6 beginning).

Two grounds are advanced for the result of the treatment, which is that the equal is not a contrary to those it is opposed to. The first is the same that has been mentioned. The equal is opposed to the greater and the lesser, or to the unequal, which signifies at the same time both of them; but it is impossible that one is a contrary to two (1056a3–11; compare a15–20). (This first ground would not prevent the equal from continuing to be understood as derivative from the one: compare 1056a1–3.) The second ground is drawn from the discussion in the second half of I4. The equal appears (to be) an "in-between" between great and small; but contrariety neither appears (to be) an "in-between" of anything nor, by its definition, is this possible for it; rather it has always itself some "in-between," that is, something between the contraries (1056a12–15; contrast I4 1055b1–2 as well as I7 1057a18–19).

A remark at the end of the chapter indicates that opposites between which there is some "in-between" or there is naturally some interval, or of which there is a difference (diaphora), are in the same genus, so that their substratum is one.

The perplexity as to whether the one and the many are opposed as contraries—not to say, as the first and the genera of the contraries—is handled in I6 somewhat more delicately than the admittedly similar perplexity about the equal was handled in I5. Aristotle opens the discussion by remarking that, if the many are simply opposed to the one, several impossibilities result (1056b4–5). In the sequel, he spells out the difficulties, which prove to be more apparent than real; and, in the course of removing them, he introduces that discussion of the one and number to which we had recourse in attempting to understand I1. As he admits in this context, it is only as number that the many are opposed to the one (1056b19–20). Opposed in what way? The answer is supplied piecemeal, in statements that are separated from one another by other remarks. According to the first (1056b32–1057a1), the one and the many are opposed as what are "towards something" (pros ti), or rather as some of these are. Aristotle claims to have distinguished elsewhere, presumably in D15, between the "towards something" which are opposed as contraries and those which are opposed as knowledge is towards the knowable. (As Ross observes here, there is no mention of contraries among the "towards something" discussed in D15.) According to the second statement (1057a3–6), the one and number are somehow opposed, not as contrary (is opposed to contrary) but "as has been said" as some of the "towards something" are. But have not some of the latter been said to be opposed as contraries (1056b35–36; compare I7 1057a37)? The doubt is removed in the third statement (1057a12–17), which specifies the way in which multitude, as number, is as a "towards something" (opposed) to the one: (it is opposed) as knowledge is to the knowable. It is true that this last statement of I6 claims also to find some contrariety in the relation of multitude to the one—in the way that it had allegedly been found at the beginning of I3, as the divisible to what is indivisible. But would such a pair be any more capable of possessing an "in-between" or of sharing the same genus than are, according to I7 (1057a37–b1), what are "towards something" in the manner of knowledge and the knowable?

What is at stake in the perplexity concerning the one and the many as contraries, as I7 will again make clear, is their alleged role in coming-to-be; but that, in turn, bears on the question of the intelligibility of coming-to-be, if not of all change, its reducibility to intelligible principles (compare I4 1055b27–29). And from this we can perhaps understand why, in both I1 and I6, which share the task of disclosing the truth about "one," the theme of knowledge as the measure of things (I1 1053a31–32) is broached—and why both chapters point to the limits of that measure. (On I6 1057a9–12, in particular, see pages 205 and 208 above.)

* * * *

"Since there admits of being some in-between between contraries and, between some (of them), there is (an in-between), it is necessary that the in-betweens be from the contraries" (1057a18–19). As we see from the beginning of I7, this chapter continues to ascribe responsibility for what are between them, that is, for what are in the same genus as they are (1057a19–30 and b2–4), to the contraries. This is consistent with what we have heard in I4 (1055a6–10): that the comings-to-be for what differ in species (eidos), that is for what share the same genus, are from the contraries as extremes (within the genus: see I4 1055a23–30 as well as I7 1057b22–30). But I7 no longer speaks of the one and the many in this (or any other) connection. (Compare I4 1055b27–29 with I7 1057b16 and context as well as b32.) It no longer speaks of the one and the many, unless one is to take its observation about what are "towards something" in the manner of knowledge and the knowable (which do not, since they are not in the same genus, have an "in-between") to be a reference to them (1057a37–b1).

Having reached this point, moreover, or rather while reaching it, I7 begins to question what it can mean to be from the contraries. And this questioning, which is corrected in part but also carried forward in I8 (and completed, perhaps, only in I9) goes so far as to cast doubt on the very notion of a coming-to-be from contraries. The questioning appears to be provoked by the observation that, if the "in-betweens" are in the same genus as the contraries, they necessarily are composed (sunkeisthai) from those contraries (1057b2–4; compare b22–30). For is not each of the contraries itself composed of the genus and the relevant differentia (diaphora), neither of which can be said to be in the same genus as the contrary (1057b4–11 and 20, I8 1058a21–22)? And must not the same be true of the "in-betweens" (1057b12–22)? Moreover, the differentiae of which the contraries within the genus, the contrary species (1057b6–7), are composed may themselves be said to be contraries (1057b5–11). From which contraries then—these prior contraries (1057b20–22 and 31–32) or those within the genus (1057b2–4 and 22–30)—are the "in-betweens" composed? And, above all, what sort of composition is at issue here?

It is true that, in raising these altogether legitimate questions, I7 argues on the basis of an erroneous premise: that a genus is something apart from its species (1057b4–7). The error is corrected in the first half of I8 (1057b35–1058a8: at 1058a5, the singular "hauto" should be read with mss.EJ, rather than the plural "hauta"; see also I2 1053b21–22). I8 goes on then, in its second half, to argue that otherness in species, that is, difference (diaphora) of or within the genus, is as such contrariety (1058a8–9, 16–19, and 26–28; contrast I3 1054b31–32, as well as I4 1055a3–5). Here again, the inadequacy of the argument that purports to show this should not tempt us to take any the less seriously the question that its conclusion raises. If every difference in species is a case of contrariety, there will be no "in-betweens," no intermediate species, to be (in whatever way) from the contraries, the contrary species (for as 1058a17–21 as a whole makes clear, the "in-betweens" referred to at a20 are not intermediate species). What becomes then of the much discussed coming-to-be from those contrary species?

The general theme of I8 is "otherness in species"—in what it consists—and the discussion of this theme is officially concluded only at the end of I9 (1058b24–25; compare I8 beginning). The thesis of I9 is that the contrariety of female and male does not constitute a difference in species. Aristotle refrains from referring explicitly to the undeniable responsibility of this pair for some coming-to-be (see 1058b23–24).

* * * *

I9 is thus joined officially to I8, and therewith to the pair I7–I8. Could it have also, in accord with the plan which we believe we have discerned in the last portion of Iota, a connection with I10? The perplexity with which I9 opens and which it addresses for the most part in terms of the relation of female and male, concerns more particularly that of woman and man (I9 beginning). And I10 as well, in addressing generally the question whether the perishable and the imperishable can be the same either in species or even in genus, is concerned more particularly with the question whether there can be an imperishable human being, as the Platonic doctrine of ideas or forms would seem to have entailed (I10 end). It answers that question in the negative. Perishability belongs necessarily, not accidentally, to each of those to whom it belongs: it is their ousia or in their ousia. In the case of man, as we can add, not just perishability but the consciousness of it is constitutive of what he is: a "man" lacking altogether in this awareness would no longer be a man. According to a Platonic doctrine of which the juxtaposition of I9 and I10 could remind us—and which is not rejected, nor indeed mentioned, here—consciousness of our mortality shapes the eros which is that in us which communicates with the divine (Symposium 202d7–203a8, 206a3–c8 and e2–207a4).—The connection of I10, at least, with the theme which forms the background of the discussion in Iota as a whole, is indicated also by Thomas (Commentary on Aristotle's Metaphysics, para. 2140).

K1) We have taken our bearings hitherto by the hypothesis that the Metaphysics is Aristotle's introduction to a philosophic science. But has not the case for or against such a science been completed by the end of Iota, at the latest? Or is the term "philosophic science" capable of more than one application, that is, of an application other than the most demanding one?

According to the lines which open and introduce us to Kappa, "That wisdom is some science about principles," is clear from the first (parts of the Metaphysics) in which the perplexities entailed by what the others have said about the principles were gone through. The reference is not to the very first chapters of Alpha (A1–2), nor even to the first of those devoted to the examination of what the others had said about the principles and causes (A3–7: see A3 983b1–6 and A7 beginning), but rather to the two which follow these (A8–9: see A7 end). And it is therefore a puzzling one, since "that wisdom . . . is a science," a science about some principles and causes, was said to be clear as early as the end of A1 (982a1–3). But this was not yet clear to "all" (compare Al 981b27–29 in the light of 981b23–27 and A2 982b28–32).

The readers to whom Kappa is primarily addressed are then among those for whom it would not have become clear before they had read A8–9. (See, in particular, A8 beginning, retaining the words omitted by ms.Ab at 988b25–26, as well as 989b21–33, 990a5–7 and 29–32, but also 990a7–8 and following, together with the corresponding critique of the ideas or forms in A9: 991a8–10 and following and b3–5 and following, 992a24–26 and b8–9.) Now, readers such as these will have been disappointed in the result, or at the lack of result, of the investigation of ousia in Zeta and Eta, at its failure to reach its announced goal (Z2 1028b27–31, Z17 1041a6–9)—a failure that is unlikely to have been redeemed for them by anything which they may have gathered from the treatment of potentiality and truth in Theta or of "the one" in Iota. And in this situation, as if to make a new beginning, Kappa returns to those books of the Metaphysics which took the character of the science being sought for as their explicit theme (B1 995a24–b2, G1 1003a21–28 and 31–32, E1 1025b3–10 and 1026a10–25). In its first seven chapters and the greater part of the eighth, it repeats portions of these early books. By reminding its readers of certain points, it sharpens their awareness of a problem which they will already have felt and which the sequel will, somehow or other, have to solve, if they are to retain the conviction that they came to only in the wake of A8–9. Some of the points may have become clearer to them in the cold light of the intervening books; in the case of others, that light will have proved to be of no avail to them. But this means that the repetitions—which need not reproduce verbatim the passages that they recall to their memory and which are, in fact, adapted to their needs—provide indication of how an important class of those to whom Aristotle addresses himself will, as he expects, have read his text to this point.

For example, it is clearer to them now (after I3–10) than it had been in Beta that the principles are not contraries (1059a22–23; compare B2 996a20–21 as well as G2 1004b27–1005a5). Nevertheless, they are inclined to the view that wisdom is one science rather than many ("tautēs" at 1059a25). They are clear that it is a science of the ousiai, which they regard as what are first (1059a33–34), but not as to whether it is of all of them (1059a26–29). Or, rather, they think that it cannot be of the perceptible ousiai, for they are perishable (1059b14; K2 1060b25–26), and that it must therefore be of some different (ousiai) (1059a38–b1), which they are inclined to conceive of as free from motion or change (1059a38 and context); but then (as they fear) it would be of the (Platonic) forms or the mathematicals (1059b1–2), and they are clear that the forms are not (1059b3; compare Z16 1040b27–34 as well as A9 990b8–9 and following) and that none of the mathematicals is separable from the things here (1059b12–13 and context). They recognize, if not in the precise terms in which it was posed earlier (B2 997b34–998a6 and pages 43–44 above), the question that this last point raises as to the identity of the objects (1059b9–12) or the subject matter (1059b15–16; compare K4 1061b21–22) of the mathematical sciences. And they can conceive that the science which ought to go into that perplexity and make the (required) investigation concerning those objects is none other than the philosophy now under discussion (1059b14–21; compare 1059a29–34 together with Nicomachean Ethics Z3 1139b31–32). They know that, if the genera are to be held to be the principles of concern to the science being sought, it must be as the universals that comprehend the composite beings rather than as their elements (compare 1059b21–31 with B3 998a21–25); but they know also that difficulties stand in the way of regarding either the broadest classes or the narrowest as those principles (1059b31–1060a1).—At this point, Aristotle pauses in this enumeration of the perplexities which beset that science, that is, in his repetitions of Beta, only to resume it at once (in K2).

K2) When he does so, it is to draw, as definitive, the conclusion merely suggested by the difficulties mentioned at the end of K1 (K2 1060a5–7).—And thus his pause there may have been intended to allude to the further grounds which such a conclusion would require and which he has perhaps reserved for later mention here (for example, at 1060a36–b3: compare 1060a6–7 with K1 1060a1–2).—The gravity of the conclusion is traceable to the facts that the science being sought cannot be of the particulars, which are limitless (in multitude), and that besides the particulars there are only (their) genera and species (1060a3–5). Perhaps then its finality is less certain to Aristotle himself than to his immediate addressees (compare 1060b19–23 and K1 1059b24–26 with 1060b2–3 and context).

The new chapter's second depiction of a perplexity mirrors its first. It speaks now of "the perceptible ousiai and those here" rather than "the particulars" and of "wisdom" rather than "the science being sought"; but it raises again the question whether the latter can be about the former (however both are to be called). But whereas it had earlier acknowledged, besides the particulars, only (their) genera and species, it now asks—and its purpose now is to ask—whether one must assume there to be, besides the perceptible ousiai and those here, some ousia which is separate. "For we seem to be seeking some other (ousia), and this is what is under discussion for us: I mean, to see if (there is) something separate, by itself, and present to none of the perceptibles" (1060a10–13). To the distinction that Aristotle quietly draws between the "we" or "us" and the "I" may be traced also the fact that the question as to which the ousiai are is spoken of here as equivalent to the question as to which the beings (onta) are (1060a9).

The readers whom he addresses in this way are aware that it would be no easy task, if there is besides the perceptible ousiai some different ousia, to determine besides which of them one must posit this (ousia) to be (1060a13–16; compare H3 1043b18–23 as well as Z11 1036b22–32) and that to fabricate permanent (ousiai) different from the perceptible and perishable ousiai but equal to them (in number) would seem to fall outside the bounds of plausibility (1060a16–18; compare A9 990a34–b8). They understand that matter is not a thing—something that could be appealed to as a permanent substratum of all change—but rather the particular potentiality that belongs to each thing as the (perishable) thing that it is (1060a19–21; compare Z7 1032a20–22 together with H1 1042a27–28). And they know or have heard that the form and the shape of the bodies (or things), which would seem to be more of a principle, more authoritative than their matter, is perishable (1060a19–23; compare H5 1044b21–22, which removes the doubt that was left at H3 1043b14–16). "So that there is not at all (any) permanent ousia, separate and by itself. But (this is) absurd, for there seems (to be) and it is being sought by (all) of the refined, just about, as if there is some principle and ousia of this sort. For how will there be order, if there is not something permanent that remains separate?" (1060a23–27, omitting the second "kai" at a26 with ms.E)

This question perhaps suffices to explain why, towards the end of the chapter, Aristotle returns to that of whether there is something besides what he now calls the composite whole or not: "I mean the matter and what is with it" (1060b23–25). For if there is not, (nothing is imperishable, since) the things in matter are all perishable; but if there is something, it would be the form and the shape (1060b25–26). In other words, he reopens the door which he had just closed (1060a21–23), with only a reminder that it is difficult to distinguish the cases in which this is possible from those in which it is not: for in some the form is clearly not separable (1060b26–28; compare 1060a13–16 as well as L3 1070a21–26). He must have assumed that any acquiescence to that earlier step on the part of his immediate addressees would have been only half-hearted. And that this later one is a concession to them is confirmed by the passages which surround it and which point, each in its own way, to the necessity that the principles of knowledge be not ousiai but universals (1060b19–23 and 28–30; at b30 "tauta" should be read with ms.Ab: compare B4 999b31–1000a4). In the interval between the statement we have been considering and the earlier one that it rescinds or modifies, Aristotle had made clear that "we are seeking" such permanent first principles as (would be), each of them, some this and an ousia: "how else will they be separate (or separable) and by themselves?" (1060a37–b3)

The readers for whom this and other such concessions are intended are not unmindful, however, of how difficult it will be to establish the connection they anticipate between such an ousia and principle as "we are now seeking" and that order, especially, that prevails among the perishable things (1060a27–36 in the light of a26–27). They have learned that lines and points and the like cannot be such principles (1060b12–17; compare B5 1002a4–8); and they know or have heard that there is a coming-to-be of every ousia (1060b18–19). On the other hand, it is not clear to them how the oneness of each of the numbers is to be grasped or understood (1060b10–12; compare I6 1056b23 as well as D14 1020b7–8).

K3) We come now (in K3–6) to the central set of these repetitions, those of Gamma. It is a question in this first chapter of whether what it calls "the science of the philosopher" (1060b31; compare 1061b5–6) is one science (1060b31–36, 1061b11–17). This is said to require, if not that the intended objects comprise one genus (compare 1060b34–35 with 1061b15–17), at least that the name by which they are called refer to something common which they share, that it not be applied to them homonymously (1060b33–36). But the philosopher's science is said to be "of being as being universally, and not partially" (1060b31–32; compare G1 1003a21–26); and "being" (tò on) is spoken of in many ways and not after one manner (1060b32–33).

The discussion that addresses this difficulty must indicate in the course of doing so—and this is its real interest—what Aristotle expects the readers with whom he is now concerned to understand by a science which is of "being as being universally, and not partially." Gamma had suggested this contrast: the mathematical sciences pursue theoretically some part of being, what accrues to it, which they have cut off (apotemomenai) (G1 1003a23–26). And here in Kappa the theoretical pursuit of the mathematician is said to be about objects that he has obtained by abstraction, by having taken away (perihelōn) from the objects of perception all of their perceptible qualities, leaving only the "so much and continuous," in one, two, or three dimensions (1061a28–35). His pursuit is partial, then, not in restricting its attention to some class or classes of beings, to the exclusion or neglect of others. Rather, its attention extends to all of perceptible being, but only to some aspect or aspects of it. So, too, to physics one might assign the theoretical pursuit (of all perceptible beings) not as beings but rather as they share in motion (1061b6–7). If, then, the contrast proposed in Gamma were still intended here, the suggestion would be that to pursue theoretically being as being universally, and not partially, is to attend to all of it, not merely to some aspect or aspects; and the science of the philosopher would have to include both mathematics and physics (compare K4 end). But instead of contrasting that science here, in its universality, to these partial sciences, Aristotle now likens it to them in precisely the respect that has been mentioned: the same holds about being, for it belongs to no other science than philosophy to pursue theoretically what (pl.) accrue to it so far as it is being, as well as the contrarieties of it as being (1061b3–6).

In the meantime, he has begun to answer the question whether the term "being" is used homonymously, his answer proceeding apparently along the lines of that which he had given in G2. The new statement fails to adhere to the distinction between "pros hen" and "kath' hen" that the earlier one had insisted upon (G2 1003a33–34, b5–6 and 12–14; compare K3 1060b32–36 and 1061b11–12 with 1060b36–1061a3 and a10–11). But perhaps this distinction is not so clear-cut as it had there for the most part appeared to be (compare G2 1003b14–15). The earlier statement had explained, and thereby justified, the application of the term (tò on) to what are called beings (onta) by recourse to the relatedness in which they severally stand to the ousiai (1003b5–10). The new one explains the application of the term to "all being" (1061a8, 10–11, and b11) by recourse to a relatedness to what it calls "being as being": that is, according to it, a quality or state or disposition or motion, or any of the other such (beings), is said to be a being because it is, for example, a motion of "being as being" (1061a7–10). Must it not be, then, the ousiai to which this statement, too, refers the beings, differing from its predecessor only in calling them, the ousiai or things, "being as being"? (Compare Physics G1 200b32–33: there is no motion besides, that is, apart from, the things [ta pragmata].) Must we not conclude, in other words, that this difference, too, between the two statements is more apparent than real? But this would be to ignore what we were forced to infer from the analogy that the chapter goes on to draw between mathematics, as well as physics, and a science of "being as being." If, just as mathematics studies the perceptible beings only as they are "so much and continuous" and physics studies them as they share in motion, the science in question studies what accrues to them insofar as they are being(s), then what it, too, studies (as "being as being") is some aspect of the perceptible beings or the ousiai. And "being as being" is that aspect of them, and not the ousiai tout court.

"Being as being" must be the ousiai; "being as being" is not the ousiai. What can this mean, both in itself and as it constitutes a real departure from the statement in Gamma? That statement, to repeat, had traced our use of the term "being" to a relatedness (of what we apply it to) to the ousiai: in calling something a being, we have in mind its relation to something else, namely, to an ousia or thing. It is the latter, the ousia, which serves as foundation to the being of the former, a foundation that makes it meaningful to say of it that it is. There was only this difficulty in Gamma: the fact that the ousiai themselves are called beings, which it acknowledged (G2 1003b6), could not be explained in this way. And this led us to wonder whether they are called beings meaningfully (pages 64–65 and 100 above). But the thought that the foundation is merely given, that it lacks itself a knowable foundation, is admittedly difficult from more than one point of view. Some might be tempted, therefore, also for the sake of science, to find the missing foundation in a so-to-speak beingness of the beings, in "being as being." And not the least of the advantages such a step would confer on those who took it would be the ability to explain their application of the term "being," in accord with customary usage, also and especially to the ousiai or things. (Compare John Locke, An Essay Concerning Human Understanding, Bk. II, ch. 12, §6 beginning.)

In attempting to supply content to a science of "being as being," Gamma had had recourse to the near identity of being (tò on) and "the one" (G2 1003b22–26 and context). The contrarieties of "being as being," for example, which are still included in that content here (K3 1061b4–6), were attributed there at least as much to "the one," or to the one and the many, as to being (G2 1003b33–1004a2, a9–10 and 17–24, b27–1005a5). What Aristotle expects his readers, including those with whom he is primarily concerned now, to have learned from Iota about contrariety and the one, has led him to place less weight here on such an attribution (compare, with K3 1061a15–18, a10–15).

K4) As we have seen, K3 wavered as to whether "all being" or all beings are so called by virtue of something they are towards (pros) or by virtue of something proper to them (kath'). Perhaps it did so to reflect the wavering of a thought impressed equally by the dependence of the others on the ousiai and by what it conceived of as the dependence of the ousiai, and through them of the others, on "being as being" (compare K2 1060a36–b6). But however that may be, it is presumably "being as being," as what is common to all the ousiai, that permits them all to be treated by one science, as the conclusion of K3 affirmed that they can be. (That the beings, differing in genus, of which that conclusion speaks, are in fact the ousiai, is indicated by the perplexity to which it refers as having been mentioned "at the beginning," the perplexity whose solution it professes to state: see K1 1059a26–29.)

The chapter to which we now turn is a repetition of the first part of G3 (1005a19–b2). Some changes which it makes to the argument of that earlier passage bring into sharper focus a development within Kappa that was already discernible in K3. K4 can thus be considered to be an appendix of sorts to K3.

The question addressed in Gamma (G3 1005a19–22) and again here (1061b17–19) is whether it falls to the science of the philosopher (or to what K4 calls "the first philosophy" or "the first science") to investigate the so-called axioms (or principles) of mathematics. The ground of the positive answer that both passages give to the question is, as it is stated in Gamma, that those axioms pertain to all the beings, that they are not the proprium of some (one) genus apart from the others, that as axioms of "being as being" they belong to each genus as (a genus of) being (1005 a22–25). As that ground is first rendered here, however, the principles in question are said to be common to all the (beings that are) "so much" (1061b19–21; compare K3 1061a28–33). Why, then, should it not fall to the universal mathematics to investigate their validity? In order to avoid or evade this awkward question which it has brought upon itself, our chapter has, in effect, to deny the existence of such a science (compare 1061b21–24 with E1 1026a25–27). That its slip, of which there is no trace in the passage in Gamma, is however a deliberate one—as that evasion already indicates—is confirmed by a second change that it makes in the argument of the earlier passage.

G3 had referred to nature as merely "some one genus of being," and it had in the same context spoken of the superiority to the physicist of the philosopher, as one whose theoretical pursuit is not only universal but also concerns "the first ousia" (1005a33–b2; contrast 1005a31–33 together with A8 990a3–5). There is no mention in K4 of this "first ousia"—nor, indeed, of any beings other than those which the physicist (or the mathematician) studies. And it is therefore these that the philosopher, too, is said here to study (1061b31 and b27). Not, of course, as the physicist (or the mathematician) does, but insofar as the substrata of the aspects which they study are beings (1061b30–32 and b25–27). In speaking, then, of the principles of mathematics as common, not to the beings, but rather to what are "so much"—in substituting the latter for the former—what our chapter meant perhaps to suggest is that these are the beings (in one of their aspects), that there are no others. And therefore, as it adds by way of conclusion, physics and mathematics are parts of wisdom (for they, too, study aspects of the ousiai).

But what becomes, then, of the hope for some ousia that is separate or separable from the perceptible ousiai (K2 1060a10–13 and 24–27)? Or is "being as being," which has been suggested to be some one thing that is common (to all of them), also the very thing that is separable (from them all)? (Compare K3 1061a10–11 and b11–12, as well as K2 1060a36–b6, with K7 1064a28–29.)

K5 & K6) These chapters treat in brief compass the denial that nature is such as to be comprehended by reason in any substantive and reliable way (compare G4 1008b2–5, retaining "mē" before "alētheuei" at b4 with ms.Ab and Alexander). That denial had been treated at much greater length in Gamma, the discussion of it extending from the middle of the third chapter through the eighth and last. It was, after all, put forward and articulated by a number of Aristotle's most formidable predecessors and wrestled with by all of them (compare Plato *Theaetetus* 151e6–153a4). Next to the disparity in length of the two treatments, and not unconnected with it, the most obvious difference between them is the absence from Kappa's of any acknowledgment of the weightiness of the challenge thus posed to science, to its very possibility (compare G5 1009b33–1010a1 and context). The author expected of his primary addressees here an easy, not to say dogmatic, acceptance of his rejection of *this* challenge to science as an invalid one (see, for example, K6 1062b30–31 and 33–35, not to mention K5 1062a31–35). And this was something that he had neither expected, in the same degree, nor even wished from his addressees in Gamma. For he knew that an easy or dogmatic acceptance of a position is, as such, a weak acceptance of it: that those lacking an adequate grasp of the difficulties besetting a position they hold—in this case, as to the possibility of science—will lack also a grasp of the grounds on which any genuine response to the difficulties must rest (B1 995a28–30). And it becomes then a question hardly to be avoided how their adherence to the intrinsically sound position is to be maintained.

As it is considered in both Gamma and Kappa, the denial that nature is such as to be comprehended by reason takes the form of a contesting of the principle of contradiction and of the assertion, attributed in each book to Protagoras, that whatever anybody opines to be so, is true. The discussion in each centers therefore on these contentions, which are understood in both of them to amount very nearly to the same point. (Kappa is somewhat more cautious in this regard than Gamma: compare K6 1062b12–19 with G5 1009a6–16.) The principle of contradiction is said in Gamma, but not in Kappa, to be the firmest of all principles (G3 1005b8–23; compare K7 1064a36–b1 in the light of K2 1060b19–23). At the same time, Gamma is somewhat clearer or more explicit than Kappa about the defectiveness of the only sort of demonstration the principle is susceptible of (compare G4 1006a5–26 with K5 1062a2–16 and 30–31). The assertion of Protagoras is explicitly identified in Kappa, and not in Gamma, with his saying that "man is the measure of all things" (K6 1062b12–15; compare G5 1009a6–8). A very different interpretation of that saying had been offered by Aristotle, in the meantime, in the first chapter of Iota (1053a35–b3). He clearly did not expect the readers of primary concern to him here to have grasped the far-reaching implications of that interpretation, which he had refrained from fully spelling out even in Iota. (In this connection, one might compare what is said or suggested about "ta aisthēta" in K6 1063a35–b6 with what was said or suggested about them in G5 1010b30–33 and following.)

Gamma had spoken of "ta aisthēta" (the perceptible beings) in places where Kappa avoids this expression (compare G5 1010a25–32 with K6 1063a10–17, as well as G5 1009a22–23 and 38–b2 with K6 1062b20–24). It traced the cause of the opinion which both books combat to the conviction, of those of Aristotle's predecessors who professed it, that the perceptible beings are the only ones (G5 1010a1–4); and it therefore called upon them to accept that there is also some other ousia of the beings, to which neither motion nor perishing nor coming-to-be at all pertains (G5 1009a36–38), or some unmoved nature (G5 1010a32–35); it went so far as to speak of an unmoved first mover (G8 1012b29–31). What we have seen thus far of Kappa suffices to explain the absence of a comparable demand in our two chapters. It would no longer, or not yet, appear to be justified: this is the very point that is now at issue (K2 1060a10–13; compare K7 1064a33–36).

On the other hand, Kappa is less willing than Gamma had been to grant to those whom it calls "the physiologists" (K6 1062b21–22) the instability of the perceptible or bodily realm (G5 1010a1–5; compare a22–25 with K6 1063a23 and context; see also 1062b33–1063a3). Where Gamma had conceded that the place (or part) of the whole heaven (of the perceptible whole: compare A8 990a4–5) which is around us is continuously (involved) in perishing and coming-to-be (G5 1010a28–30), Kappa concedes that the things here appear changing and never remaining in the same (states) (K6 1063a10–12); and it explicitly exempts the things in what it calls "the cosmos" not just from perishing and coming-to-be but from any change whatsoever (compare K6 1063a13–15 with G5 1010a25–32). But this only means that the willingness thus presupposed in its readers to accept that there is a stable perceptible order for reason to comprehend will have been accompanied, on the part of many of them, by an expectation or hope of discovering the imperceptible basis on which any such order must presumably rest.

An anomalous passage, anomalous in this context, troubling to editors and misread by Ross among others (Vol.II, p.319), casts a very different and not untrue light on the relation between reason and the phenomena it attempts to grasp. Aristotle may have intruded it here (K6 1063a17–21: there is no parallel passage in Gamma) to serve as an elliptical reminder of the deeper strata of the problem under discussion.

K7) "This chapter answers to E.1 much more closely than the preceding chapters answer to B and G" (Ross Vol.II , p.321). All the more striking, and perhaps important, are then the departures that the new chapter makes from the one which it repeats. Physics or the science of nature, for example, is not said here, as it was in E1, to be a science about some genus of being (1025b18–21; see also G3 1005a33–b2). This is consistent with the fact that the statement with which the chapter opens about the limitations of the sciences—each of which is said to confine its activity to some genus that it has circumscribed for itself—is generalized in such a way as to place physics outside of its reach (compare 1064a1 with 1025b6, the relevant line of the comparable statement in E1). When the opening statement goes on, therefore, to make a further criticism of these sciences, of the failure of each of them to concern itself with the being of the very genus that it is concerned with as (on the assumption that it is) present and (a) being, adding "but this is some different science, besides these sciences" (1064a3–4), it is not yet excluded here that the different science which does this, which concerns itself with the objects of the sciences as beings because it conceives of them as beings, is physics (compare G3 1005a31–33).

Physics is described, here as in E1, as a theoretical science concerned with what have in themselves a principle or beginning of motion. And it is made clear in both chapters, via a discussion of definition in the sciences, that the objects of physics, as moving or capable of movement, have matter. They are, in other words, the natural bodies. Having made this clear, however, indeed immediately after doing so, the new chapter poses a question that was not raised in E1: "since there is some science of being as being and separable (or separate) (compare 1064a3–4), one must investigate whether this is to be posited to be the same as physics or, rather, different" (1064a28–30).

By posing this question where it does, as one still in need of investigation, the chapter suggests that the fact that the primary objects of physics are the natural bodies is no objection to its being also the science in question (compare K4 as well as pages 232–233 above). Yet this very fact appears to be made the basis of such an objection in the immediate sequel. What precisely is it, then, that is alleged here? Physics is said again to be about (objects) that have a principle of motion in themselves. Mathematics, too, is said to be a theoretical science: about (objects) that remain (unmoved) but are not separable (or separate) (compare E1 1026a7–10 and 14–15 with K1 1059b12–13). Concerning the being which is separate (or separable) and without motion (compare E1 1026a10–11 and 15–17, but also K2 1060a23–24 and b2–3), there is said to be, therefore, some (science) which is different from both of these sciences—"if indeed there is some such ousia, I mean (one that is) separate (or separable) and without motion, which (is the) very point we will attempt to show" (1064a34–36).

The fact that the primary objects of physics are the natural bodies is understood then to be an objection to its being also the science of being as being and separable (or separate), on the condition, admittedly still to be established (see also 1064a36–37), that there is an ousia of the sort indicated. An ousia or nature of that sort would be the seat of the divine (1064a36–37; compare E1 1026a19–21):

in other words, as the new chapter adds, it would be (the) first and most authoritative principle (1064a37–b1; compare K2 1060a23–27 and a36–b3). And the theoretical science that concerns itself with it is theology, which is of course the first of the sciences (1064b1–6; E1 1026a18–23). Nevertheless, it remains the case that here, as in E1, some consideration is given to the alternative that physics is the first of the sciences. But the physics that threatens to usurp the place of theology may be differently conceived in the two chapters; and this difference, in turn, may affect the ultimate outcome of the contest (between these sciences) in which the Metaphysics can be said to culminate.

The condition under which physics would be the first science (E1) or the first of the sciences (K7) is, as E1 has it, that there is not some different ousia besides the naturally constituted ones (1026a27–29) or, as it is put here, that the natural ousiai are the first of the beings (1064b9–11). The condition is stated, in each chapter, in the course of its consideration of another question that someone might be perplexed about: as it is put in E1, whether the first philosophy is (a) universal (one) or (rather) about some genus and some one nature (1026a23–25); as it is put here, whether one must posit that the science of being as being (is a) universal (one) or not (1064b6–8). Now, if the naturally constituted ousiai are the only ones (the condition as stated in E1), there is no reason why the physics that studies them should not be the universal science. (The objection made earlier in that chapter, that the concern of physics is limited to some genus of being, would effectively have been withdrawn.) As these ousiai need not be conceived of as beings however (see pages 230–231 above), there is no need for physics to study them as beings. Nor is there any suggestion in E1 that it does so. It is only theology which is said there, if there is such a science, to study being as being (1026a27–32). In the new chapter, however, the argument which we have traced carries with it the implication that in the absence of the condition under which theology is a science—in other words, if the opposed condition, under which physics is the first of the sciences, prevails—the objection to physics being also the science of being as being and separable (or separate), the only one raised here, is removed. And just as it made sense that the physics considered in E1 not be suggested to be (also) a science of being as being, so it makes sense that the physics considered here, if it conceives of its objects as beings, is suggested to make the attempt to study them, or to put itself in a position to study them, as beings. But this also means that, if the condition under which theology is a science prevails, the physics considered here is deprived, relieved rather, of its additional burden. The science which would then claim as its prerogative the study of being as being, because all being must be understood in the light of that highest ousia that is its special concern (E1 1026a29–32; K7 1064b6–14), would in this way leave or restore physics to its own proper objects (which it will still conceive of as beings).

K8) The first and largest part of this chapter consists of repetitions of the remaining portions of Epsilon, which is the last of the books of the Metaphysics to be repeated in Kappa. Aristotle turns first to the treatment of accidental being in E2 and E3. He says in effect here (1065a8, 12, 15–16, 21), as he had there (E2 1027a12–13, E3 1027a30–31), that if the accidental is not, everything will be, or come to be, of (or by) necessity. Yet he passes over in silence now the question of principle that he had raised in this context in Epsilon: whether it is the case that there is nothing which is either always or for the most part (as it is) (E2 1027a15–16; compare On the Heaven G2 301a4–11). And thus there is no allusion here to the further question of the character and source of a necessity that would hold even in that case. He is silent now also on the question whether there is that which is for the most part but nothing that is always, a question which he had called attention to in Epsilon as requiring later investigation (E2 1027a17–19). But he does repeat here, if somewhat less distinctly, the admission of Epsilon that all science is either of what is always or of what is for the most part (1065a4–5; compare E2 1027a20–21; compare also Prior Analytics A13 32b18–21 and context).

More important, perhaps, even than what Aristotle suggested by his silence on that question of principle (E2 1027a15), is what he suggests at the end of this part of Kappa by the brief repetition of E4 with which he brings his repetitions of these early books to a fitting close. He associates accidental being here, as he had there, with being as truth. The latter, in turn, is again distinguished, as belonging to thought (1065a22–23; 1027b27, 30, 34–1028a1), from the things (1027b25–26, 30–31) or from what is called here "the being (which is) external and separable" (1065a24; compare 1028a2), that is, separable or separate from us. Now E4, even while insisting on the subordination of being as truth to this different being (1027b31), had at the same time called into question that judgment, and therewith the distinction on which it was based, by saying that being as truth (it, too) requires later investigation (1027b28–29). In the meantime, a further investigation of it has in fact been carried out (see Th10 and pages 205–208 above). Has that investigation made any impression at all on the readers of Aristotle's primary concern here? At any event, he gives no sign of a desire to remind them of it. To do so would have been to run the risk of undermining their confidence in the exteriority of the objects of the science that he is attempting to prepare them to engage in, either actively or by way of looking upon it with favor, with a sympathetic understanding.

* * * *

In E4 Aristotle had contrasted both being as accident and being as truth with the being (or nature of being) that is external, which he also called there "being itself" (1027b33–1028a4); here in K8 he contrasts only being as truth with the being that is external and separable (1065a21–25). In E4 he had referred to the cause of accidental being as indeterminate (1027b33–1028a1); in K8, although he has described such being as "not necessary but indeterminate," he says of its causes rather that they are "without order and without limit" (1065a24–26; compare K2 1060a34–36 and context). These facts may be connected with the mention in K8, but not in Epsilon, of an eclipse (1065a16 and following). An eclipse would seem to fit the definition of the accidental that has been offered here (1065a1–3), despite the fact, which an earlier treatment of it has made clear, that it is a natural occurrence, whose cause can of course be inquired into (compare H4 1044b8–15 with 1065a6–8 as well as E3 1027b11–14 and D30 1025a21–25). Its mention in this context therefore suggests that, between the natural in the sense of what is or occurs for the most part, if not always, and the accidental in the sense of the merely coincidental (E2 1026b37–1027a2; D30 1025a14–21), there is an accidental whose naturalness cannot be denied, even though it, too, occurs neither always nor for the most part. (Compare also the beginning of the Meteorologica.) And before turning from his repetitions of the Metaphysics itself to a series of repetitions of passages in the Physics, the chief of his works on nature, Aristotle apparently wished to remind some of his readers that this is the case.

According to Ross, "An examination of the first part [of K] shows that it is no mechanical paraphrase of BGE such as a disciple might have made but an independent handling of the same topics, omitting much . . . , rearranging much, and inserting not a little of its own. . . . The latter part of K," on the other hand, "stands on quite a different basis. It consists of excerpts taken almost word for word from the Physics; there is no independence of treatment." (Vol. I, pp. xxv-xxvii) But are such changes as were to be found in the first part of Kappa, in its repetitions of the Metaphysics, needed here? If those changes have indeed prepared an approach to the study of nature such as the Physics by and large presents, the answer must be "no": the passages now to be repeated from it, with little or no alteration, need serve only to illustrate the approach in question. This is not to deny, however, that they may well appear in a new light to readers already familiar with them (consider K1 1059a34 and K6 1062b31) who have noticed the way or ways here in which they have been (re)introduced.

The repetitions of the Physics begin, in the second part of K8, with a few brief excerpts from the treatment (in Physics B4–6) of a question that concerns the fundamental premise of (the) science: what is the cause of, or what is responsible for, the heaven (that is, the perceptible whole: compare A8 989b33–990a5, as well as

Physics B4 196a24–28 and B6 198a9–13)? And the answers to it which are considered, both in the original discussion and in its fragmentary repetition, are on the one hand chance or spontaneity (the difference between these two can be disregarded for present purposes, as it is in the repetition) and on the other mind and nature. Do these answers exhaust the alternatives that must be considered in this connection? Nature is understood in the context, along with thought, as a cause that acts for the sake of something. At the same time, nature and thought are suggested to be correlates of accidental causation: it is when something which might have been brought about by nature (or from thought) comes about by accident that it is ascribed to chance. And the answer which is finally given both here and in the Physics to the question of concern to us depends on this correlation. Or, rather, it depends on the simple identification of accident with chance (compare 1065a1–3 with Physics B5 196b10–17)—on the reduction, we can say, of accident to chance and spontaneity, which are in turn correlates of nature so understood (and thought). But, in fact, the range of the accidental extends beyond that ascribed in this context to chance and spontaneity (Physics B5 196b19–21, 197a32–35). And, as we learned from the first part of K8, we find in that portion of the accidental with which chance and spontaneity do not coincide occurrences that are natural, and are so in a sense not acknowledged in the chapter's second part. (Compare 1065a16 with H4 1044b12 and context.)

K9–12) The repetitions of the Physics to which these remaining chapters of Kappa are devoted, along with the second part of K8, are of passages that, by what must be regarded as a curious coincidence, have been drawn exclusively from books BGE of that work. What principle did, then, govern the selection of the passages? They all belong, to make use of a distinction pronounced early in the last book of the Physics (Th1 251a5–8), to the theoretical pursuit concerned with nature, rather than to the investigation concerned with the first principle, to which the last book itself is devoted. But they may have been chosen for their special relevance to that investigation or to the task alluded to in the first part of Kappa (K2 1060a10–13 and 23–27; K7 1064a33–36) and taken up in the latter part of Lambda: consider Physics Th1 251a8–11 in connection with K9, for example, and Physics Th10 267b20–22 as well as L7 1073a8–11 in connection with K10; and see pages 83–85 above. But there are surely other Physics passages, not repeated here, for which such relevance could be claimed: that referred to at Physics Th5 257a33–b1, for example. And this means that the question of principle regarding the selection cannot be settled prior to completion of a thorough study of the first seven books of the Physics in their relation to the last book, as well as to the latter part of Lambda. Pending the results of such a study, we will therefore consider briefly what the selected passages, or some of them, may have to teach us about the science that the first part of Kappa sought to prepare its readers to engage in: that is, we will assume, as our working hypothesis, that they have been chosen not least for the light that they may shed on that science.

The passage repeated in the second part of K8 treated a question that concerns what we called the fundamental premise of the science. The first topic of the passages repeated in K9–12, and the topic treated most extensively in these passages, is motion. The Physics, perhaps together with other works, had been referred to in Th8 as "the (remarks or writings) about motion" (1049b36). As for the other topics treated in the passages repeated here, it is not impossible that their inclusion is due to a connection of one sort or another which their treatment has with the repetitions' treatment of motion.

Motion (kinēsis) is the motion of things: "there is not any motion besides the things" (K9 1065b7). It would follow already from this, though the conclusion is not drawn in this context, that coming-to-be is not motion (K11 1067b30–34): coming-to-be is admittedly change (metabolē) of some sort (K11 1067b14–23; compare K9 1065b7–14). Others, in attempting to define motion, had been influenced by what they took to be its indeterminateness (K9 1066a7–17). Aristotle makes it determinate by tying it to the (limited) potentiality (dunamis) for motion of particular things: "the actualization (energeia) of what (is) in potentiality, insofar as (it) is (in potentiality), I call motion" (K9 1065b16; compare Physics G1 201a10–11). The "insofar as" proves to be in need of clarification. "I mean (it) in the following way: the bronze is in potentiality a statue; but nevertheless (it is) not the actualization (entelecheia) of the bronze, insofar as (it is) bronze, (that) is motion; for (what it is) to be bronze and to be some potentiality (is) not the same; since, if it were simply the same . . . , the actualization (entelecheia) of the bronze would be some motion" (1065b23–27). As goes almost without saying (1065b28), bronze is not motion (compare A6 987a32–b1). What is motion, is rather the actualization of its potentiality for being formed into a statue. And it follows, therefore, that there is motion whenever there is this actualization, "and neither before nor after" (1065b20–21 and 34–35). Departing again from its model, the repetition makes this statement twice: shortly before, as well as after, the discussion of the bronze (compare Physics G1 201b6–7 and context).

The same point, perhaps, is conveyed later on by the insistence that there is not motion of a motion, nor, more generally, change of a change (K12 1068a14–16 and following).—Soul is spoken of in this context as something which, in distinction from motion, can undergo change (1068b10–12).—Similarly, the terms or endpoints of motion are not motion (K11 1067b9–12; compare Physics E1 224b13–15 and context).

At first glance, there may not appear to be in K10, which repeats a rather small portion of the Physics' treatment of the limitless or infinite, anything that bears in a noteworthy way on this discussion of motion. Aristotle contests here the existence of an actual infinite by arguing that it could be neither itself some ousia (1066b1–21) nor an attribute of a perceptible body or bodies (1066b22 and following). But did those physicists who speak of the infinite as the source from which they generate the elements (1066b34–35 and 1067a5–6) conceive of it as a perceptible body? Or would "imperceptible body" be a contradiction in terms? Aristotle dismisses their suggestion of the existence of a further body besides the elements, at any rate, by saying (in part) that no such body appears (1066b36–1067a1). In the same context, he rejects the derivation of "the all" from any single element by appealing to the presumably observable fact that everything which changes does so from a contrary, as from warm to cold (1067a1–7 together with K11 1067b12–14). Finally, the definitions in the latter part of K12 (1068b26 and following), with which the repetitions of the Physics conclude, provide still further evidence of the orientation by (perceptible) body that we have observed—or by its mathematical idealization (compare B2 997b34–998a6 as well as M3 1077b17–22). In judging of this orientation, however, we should keep in mind that it is perhaps in what is most manifest to us that the necessity sought by science is to be found in its least questionable form. (Compare page 195 above.)

L1) Aristotle, or his philosophic editor, regarded the first five chapters of this book as an appropriate bridge between Kappa and the latter part of Lambda. Let us try, then, to see how these chapters prepare the primary addressees of Kappa, but not only them, for appreciating what awaits them there.

They begin with the assertion that "the theoretical pursuit (of concern to us) is about ousia"; the principles and the causes that are being sought are those of the ousiai. For, whether or not "the all" is a whole, a question which is left open for the time being (compare L7 1072b13–14 with K2 1060a26–27), ousia has the first place within it. The questions "what is ousia?" and "which are the ousiai?" are no longer, or not yet, raised here. Rather, answers to them are presupposed. A distinction is first drawn between ousia and what are designated by the other predications: what the others designate are, strictly speaking, not even beings. In other words, it is the ousiai which are beings, the beings. And appeal is then made to the philosophers "of old" who bore witness in deed to what has been said or implied. It was ousia that they sought principles and elements and causes of; and they posited as ousiai—not universals, as do "those now"—but the particulars, which are as such not merely bodies, but bodies of particular sorts, like fire and earth.

The answer presupposed to the question "which are the ousiai?" is then too harsh to be left without qualification. The qualification which comes at once is in the form of a statement that, in accord with our practice, we will try to understand as it has been transmitted to us by the manuscripts upon which our text of the Metaphysics chiefly relies. According to this statement (1069a30–b2), there are three ousiai (that is, classes of ousiai). One (mia men) is perceptible, of which (that is, of perceptible ousiai) this (hē men) is everlasting and that (hē de), as to which all agree, is perishable, like the plants and the animals. And that (hē d' [answering to "mia men"]) is everlasting, the elements of which there is a necessity to grasp, whether they are one or many. And another (allē de) is without motion, and some say that this (ousia) is separate (or separable).—The central ousia or class evidently differs from the everlasting subclass of the first in being imperceptible; and from the third in not being without motion, if not also (compare L3 1070a24–26) in not being separate (or separable).—. . . Finally, those (ousiai or classes) belong to physics (to study), for they are with motion (compare E1 1025b34–1026a6), but this (ousia or class) to a different (theoretical pursuit), if there is no principle common (to the beings in question).

The general question with which the statement leaves us is that of whether there is, as it appears to suggest, motion (or change) of imperceptibles (compare K9 1065b7–8) and, if so, how that imperceptible or those imperceptibles are to be understood. But the conclusion of the chapter speaks rather of the change to which (all) perceptible ousia is subject. Yet, in doing so, it calls attention to the fact that, as the contraries between which the change occurs do not change, there is a necessity that there be something underneath (the change), namely, that which changes to or towards the contrary.

L2) It is left to the new chapter to say that this third something, besides the contraries, is matter. It has in the meantime been said here to be what, unlike the contrary, remains (throughout the change). As what does it remain? Not as the contrary (or in-between) that it was and is no longer; nor as the contrary (or in-between) that it was not but has now become. As what then? It may well be identifiable both as what it was before the change and as what it is afterwards (but compare K11 1067b12–14 and 1068a1–4 together with 1067b21–25). But as what is it identifiable in the course of the change? Or, rather, is it identifiable then? Perceptible matter (D24 1023a36–b2; E1 1025b32–34), something by itself a thing in appearance or as it seems (L3 1070a9–11 and 18–20; Z16 1040b5–10) yet potentially part of a more genuine whole, may retain its looks, at least, while coming to be or ceasing to be part of that whole (see D11 1019a4–11). But is this the case with all matter (compare H5 1044b34–1045a6)? With matter as it is intended here?

The reintroduction of matter (compare K2 1060a19–21 and pages 227–228 above) occurs in the course of the discussion, introduced in L1, of the change to which perceptible ousia is subject. We had heard little of matter in Kappa's repetition of the Physics' account of such motion or change (consider in this connection the criticism of Bonitz with regard to Physics E1 225a3–7, a passage repeated at K11 1067b14–18, which is made by Ross in his commentary on the Physics ad loc.), though what we did hear of it (K12 1068b10–12) anticipated in a way the more particular question which the statement in L1 has left us with. Yet matter is brought back here.—In accord with this, little or no attempt is now made to distinguish coming-to-be from the other changes or the motions (compare 1069b9–15 and 24–26 with K11 1068a1–5 and K12 1068a8–11); the tendency is rather to understand the others, that is, all change as a coming-to-be (compare 1069b15–20 and 26–28 with K11 1067b25–34).—Why, then, is it brought back? Why in this context?

Some light is perhaps cast on this question by the excursus on Anaxagoras and others that immediately precedes the conclusion of the chapter and takes up a not negligible portion of it (1069b20–32). Anaxagoras had spoken of "the one" in (or as) which "everything (was) together" prior to its articulation by mind (nous). And others had spoken of "the mixture" or of when "everything was for us (hēmin, with the mss. at 1069b23) in potentiality but not in actuality." And, according to Aristotle, what they had touched on (or dimly grasped) in this way is matter. At this point, he reminds us that everything which changes has matter—is the "everything" (panta) of which Aristotle speaks and which could presumably be rendered by "all things" the same as the "everything" (panta) of which Anaxagoras spoke?—but a different matter. If something is in potentiality (something else), it is not (the potentiality) for anything that may chance (to emerge), but what is different (comes) from what is different. And, on this basis, he makes a correction of Anaxagoras. That everything (was) together is not sufficient, for there is differentiation in the matter, which accounts for the fact that what came to be is without limit (apeira, pl.) rather than one. Mind is one, so that if the matter, too, were one, that (alone) would have come to be for which the matter was in potentiality.

The correction implies a measure of agreement (compare A8 989a30–b21). The matter, which is in potentiality but not in actuality (compare 1069b15–20), is nevertheless not nothing. Indeed, it has according to Aristotle an inner articulation of sorts. One may even have to go so far as to ascribe to it motion (or change). (Compare Physics B9 200a30–32.) This much, at least, may be inferred from the conclusion of the chapter (1069b32–34) where, departing once more from Anaxagoras, Aristotle speaks of matter and the two contraries as the causes or principles. But this would not yet be the motion of things. To tie motion to the things, as Aristotle would like to do (see pages 243–245 above), makes it indeed determinate, or intelligible, but leaves us with the question of how motion comes to an "all" whose parts are intrinsically inert (see pages 13–14 above). And this difficulty can be avoided by recourse to a "matter" that is no more thing(s) than it is motion—though admittedly at the price of the intelligibility of the latter. (The development we have been discussing may have been anticipated by the addition which K9 1065b5–6 makes to its model, Physics G1 200b26–27. Compare, on the other hand, On Generation and Corruption A5 322a4–6 as well as On the Heaven G2 302a3–9.)

L3–L5) At the end of L5 (1071b1–2), Aristotle claims that it has been said (in L1–5) which and how many are the principles of the perceptibles—principles which, as perceptible ousia is subject to change (L1 1069b3), must be able to account for that change. Yet his discussion has barely touched on the motion of those perceptible ousiai that he has called everlasting (L2 1069b24–26; compare L1 1069a30–31). He could hardly have treated their motion without answering the question to which he had alluded towards the end of L1 (1069b1–2; compare E1 1026a15–18). For the same or a similar reason, at the very beginning of L3 he puts in the place of the triad of causes or principles on which he had insisted in the conclusion of L2—and with which he had intrigued some of his readers—a new threesome, which overlaps in part with the old. (Note the break indicated by the repeated "after these [remarks]": 1069b35, 1070a4.) The most obvious difference is the substitution, for privation or the contrary from which, of what is called "the first moving (cause)." And, when privation is later on restored (L4 1070b10–13 and 18–19), the number of causes or principles is also revised upwards, from three to four (L4 1070b22–26; compare L5 1071a33–34).

The moving cause, which we are entitled here to call a new one, is understood to be external to what is moved (L4 1070b22–23; L5 1071a13–17). The context in which it is first introduced (L3 1069b35–1070a4) suggests that Aristotle has in mind in the first place the proximate moving cause (Ross at 1070a1); and this raises the question of what moves that moving cause (see again L5 1071a14–16). "First principles of everything are what is in actuality the first 'this' and something else which is in potentiality" (L5 1071a18–19). But it may be only the ousia composite of form and matter which is in actuality "some this" (L3 1070a9–18 and 21–26; L5 1071a8–11; compare D8 1017b23–26), which is as much as to say that every "this" is both in actuality and in potentiality (compare L5 1071a6–7). That is not a problem—in particular, it does not require one to posit the existence of the ideas (L3 1070a26–27)—since each composite ousia comes to be from or by the agency of an ousia of the same name or kind (L3 1070a4–6):

man generates man (L3 1070a8 and 27–28). This would seem to require however that the order in which this process can and does occur be everlasting—or that "the all" be a genuine whole (L1 1069a19–20) or that the causes or the principles of all things be in some sense, at least so far as the highest causes are concerned, the same (L4 1070a31–33 and following [compare L5 1071a19–24]; L5 1070b36–1071a2 [compare 1071a24–29]; and 1071a29–b1). There is indeed a sense in which man could be understood to be the single highest cause of all things and even their moving cause (L4 1070b30–31, keeping to the single "anthrōpos" with mss. JAb; 1070b34–35, keeping to "hōs to" with the mss.; L5 1071a1–3; and L2 1069b23). And one could even claim some Anaxagorean support for the suggestion that it is the mind whose home is man which is the first moving cause, insofar as it is responsible for the articulation presupposed by all perceptible change (see again A8 989a30–b21 together with page 25 above; compare also On the Heaven G2 301a11–13). But apart from other difficulties here (compare L2 1069b30–32), there is that of the finitude of man (L5 1071a6–7; compare Physics D14 223a21–26), that is, of our dependence on external causes or conditions (L5 1071a13–17).—Other passages as well (for example, L4 1070a33–b4 and b5–9, as against L1 1069a18–22: compare pages 64–65, 100–103, and 108 above) have impressed upon us the sobriety with which the first five chapters of Lambda have in general carried out the task assigned to them in the argument of the work.

L6–L10) In these remaining chapters of Lambda, Aristotle undertakes to argue or to say—as he says that one must argue or say (L6 1071b3–5; but compare K7 1064a34–36)—that it is necessary that there be some everlasting (or permanent) ousia without motion (compare L7 1072b11–13): "it is upon a principle of this sort that heaven (the perceptible whole) and nature depend" (L7 1072b13–14; compare K2 1060a26–27); and the ousia in question is to be identified with or as God (L7 1072b14–30; L8 1074a38–b10; L10 1075a11–15 and b37–1076a4). In accordance with this, the words which he devotes to it here are among the most moving and the most justly prized of the work. Nevertheless, we will depart so far from his injunction (L6 1071b3–5) as to refrain from adding to them, elliptical as they are. We would be even less capable of doing so than the prophet who, after his manner, has warned us against any such attempt (Proverbs 30.1–6). Instead, we will merely note several points that bear on the discussion hitherto.

At the end of L5, we found the claim that the principles of the perceptibles had been stated—presumably in the course of Lambda's first five chapters, but at any rate prior to the treatment of the theme of its last five (see L1 1069a36–b2). Since perceptible ousia is, as such, subject to change (L1 1069b3), those principles must be also, or include, the cause or causes of its motion or change. The situation at the beginning of L6 is thus as follows: of the three ousiai called to our attention in L1 (1069a30–34), the first has already been treated (in L1–5) and the third is about to be treated (in L6–10). What, then, of the second, whose elements Aristotle had said that it is necessary to grasp (L1 1069a32–33)? Is his silence in its regard, as he effects the transition from the first to the second part of Lambda, meant to suggest that it has not and will not be treated in the book (in other words, that its treatment, too, is not required for an understanding of the principles of the perceptibles)? Or is that silence rather a pointer to the attention, understated as it has been, which has already been accorded this "ousia"? (Consider L2 1069b20–34 as well as pages 247–248 above.) We do find in L6 the remark that "the matter will not move itself" (1071b29–30); but, as the immediate context makes clear, the matter in question is wood, as it is worked upon by the art of carpentry.

The remark's broader context in L6 is an exposition of the impossibility of what the theologians who "generate (all things) from night" argue or of what the physicists say, "that all things (were) together" (1071b26–28 and following; compare L2 1069b20–24 as well as L10 1075b24–27). After contending in L6 for the admissibility (L7 1072a19) of the solution to the problem of motion that he has begun in the chapter to adumbrate, Aristotle indicates at the beginning of L7 that, if the problem is not solved in this way, "(all things) will be from night and everything together and from nonbeing" (1072a19–20). Appeal might be made, for the rejected alternative, to an alleged priority of potentiality to actuality (L6 1071b22–26). Aristotle has contended in Th8 for the priority of actuality to some sort or sorts of potentiality (1049b5–12 and 1051a2–3; compare L6 1071b12–19): as he indicated in Theta more broadly and admits again here (L6 1072a3–4), there is a sense in which potentiality (of some other sort) may be regarded as prior. (Every genuine potentiality is a potentiality of something actual, but the actuality in question need not be the actuality belonging to an ousia or thing, that is, to what is actual in the fullest sense. Consider, again, in this connection K9 1065b5–6.) But, as he continues now (L6 1072a4–7), even Anaxagoras and Empedocles (among others) bear witness to the priority of actuality; "so that there was not, for a limitless time, chaos or night but the same (things) always, either periodically or otherwise (that is, simply)" (1072a7–9). Since it is more particularly the periodic return of the same (thing) that Aristotle considers here (1072a9–10), the reading of mss.EJ at 1072a11–12 should be preferred to that chosen by the editors.

This is not to deny, of course, that the argument aims finally not only at the permanence of "the first heaven" (L7 1072a23)—that is, the outermost part of the one and only heaven (L8 1074a31–38) or of the whole (L10 1075a11–25)—but also at that of the order of coming-to-be and perishing, as we know it, within that heaven (already at L6 1072a15–18). What there is only periodically is the level of understanding among human beings that is required for realizing that "the divine embraces the whole nature" (L8 1074b3) or that it secures what Aristotle also calls "the nature of the whole" (L10 1075a11–15). For it is to be assumed that after each art and each philosophy (or science) has been discovered and brought to its peak, they have again perished and that this process of discovery—given the permanence of the order which it presupposes—has occurred, as Aristotle says in this context, "many times" (L8 1074b10–12). (Compare Politics H10 1329b25–27 as well as On the Heaven A3 270b19–20 and Meteorologica A3 339b27–30.)

By referring to the political function that is served by the mythical additions to the inherited core of truth about the divine (L8 1074b3–5), the truth which must again and again through the greatest intellectual effort be reacquired, Aristotle indicates that his own doctrine is not meant to serve a political purpose. In accord with this, he does not squint at its difficulties (L9, as a whole, together with L7 1072b19–24 and 26–30). Now, these difficulties raise questions that must be answered if even the life which is best for human beings (L7 1072b14–16 and 24–26; L9 1075a7–10), the theoretical life, is to achieve self-understanding, in other words, if it is truly to be lived. It will be necessary then, also for those who (perhaps like Anaxagoras) trace such order as there is solely or chiefly to a human mind, to take them into account.

Indeed, Aristotle brings Lambda to a close by reminding us of the numerous (other) difficulties or rather "impossibilities or absurdities" that confront the proponents of alternative doctrines (L10 1075a25–27 and following: the passage's introductory sentence, which we have rendered only in part, is perhaps somewhat misleading). Only Empedocles and Anaxagoras are mentioned by name. Aristotle's doctrine comes to sight in this passage as distinguished by its recognition of matter on the one hand (1075a31–34) and the good on the other (1075a36–b1; compare L7 1072b3–4): that is, by the distinction that it maintains between them. Empedocles, by contrast, had "absurdly" made love or the good a principle both as that which moves (what is moved) and as matter, although the latter are distinct, at least in their being (or definition) (1075b1–6).

A Note on Mu

If Kappa and Lambda belong together in the place where we have them in the transmitted text of the Metaphysics (on the character of the necessity that binds them to one another and links them with the argument of the preceding books, see pages 224–225 and 236–239 together with 232–233 above), what is one to make of Mu? The beginning of Mu (1076a8–16) conveys the impression or suggests that the investigation as to whether or not there is, besides the perceptible ousiai, some ousia that is without motion and everlasting, and if there is which it is, is about to begin in earnest: "first" to be considered are what the others have said about these questions. Can the author of Mu have been ignorant of the most manifest result of Lambda (L7 1073a3–5)? It is true that Lambda, in reaching that result, had disregarded the opinions to be taken up now and that it had done so after calling them to our attention, in the same configuration in which they are presented here, in its very first chapter (1069a33–36; compare 1076a16–22).—They were returned to, briefly, only in the latter part of its last chapter, where Aristotle adumbrated his authentic position by means of comments directed to virtually all of his predecessors in turn, to what they had said or failed to say.—But has not the gap in the argumentation of Lambda that this disregard could be thought to constitute been filled in advance by the criticism that the opinions have already been subjected to in Alpha and Beta (some portions of which Mu recalls, while it repeats, more or less literally, others)? And, above all, if Mu is intended by its criticism of the opinions that it considers, of the answers that they represent to the questions which it once again raises, to support the answers supplied to these questions in Lambda, if it is intended, in short, to support the manifest result of Lambda, why is there no mention of that result here?

There remains, however, the alternative that Mu is addressed to readers who were unable to accept Lambda's result (its silence constituting a tacit acknowledgement of their judgment in that regard) and who have retained, whether for good reasons or bad, an interest in the ideas and the mathematicals (compare K1 1059a38–b3 and b12–13). Moreover, the criticism to which Aristotle subjects the ideas and the mathematicals here is not simply or even for the most part repetitive of what he had said in Alpha and Beta. Above all, he indicates now, that is, in a context in which he will more clearly distance himself than he had before from the proponents of one of the doctrines in question (see page 27 above), a concern to uncover any ground that he may share with them in particular (M1 1076a12–16 together with M10 1086b14–16; compare L10 1075a25–27). And it is, as we anticipate at least, against the background of this shared or common ground that the distinctive contribution of Mu to the argument of the Metaphysics as a whole will have to be understood.

* * * *

According to the beginning of Mu, or to the beginning of that beginning, which or what (ms.E at 1076a8) the ousia of the perceptibles is has already been stated: (first or partly) in the inquiry (methodos) of the natural scientific (writings) about matter; later (in the inquiry) about that (ousia) in actuality (kat' energeian). (1076a8–10) By the latter inquiry, that which has been carried out thus far in the Metaphysics itself may well be meant (see, for example, H2 1042b9–11). When Mu comes, however, in the latter part of its ninth chapter (1086a21 and following) to speak, by way of a new beginning, of the first principles and the first causes and elements—of the beings (1086a28)—, it outlines a program which differs in more than one respect from the program which it had outlined in its first chapter. The guiding question here is of a disclosure not of ousiai or beings but of their first principles (compare M1 1076a29–32, which points ahead to M6 1080a12–14 and following, with M9 1086a21–22 and, especially, 26–28), and not of the principles themselves but only of what is said about them by two classes of thinkers. (The classes appear to be exhaustive.) What is said by those who draw distinctions (or lay down definitions) about perceptible ousia alone has been stated, in part, in the (writings) about nature. The other part of what these thinkers say does not belong to "the present inquiry." If the latter phrase refers here (1086a24; compare N3 1091a20) to the inquiry carried out in the Metaphysics as a whole, this would mean that Aristotle has not and will not state in the work that portion of what any member of this class says (or thinks) about the first principles which has not already been stated in the writings about nature. He turns instead (in the latter part of Mu and in Nu) to what is said about them by the thinkers of the second class, who assert that there are, besides the perceptible (ones), different ousiai: "since some say that the ideas and the numbers are of this sort and that the elements of these are elements and principles of the beings, one must investigate . . . what (it is that) they say and how they say (it)" (1086a26–29). This is the investigation the pursuit of which "follows next upon" (echomenon: 1086a25–26) what has been said (in the earlier part of Mu).

The suggestion that it does so is somewhat surprising. The most manifest result of the first part of Mu has been to establish the untenability of the various theses about the ideas and the numbers, or the mathematicals more broadly, advanced by those thinkers (compare, in particular, M6 1080b4–11 and 30–35 with 35–36). And its declared intention is to persuade readers open to persuasion of their untenability (see the statement at M9 1085b34–1086a21 with which this part of Mu concludes). But perhaps its most manifest result is not its most important one. In that case, the suggestion which we find surprising would have to be reevaluated and, in the first place, understood, on the basis of a prior determination of that less manifest but, in the context at least, more important result.

* * * *

The first part of Mu consists of three sections (M2–3, M4–5, and M6–9 1086a21), as it follows to this extent the plan spelled out in M1 (1076a22–32). The third of these sections, which is also by far the longest one (compare M1 1076a30), turns out to be devoted to a largely immanent critique of "the numbers," which is also a critique of the ideas—if the ideas are not "numbers," they cannot be at all (M7 1081a12–13)—, and to an equally immanent critique of the other mathematicals (M9 1085a7 and following). (By an immanent critique, I mean one that argues on the basis of the premises or principles of the position under scrutiny. See, for example, M7 1081a13–17, a35–b1, b29–33, 1082b19–23, b24–33; M8 1083a17–20, a20–36, b23–36; M9 1085a9–19, a31–b4, b12–22, b27–34.) It is a question in this section almost exclusively of the impossibility of number and magnitudes being separate (from the perceptibles) (M9 1085b34–36 together with M8

1083a36–b1, b19–23, b36–1084a1 and following, M9 1085a23–31; compare M1 1076a29–32 as well as M6 1080a12–14).

In the much shorter first section, however, Aristotle had treated the mathematicals, by themselves and in separation from the question of the ideas (see M1 1076a22–26), more comprehensively. As he had put the question at the end of M1 in introducing the section: (it is a) necessity, if indeed the mathematicals are, that they be either in the perceptibles, in accord with what some say, or separate from the perceptibles, as some also say; or, if neither (is the case), either they are not or they are in another manner, so that the dispute "for us" will be not about their being (or whether they are) but about the manner (of it).

He argues then in M2 that it is impossible for them to be in the perceptibles (1076a38 and following) and, at somewhat greater length, that for there to be such natures separate (from the perceptibles) is not possible either (1076b11–12 and following). (Both arguments use a combination of old and new points, as he acknowledges by referring in each to the earlier passage in question: at 1076a39–b1 to B2 998a7–14 and at 1076b39–1077a1 to B2 997b14–24. The recalled passages surround another passage in B2 that raises a problem which will receive its resolution only in this section of Mu: see pages 43–44 above.) But to this anticipation, in the latter argument, of the result of the third section of Mu, he adds here that to posit that the mathematicals are, in such a way as to be some separate natures, entails—if they are in that way—that they are prior to the perceptible magnitudes, which is contrary both to the truth and to what it is habitual to accept (1077a14–18). And the argument by which he seeks to show that they are neither ousiai more than the bodies nor prior in being to the perceptibles, but only in speech, is thus incorporated into that which establishes the impossibility of their separate existence: it becomes part of the adequate statement of the latter (1077b12–14).

According to what he says in this connection, it is only body that comes to be ensouled (1077a28–29; see also a18–20). And it is apparently only by recourse to soul or to a part of soul (and hence to body) that one can explain how the mathematical magnitudes themselves are each one. The explanation is admittedly valid only for such magnitudes "here": as for "those," that is, those allegedly separate, what cause can be given for their each being a one that remains? (1077a20–24; compare the reductio ad absurdum at 1077a1–9) That a line or a plane should come to be ensouled would be an expectation beyond (what is warranted by) the perceptions of our senses (1077a29–31; Aristotle disdains even to allude in this context to mathematical solids, which had been mentioned rather frequently earlier in the chapter: see, in particular, 1076b19–20). Body is some ousia, which lines are not, not even as matter, since it is apparent that nothing can be compounded from them or planes or points (1077a31–36). One may grant, therefore, that the latter are prior in speech, insofar as definitions (of ousiai or things) may presuppose their definitions. But priority in speech does not coincide with priority in ousia or in separate existence. (1077a36–b4)

The powerful passage which we have tried in this way to summarize must place its stamp, clearly, on everything that follows. But the immediate problem or question with which it confronts us is that of how to understand the mathematicals. For, if it has now been shown adequately that it is not possible for them in separation (from the perceptibles) to be, neither is it admissible for them to be in the perceptibles. After reminding us of this result of its first argument—which some parts of the summarized passage (1077b4–9, for example) might have caused us to wonder about—M2 ends therefore with this restatement of the problem, whose solution it leaves to M3 to adumbrate: either they are not at all, or they are (only) in some manner and on this account are not simply, for we speak of "to be" (tò einai) in many ways.

The new chapter begins from what has already been granted, or at least assumed, regarding universal propositions in mathematics: that they are not about anything besides or separate from (for example) magnitudes and numbers (compare M2 1077a9–14). Rather, it continues, they are about these but not insofar as they are such as to have magnitude or to be divisible (or divided). And it is likewise clearly admissible, it suggests, that there be speeches (logoi) and demonstrations about perceptible magnitudes (that is, bodies) not as they are perceptibles but rather as they are magnitudes. For there are many speeches (about them) also only as they are in movement, apart from what each of them is and what accrue to them (as what they are); and there is not, on that account, a necessity that there be something in movement which is separate from the perceptibles or that there be in them some nature distinct (from them). And likewise, in the case of what are in movement (that is, the perceptible magnitudes or the bodies), there will also be speeches and sciences (about them) not as they are in movement but rather only as they are bodies (or solids: compare M2 1076b19–20 and context), and again only as they are planes and only as they are lengths, and as they are divisible, and as they are indivisible but have a position and as they are indivisible only. "So that, since it is simply true to say (haplōs legein alēthes) not only that what are separate (that is, the things) are but also that what are not separate (or inseparable) are, like what are in movement (considered only as in movement), it is true to state simply (haplōs alēthes eipein)," according to the conclusion now drawn, "that the mathematicals, too, are and (that they are) such as they say" (1077b31–34; compare M7 1081a19–21 and context).

The conclusion that we have quoted is drawn well before the chapter has reached its midpoint. It is indeed sufficient for the purpose of guiding scientific work—in the mathematical sciences in the first place (see 1078a17–25), but not only there (compare 1078a5–8). And it is therefore an important one. Yet its content is also "simple" in that it is insufficiently precise as to the manner of being of the mathematicals (compare M2 1077b16–17) and for that reason fails to make clear what the mathematical sciences, in particular, are ultimately about.

They are certainly about the perceptibles. This much is made clear in the passage immediately following the quoted one. The new passage (1077b34–1078a5) culminates in the assertion that it is not (ouk) the case, "if what they are of happen to be perceptibles but they are not (of them) as they are perceptibles, that the mathematical sciences will not (ou) be of the perceptibles—nor, all the more, (will they be) of other separate (things) besides them." (Editors and translators who disregard the force of the second "ou"—which Jaeger, at least, has the consistency to bracket—are asked to compare 1078a35–36 in the same chapter. Regarding the "ou mentoi oude" that introduces the final clause, one should compare Denniston, pp. 29 and 30, on "ou mēn alla" and "ou mentoi alla." The understanding of the passage as a whole has been much impaired by the emendations accepted by editors at 1077b36–1078a1: the text as transmitted by mss.EAb is difficult but not impossible to construe. A prerequisite for doing so is the proper rendering of "tou sumbebēkotos" at 1077b35: compare 1078a17–18 and, above all, On the Soul B6 418a20–23.—In speaking here of "the mathematical sciences," Aristotle has particularly in mind geometry, as he indicates at 1078a2. For the significance of this, compare M2 1076b39–1077a4.) But how or in what way are they of them?

According to the passage that we are considering, they will be of the perceptibles insofar as their primary objects are what the perceptibles or things, in one or more of their aspects, are. A science whose primary object is health, for example, will be also of "the white thing" (a human being or other animal), as that thing is healthy or insofar as health belongs to it. And much accrues to the things, as the continuation (1078a5–9) has it, as each of such aspects is present to them. There are particular qualities or affections of an animal as it is female or as it is male; and there is not something female or male separate from animals but—as we can add—one or the other of these is an aspect of each of them. "So that" (the same can be said of the perceptibles), as they are only lengths or as they are planes.

But at this point mention is made of the problem of precision (1078a9–17). And this reminds us of the question of whether the aspects of the perceptibles that we regard as lengths (of a certain sort) or planes are truly lengths or planes as the mathematicians understand them (compare B2 997b34–998a6). So far as the problem bears on scientific practice, it is easily solved, as Aristotle indicates in the passage to which we have already referred and which forms here the immediate sequel (1078a17–25). But there is a question also on the level of principle. If the mathematicals are not, after all, aspects of the perceptibles, of the things, what are they truly? And what entitles them to be called the beings that they were earlier (1077b32–34) stated to be?

Some light is cast on these questions, and therefore also on that of the way in which the mathematical sciences are of or about the perceptibles, by the last passage that we will consider in the chapter (1078a25–31). It is a continuation of sorts of the instruction to the sciences which precedes it; but, at the same time, it raises the discussion to another level. According to that instruction, the proper procedure is to posit as separate what is not separate from the being in question and then to consider what accrues to the being insofar as what has been separated in thought is an aspect of it (1078a17–22). And this is said to be what arithmeticians and geometers do. But the difficulty, as we have seen, lies with the cases where what has been "separated" is not truly an aspect of the being under scrutiny. And it is in this context that Aristotle says, in the continuation that we are considering, something further about the geometers, in particular. The case in point is that of a man, who is of course, as man, indivisible; but the geometers consider him, not as he is (a) man, nor as he is indivisible, but as he is (a) solid—and hence not indivisible. What would be present to him then—that is, what is possible for him, or for the thing that he also is, as not indivisible—clearly admits of being present to him. (Christ correctly refrains from bracketing "tò dunaton" at 1078a28.) "So that, on account of this, the geometers speak correctly; and (what) they converse about (are) beings; and (what they consider) are beings. For being (tò on) is twofold: the one in actuality, the other by way of matter (that is, in potentiality or as possible)." (1078a28–31) The beings about which the geometers converse are the things; and the beings which they consider are mathematicals—which are, as potentialities or possibilities of the things. These mathematicals, too, are then beings. And they are even, in a sense, prior to the things (compare M4 1078b7–9, which looks back to this discussion as well as to that of the latter part of M2 [1077a14 and following], together with D11 1019a1–11 and D12 1019b22–33). But their being cannot be divorced from that of the things whose possibilities they are.

The second section (M4–5) of the first part of Mu is devoted to the ideas. Most of it is a more or less literal repetition of portions of A9. (With M4 1078b34–1079b3, compare 990b2–991a8; with M5 1079b12–1080a8, compare 991a8–b9. The critique of the ideas that these passages convey is admittedly partial, intended—as M1 1076a29–32 had indicated—to be augmented in the third section, where the more rigorous arguments alluded to in 1080a9–11, at the end of M5, are presumably to be found.) The earlier part of M4 (1078b9–32), whose model is a portion of A6 (987a32–b9), is of a quite different character, however. Here, conspicuous departures from the model call attention to a most important implication of what has just been brought out in the first section of this part of Mu.

Mathematicals and their like (compare M2 1076b1–3), which are as aspects or possibilities of the perceptibles, will as such share the fate of the latter, all of which perish (compare M5 1079b13 with B4 999b4–5). This is the extreme term of that "flowing" quality of the perceptibles of which Plato had complained—consider A7 988b3–4 in this light—and which led him to doubt whether science is at all possible in their regard (A6 987a32–b1; M4 1078b12–17). For the same reason, he may have wondered whether Socrates had intended the universals he was seeking, or the definitions he was turning his mind to, to be about the perceptibles (A6 987b2–9). However that may be, in the wake of what has just been indicated about science and its objects in M2–3, Aristotle himself resolves any doubt about Socrates' intention by distinguishing him from Plato on precisely this ground: Socrates made neither the universals nor the definitions separate, while Plato or his followers separated them (1078b30–32). At the same time, he omits here a remark that in the earlier passage had suggested that Socrates was unconcerned with "the whole nature" (987b1–2; compare the more ambiguous remark in Parts of Animals A1 642a28–29). He suggests instead that what Socrates had reasonably sought (1078b23–25)—inductive arguments and (that is, leading to) universal definitions (1078b27–29)—is something that concerns the very principle (or foundation) of science (1078b29–30), something therefore that the physicists themselves could not afford to be indifferent to, as the best of them somehow realized (1078b19–21; compare A10 993a17–24 as well as Parts of Animals A1 642a24–28).

* * * *

We must now try to see in what way or ways the second part of Mu "follows next upon" what has been said in the first part. In taking up the program outlined at the beginning of this new part (see pages 255–256 above), Aristotle turns first to the proponents of the ideas (M9 1086a29–32). Those who had recourse to the ideas made them at the same time both universal as ousiai (of the perceptibles) and, again, as separate (from them) also particulars (1086a32–34, retaining with the mss. "hōs ousias" at a33). What was responsible for this inadmissible coupling (of universal and particular) on their part was that they did not make, for the perceptibles, the same ousiai (that is, ousiai which remain the same); they held that, whereas what belong to the perceptibles are flowing and not, any of them, remaining, the universal is, and is a different something, besides them (1086a34–b2, retaining the readings of the mss. at both a36 and 37). But the genuine solution to this problem of the instability of the perceptibles—so far as there is a solution to it—has already been pointed to in what we have seen in M2–3: as limits, the potentialities or possibilities of the perceptibles, which are so long as they are, do not "flow" as each of them does. The truth dimly grasped as "ideas" is then—adequately expressed—the "potentialities and natures" of the perceptibles (compare M2 1076b1–3 with B2 998a12–13; see also 1086b7–11 as well as Th8 1049b8–9). When Aristotle now reminds us, therefore, of what he had said before (in M4) about Socrates, he adds that Socrates was correct in thinking that what the definitions are of, are the (perceptible) particulars, from which they are not to be separated: "for, without the universal, science is not to be gotten hold of; but separating (them) is responsible for all of the difficulties that accrue regarding the ideas." (1086b2–7)

Science is possible then, even if we lack access to beings of the permanence ascribed to the ideas (compare Z16 1040b26–1041a3). We will not consider now whether this is Aristotle's final word, his deepest word on the question. It is here more important to note that, after his indication of the character of such science as is clearly possible, that is, after his reminder of the most important result of the first part of Mu, he turns at once to a perplexity that affects both those who say that the ideas are and those who do not: if one will not posit that the ousiai are separate and (are) in the manner that the particulars among the beings are said (to be), one will do away with ousia as "we wish" to say (that it is) (M10 1086b14–19). (There would, in other words, be a wish for such ousiai, a wish shared by Aristotle, even if the fate of science did not depend upon it.) For science itself must be understood; and, as a concern of man, it must be understood in light of the human concern that is deeper than it is and therefore, at bottom, its source. And the concern with life is inseparable from concern for the permanence of the whole which is home to our life, and hence for whatever would secure that permanence.

We have thus considered one part of the perplexity introduced at the beginning of M10. In introducing it, Aristotle had said not only that it is a perplexity both for those who say that the ideas are and for those who do not, but also that it had been spoken of before, "at the outset, in the perplexities (that is, in Beta)." But the part that we have considered seems to have no precedent there; whereas the other part, for which we do find precedents in Beta (with 1086b19–22 and 22–32, compare B4 999b24–25 and b27–1000a4; with 1086b22 and 32–37, compare B6 1003a5–7 and 13–17), weighs only on those who say that the ideas are (see 1086b19–21 and 1087a4–7, retaining at a6 with the mss. "kai ideas" as what are deemed to be [each of them] some one separate thing): the apparent exception (compare 1086b37–1087a4 with B6 1003a7–9 and 13–17) is, formally at least, included under the same rubric (see, again, 1087a4–7). Only, then, at 1087a7 and following, in the chapter which he has articulated in this way, does Aristotle return to arguing on the basis of premises acceptable to the deniers of the ideas.

But those premises, too, prove to be in need of correction. This becomes clear from the consideration of a perplexity which is described as the greatest of those spoken of (1087a13) although, as it is put here, it does not seem to have been spoken of before, at least in Beta. From the premise that all science is universal (1087a10–11)—that is, of the universals (1086b33; compare Posterior Analytics A31 87b28–33 and 88a5–7)—one is compelled to conclude that the principles of the beings are universals, too (1087a11–13); but, if it is necessary that those principles be universals, it will be necessary also that what come from them be universals (1087a21–23; compare 1086b33–37); and, if this is the case, there will be nothing separate (as the perceptible particulars are separate), nor (for this reason) any ousia (1087a23–24; compare B6 1003a7–9). What produces the perplexity is, as Aristotle suggests here (1087a13–15), a flaw in the premise. Science is only incidentally or in part of the universal—in the way that to see some color is incidentally to see "color" or to consider, as a grammarian does, a particular alpha is to consider "alpha" (1087a19–21 and 24–25). Science or knowledge is actual only insofar as it is, in the first place, of "some this": that is, of an ousia or thing (1087a18; contrast B6 1003a13–17 and 1002b32–1003a2 as well as pages 59–60 above). And the difference, within the Metaphysics, between the passage that we are considering here (1087a10–25) and the earlier one that it corrects (1086b32–37), is likely to be emblematic of the difference between the Metaphysics altogether and the logical works as a whole (compare Z12 as well as pages 153–154 above).

Some Notes on Nu

Nu continues and, we presume, completes the program introduced and embarked upon in the second part of Mu (M9 1086a21 and following). Having stated what he wished to state about what is said by those who assert the existence of the ideas (N1 1087a29:

tēs ousias tautēs; compare M9 1086a31–32), the author turns, as he had promised to do (M9 1086a29–30), to what is said by those who assert the existence only of "the numbers"—understood as distinct from the ideas (N2 1090a7–10) yet, like them, as without motion (N3 1091a20–22) and everlasting (N2 1088b20; N5 1092b3–5). As before with regard to the ideas (M10 1086b14–22; compare A6 987b18–20), the question concerns less what their proponents say about the numbers themselves (or the mathematicals more broadly) than what they say about the principles of them (N3 1091a20–22) or their elements (N5 1092a21–24), which are understood to be in turn—if only by way of the numbers (N5 1092b8–9)—the elements and principles of all the beings (M9 1086a26–29; N1 1087a31–32 and b4; N4 1092a5–8).

The numbers—whether understood in the strict sense already indicated or, on occasion, in other more or less related ways—are discussed throughout Nu, in passages too numerous to list. Yet it becomes clear only gradually, in the course of its first chapter, that they or, rather, their elements or principles are to be its chief theme (1087b7 and 15, 1088a18, b4–6 and 11–12). That is, the transition to the second branch of the program outlined in M9 is less sharply or unambiguously effected here than we have hitherto acknowledged. The difficulty which Nu takes up first pertains to a proposition about the principles that is made by "all": the natural scientists as well as all who concern themselves with the ousiai without motion (N1 1087a29–31 and following; compare N3 1091a18–22 as well as N4 1091b10–15). And, among other things, this means (what subsequent passages, too, will confirm: see, for example, the transition back to the numbers, in particular, at N2 1090a2 and following) that, despite the declaration with which the book opened, putting an end as it appeared to the branch of the program of M9 that concerned the ideas, what Aristotle had to say about them in this connection has not been exhausted by the portion of the discussion contained in the second part of Mu. The opening declaration of Nu must be taken, then, to point rather to the importance of the portion so contained. It forms, in fact, an indispensable component of the whole that is Mu. And because it does, a step apparently taken by some ancient editors (Ross, Vol. II, p.461) is rightly rejected: to make Nu begin at what is now M9 1086a21 would be to destroy the integrity of Mu, of a book that, by tying together several loose threads, brings the argument of the Metaphysics, so far at least as I have been able to follow it, to a fitting close.

This is certainly not to deny that, in addition to reaffirming in the way that has been indicated the wholeness of Mu, Nu itself is rich in passages that repay our attention to them, either in themselves or as reminders of earlier discussions (with N1 1087b33–1088a14, compare I1 and pages 208–215 above; with N5 1092a26–29 and context, compare Z13 1039a11–13; and with N1 1088b2–3, N2 1089a12–13, and N3 1091a12–13, compare L10 1075a25–26, together with 1075b1–2, and page 253 above). In studying these passages, we must keep in mind what Aristotle indicated in outlining the program that is still determinative here: he intends to consider what is said about the first principles and the first causes and elements by those who assert the existence of ousiai different from the perceptible ones, and not what is said about them by those who admit perceptible ousia alone (compare pages 255–256 above). The critique, however, to which he now proceeds to subject the assertions of the one class of thinkers may—it, too, given its source—with or without intending to do so disclose something of the views of the other class, as well, or of what those views should be.

In this way it emerges that none of the contraries is, authoritatively, (the) principle of all, since there is, as it appears and as reason bears witness, nothing contrary to ousia (N1 1087b2–4; compare 1087a29–31). Yet (it is a) necessity that there be some matter for each, what is potentially such (as it is), and therefore also for ousia (N1 1088b1–2; N2 1089b15–16). Can even ousia, then, be authoritatively (the) principle for all? (With N2 1089b24–28 and N1 1088b4, compare N1 1087a31–36 and N2 1088b14–16 and 25–28; and with N2 1088b26, compare 1089b30–32.) On the other hand, it is "absurd, nay impossible" to make what is not ousia an element of, and thus prior to, ousia (N1 1088b2–4). Yet there were those who sought to identify what is potentially "this" and (an) ousia (see N2 1089b16–20). Aristotle traces such attempts here, in part, to the influence of Parmenides, whose teaching that there is something which is "being itself" and "one itself" threatened to make all beings one—unless, it was thought, recourse was had, against the express injunction of the master, to another principle, other than being, from whose cooperation with being the manifest multiplicity of beings could be derived (N2 1088b35–1089a6 and 1089b4–8, together with B4 1001a29–b1). In criticizing the attempts, Aristotle makes, among others, the following points: (1) they fail to account for the actual multiplicity of beings, in its full range (N2 1089a7–12 together with a31–b2, b20–24, and b32–1090a2); (2) it is "absurd, nay impossible" that some one nature should, having come to be, be (the) cause of the multiplicity (N2 1089a12–15); (3) it is the very supposition that there is something (which is) both some "this" and some such nature (as "being" or each of the ideas is said to be) that renders questionable a multiplicity of the "this"—and therewith of the other beings—which it would otherwise be reasonable to accept (N2 1089b24–30; compare Z8 1033b19–22 as well as Z14 1039b15–16). Is, then, the cause (of their multiplicity), which Aristotle refers to here as "the same and analogous" for all classes of beings (N2 1089b2–4), the multiplicity itself, the manifest multiplicity of and within the ousiai? (Consider in this light also N5 1092a11–17.)—The primacy of the ousiai, in the sense of the things (see also N5 1092a17–20 and b23–25 and N6 1093a3–4), is not the whole word of Aristotle (compare L1 1069a32–33). But it is his first word and, to judge at least by the place of this discussion (in Nu), also his last. For the ousiai are the anchors of that given world which all truly scientific thought must take as its starting point—which, however high or deep it roams, it must never lose sight of and which it must return to in the end.